Catholics and the 'Protestant nation'

Manchester University Press

Politics, culture and society in early modern Britain

General editors

PROFESSOR ANN HUGHES
DR ANTHONY MILTON
PROFESSOR PETER LAKE

This important series publishes monographs that take a fresh and challenging look at the interactions between politics, culture and society in Britain between 1500 and the mid-eighteenth century. It counteracts the fragmentation of current historiography through encouraging a variety of approaches which attempt to redefine the political, social and cultural worlds, and to explore their interconnection in a flexible and creative fashion. All the volumes in the series question and transcend traditional inter-disciplinary boundaries, such as those between political history and literary studies, social history and divinity, urban history and anthropology. They contribute to a broader understanding of crucial developments in early modern Britain.

Catholics and the 'Protestant nation'

Religious politics and identity
in early modern England

edited by
ETHAN SHAGAN

Manchester
University Press

Manchester and New York

distributed exclusively in the USA by Palgrave

Published by Manchester University Press
Oxford Road, Manchester M13 9NR, UK
and Room 400, 175 Fifth Avenue, New York, NY 10010, USA
www.manchesteruniversitypress.co.uk

Distributed exclusively in the USA by
Palgrave, 175 Fifth Avenue, New York, NY 10010, USA

Distributed exclusively in Canada by
UBC Press, University of British Columbia, 2029 West Mall,
Vancouver, BC, Canada V6T 1Z2

British Library Cataloguing-in-Publication Data
A catalogue record for this book is available from the British Library

Library of Congress Cataloging-in-Publication Data applied for

ISBN 0 7190 5768 X *hardback*
EAN 978 0 7190 5768 7

First published 2005

14 13 12 11 10 09 08 07 06 05   10 9 8 7 6 5 4 3 2 1

Typeset in Scala with Pastonchi display
by Koinonia Ltd, Manchester

Printed in Great Britain
by Biddles, King's Lynn

Contents

Preface and acknowledgements

This book was conceived in 1997, inspired by a conference on English Catholicism at University College London that had been organised by Michael Questier and Alison Shell. The conference was explicitly intended to break free of the constraints that have traditionally bedevilled the subject matter: its largely conservative framework, the hagiographic tone of traditional scholarship, and a principally internalist narrative. Yet at the conference, despite the best intentions of both the organisers and the speakers, the audience kept bringing the subject back around to its traditional insularity: wasn't Edmund Campion *really* a martyr for his religion?; weren't recusants *really* the spiritual ancestors of modern English Catholics? It was as if an invisible force field was preventing English Catholic history from reaching out to the wider world.

At the lunch break, I suggested to my friend Anthony Milton that perhaps what was needed was a book of essays featuring not only 'Catholic historians' but scholars who had decided independently, from a range of perspectives, that Catholicism was not a discrete subject but a crucial facet of early modern English culture and politics. Anthony, with his usual directness, told me that I should edit just such a book; you hold the results in your hands.

In the many years since then, this volume has had several violent swings of fortune, and it has often looked as if it would never be completed. For a long time it was supposed to be co-edited by my friend Margaret Sena; she was instrumental in the early editorial stages and co-wrote the first draft of the introduction, but she later decided not to continue with the project. I owe her enormous thanks for her hard work and for her willingness to allow the project to continue in her absence. The book's existence now is also owed very much to the enthusiasm, perseverance, and occasional prodding of two of the contributors, Peter Marshall and Michael Questier. I also owe enormous thanks to Tom McCoog, S.J., who agreed to provide his chapter on short notice, and to Alison Wesby at Manchester University Press, who has shown enormous patience.

Most importantly, however, this book exists because of the skill and kindness of my teacher, Peter Lake, and I dedicate it to him. He is, and always will be, the boss.

Ethan Shagan

Contributors

Peter Lake is professor of history at Princeton University.

Thomas M. McCoog, S.J., is archivist of the British Province of the Society of Jesus.

Peter Marshall is reader in history at the University of Warwick.

Michael C. Questier is lecturer in history at Queen Mary College, University of London.

Ethan Shagan is associate professor of history at Northwestern University.

Alison Shell is lecturer in English studies at the University of Durham.

Johann P. Sommerville is professor of history at the University of Wisconsin at Madison.

Abbreviations

Chapter 1

———◆———

Introduction:
English Catholic history in context

Ethan Shagan

Over the last four centuries, the historical period that we call 'early modern' has more often been referred to by very different and more inflammatory names: the 'age of Reformation', the 'age of religious wars', the 'confessional era', and so on. It should thus be no surprise that historians of England were until recently bound by a high degree of partisanship in their accounts of England's schism from Rome and subsequent religious peram-bulations. The early historians of the period – from Foxe to Burnet, Strype and J. A. Froude on the Protestant side and from Harpsfield to Lingard and Gasquet on the Catholic side – were more often than not clerics whose historical writings were part and parcel of the religious politics of their own times. Protestant historians with impeccable academic credentials could unselfconsciously discuss the 'liberation of the Gospel' or the overthrow of 'superstition', while Catholic historians could write of the Elizabethan 'persecution' and of Thomas Cranmer's 'libertinism'. In recent decades such confessional tempers have largely cooled, but their legacy remains visible in the boundary that tends to separate historians of early modern English Catholicism from the mainstream of the discipline. Catholicism has become a historiographical sub-field or occasionally a ghetto, to be studied by specialists much as one might study the institutional history of a department of government or the evolution of a branch of law. Practitioners of this sub-field have produced works of remarkable depth and scholarly virtuosity, but their work remains for the most part both uninformed by the wider scholarship on early modern England and unable to influence that scholarship with its important interventions.

The purpose of this book is to continue recent scholarly trends by offering a post-confessional, post-revisionist approach to English Catholicism that combines the interests of traditional 'Catholic historians' and historians of English religion more generally to pull Catholicism back into the mainstream

1

of English historiography. It is our primary assertion that many of the fundamental issues of English history cannot be adequately understood without taking into account a Catholic perspective, while many of the fundamental issues of Catholic historiography cannot be understood in isolation from the rest of English society. This is not because of any allegedly revisionist readings that maintain that the Reformation was ineffectual in the face of English traditionalism or that stress the 'continuity of Catholicism' in the sixteenth and seventeenth centuries.[1] Rather it is because, as scholars like Peter Lake and Anthony Milton have stressed, English Protestants and Catholics defined both their identities and their political positions in response to their ideological opponents, allowing for a remarkable degree of cross-pollination of ideas, imagery, and texts across confessional divides.[2] Catholicism, both real and imagined, dominated debates in government and Church. Images of Catholicism, both positive and negative, flooded popular culture. Catholics themselves were not only the foil against which much of early modern English history occurred, but were also a vigorous and often divided community who sought to shape both their own destiny and the larger course of English history. The paucity of dialogue between Catholic and Protestant historians has thus produced a series of lapses and incongruities within the literature. Many historians of puritanism, for instance, have discussed supposedly distinctive aspects of that religious style without understanding their similarities to contemporaneous Catholic evangelism. Likewise, historians who have analysed the circulation of manuscripts and printed books as an important mode of political engagement before the Civil War have not noticed the massive outpouring of Catholic news books, ballads, and circulating letters in the same period.[3]

What we are proposing, then, is not a work of Catholic history, nor a history of English Catholics, at least as those terms are usually understood. This volume's main protagonists are of varied religious inclinations; students of early-modern Catholicism are accustomed to books with *dramatis personae* running alphabetically from Cardinal Allen to Cardinal Ximenes, but this book also boasts a wide array of Protestants and conformists among its subjects. The twin pillars of traditional English Catholic scholarship, recusancy and martyrdom, will be intentionally relegated to the sidelines, viewed as positions within larger debates rather than as subjects in themselves. We want instead to focus on subjects which contextualise Catholic experiences within the broader framework of English culture: Catholic readings of widely known texts, Catholic visions of the English nation, Catholic accommodations to the royal supremacy, and Catholic campaigns to manipulate public opinion. Even traditional notions of the term 'Catholicism' must be self-consciously de-centred and redefined; many of the 'Catholics' we will discuss in these pages would not have considered many of the others to be 'Catholics' at all, and it is exactly these fault-lines that we are most interested in exploring. We want to ask our readers to suspend their assumptions and prejudices about the nature of Catholic historiography as we attempt to explore a series of very different paths.

I

Any attempt to integrate English Catholic history with what is perhaps unfairly called the 'mainstream' of English historical writing must begin with a look at the current state of scholarship, and any look at current scholarship must begin at the point where 'Catholicism' becomes a distinct subject of inquiry: the Reformation. Until the 1970s, it was largely assumed that the history of England between 1521 and 1559 could be told through the lens of Protestantism. That is not to say, of course, that Protestantism was the whole story; many Catholic historians like Madeleine and Ruth Dodds stressed the strength of traditionalist religious sentiment, while some great works like Geoffrey Elton's *Tudor Revolution in Government* were little concerned with religious doctrine. But the meta-subject, the larger question to which even these works contributed, was always assumed to be the development of a Protestant nation. Even if historians knew perfectly well that statistically there were few Protestants in England in the first forty years after Luther's revolt, those Protestants dominated the literature because of their presumed importance in the grand narrative of national conversion. This view reached its apogee in the work of A. G. Dickens, who specialised in finding evidence of Protestant sentiment in obscure places; his detective work was masterful, and he considered no hint of reforming activity too insignificant to mention. In his 1964 *magnum opus*, *The English Reformation*, he combined the fruits of decades of such discoveries with a sympathetic account of the high politics of the period and a fair dose of cosmetically concealed anti-Catholicism to describe a rapid, sweeping, and triumphant Protestant Reformation.[4]

The Protestant-triumphalist position epitomised by Dickens was challenged effectively in the 1970s and 1980s in a series of 'revisionist' interventions by historians such as J. J. Scarisbrick, Christopher Haigh, and Margaret Bowker.[5] Most convincingly, these scholars showed that late medieval Catholicism was not a corrupt and unpopular religion which failed to fulfill the spiritual needs of the people, as much of the previous literature had argued, but rather was a vibrant and popular faith which enjoyed the massive support and voluntary enthusiasm of rich and poor alike. By extension, therefore, when Protestantism arrived on English shores it was not greeted with warmth by a population eager for spiritual renewal but was accepted only slowly and grudgingly, if at all. Similarly, these historians argued that the success of the Edwardian and Elizabethan regimes and the failure of the

Marian regime had been seriously overstated, and that it was only the vagaries of high-political factionalism and the contingency of royal lifespans that allowed the Church of England to survive; the English Reformation was never an inevitable result of larger social forces, and it could easily have been reversed on any number of occasions between 1534 and 1603. Most fundamentally, the revisionists made an observation that should have been obvious but for the dangers of hindsight: the history of England between 1521 and 1559, and indeed for some time afterwards, must necessarily be seen as a history of *Catholics*.

In the past several years these revisionist arguments have been incorporated into two large-scale, influential accounts of the English Reformation: Christopher Haigh's *English Reformations* and Eamon Duffy's *The Stripping of the Altars*.[6] These accounts are in some ways very similar: both see pre-Reformation religion in a highly favorable light, both see the Reformation itself as provoking serious resistance, and both stress the discrepancy between Protestant visions of godly Reformation and the actual situation in sixteenth-century England. The works also have important differences, however, especially concerning the Reformation's consequences. For Eamon Duffy, the Reformation's great legacy was its destructive achievements: the imagery, edifices, and communal solidarity of late medieval Catholicism – the very things which, in Duffy's opinion, made it such a vibrant and popular faith – were forever destroyed. On this reading, while England did not become in any meaningful sense 'Protestant' until well into Elizabeth's reign, the underlying foundations of popular Catholicism were nonetheless broken into ineffectual shards, and any Catholicism that emerged thereafter would necessarily be a different animal altogether. For Christopher Haigh, however, the Reformation was not nearly so significant a spiritual event; indeed much of the interpretive force of his book is intended to show that the English Reformation was more a high-level dispute over sovereignty than an example of European confessional conflict. Certainly Haigh would grant that in some areas there was significant evangelisation, but on a national basis the Reformation effected only the externals of Christian worship rather than the souls of English people. His book ends, therefore, with a vivid and moving description of how little had changed in English religion between 1520 and 1580.

These two works have dominated the literature on the English Reformation for the past decade, and both are inescapably 'Catholic' histories.[7] It thus might seem that our initial claim – that 'Catholic' and 'mainstream' histories have been needlessly separated – cannot be applied to the period before 1558. However, there are at least three ways in which the revisionist project is indeed disassociated from the mainstream of Tudor-Stuart historiography. First, its view of the Reformation as slow and ineffectual, not Protestantising the nation until well into Elizabeth's reign if at all, is hard to reconcile with the 'revisionism' practised by such historians of the seventeenth century as Nicholas Tyacke and Conrad Russell, who have found a surprisingly vigorous and mainstream Calvinist consensus by James I's reign at the latest.[8] The Reformation, it seems, is being pushed forward from the earlier period and pushed backward from the later period, so that on some readings it seems as if there must simply have been a weekend in 1588 when everyone suddenly converted. Indeed, this 'big squeeze' sometimes seems so absolute that we can barely comprehend how the Reformation happened at all.

Second, even though the revisionists rightly dominate the historiography of the Reformation itself, there is a great deal of other work on Tudor history that has proved able to sidestep their conclusions. This may be because the revisionists have sometimes appeared to repeat the mistakes of their predecessors, replacing a Protestant-biased history with a Catholic-biased one. The revisionists have enabled us to write about Catholicism in the Reformation – no small achievement – but they have ironically limited debate by making it difficult to talk about Protestantism in the same breath. If the English Reformation was neither a 'real' Protestant Reformation nor a particularly successful one, why should we study a small minority who failed to lay more than a thin veneer of a Reformed Church upon the thoroughly unreformed English nation? Thus scholars like Diarmaid MacCulloch, with his magisterial biography of Thomas Cranmer, and the research group led by Margaret Spufford, with their fascinating account of popular religious dissent from the late middle ages to the eighteenth century, have constructed parallel interpretations that are every bit as interesting as the revisionist account but cannot speak to it.[9] Somehow these two literatures must be brought together, showing that there were Protestants in Tudor England, and that there was even a Protestant Reformation, without implying that Tudor history was somehow Protestant history.

Third, the revisionist account of the Reformation has paid surprisingly little attention to political issues, an odd irony given Haigh's insistence that the English Reformation was largely 'political' rather than 'Protestant'.[10] What Haigh meant by 'political', however, was not what many other scholars of early modern England mean by the term. Haigh described Reformation 'politics' as events that occurred at Westminster or the court, activities among the 'political nation' consisting primarily of struggles for power; 'political' can thus be contrasted with 'religious' or 'Protestant' (adjectives which describe spirituality) and can also be contrasted with the un- or pre-political activities of the people. This neo-Eltonian notion of 'politics' is far removed from the literature on early Stuart government and religion, with the expansive views of 'politics' canvassed by scholars like Thomas Cogswell and Alastair Bellany.[11] It is also increasingly far removed from recent Tudor scholarship. Michael Bush's masterful account of the Pilgrimage of Grace, for instance, with its complex rebel coalition consisting of all classes of people and a variety of religious, social, and 'commonwealth' grievances, would seem to exist in a different world from the simple priests of revisionist scholarship, hiding their chalices from royal commissioners.[12] The fact is that the revisionists have rarely looked beneath the surface of 'political' Reformations to see what types of ideological conflict were being canvassed on the ground; as such, they tend to see Catholics as reactive rather than as creative and as united rather than as conflicted.

II

The transition from the historiography of the Reformation, dominated by revisionist assertions of Catholic strength, to the historiography of seventeenth-century Catholicism, usually associated with the history of recusancy, is a strained one. Traditional historians of the Reformation were content to ignore the 'decline' of Catholicism, seeing it as an inevitable corollary to the rise of Protestantism; it was considered 'losers' history' of the worst sort, a tale of valiant martyrdom at its best and quaint survivalism at its worst. Among Catholic historians, however, the events of the later sixteenth century have provoked a bitter debate over the so-called 'continuity of Catholicism', a controversy which developed from a series of criticisms directed by Christopher Haigh against the work of John Bossy. In his synthetic account, *The English Catholic Community, 1570-1850*, Bossy advanced the provocative thesis that English Catholicism was best understood not as a dwindling minority Church but as a rising sect in the English non-conforming tradition; there was a fundamental difference between Catholic communities before the advent of a Protestant regime and those communities afterwards, when Catholic practices necessarily carried with them certain legal, social, economic, and cultural baggage. Bossy suggested that the parish-based piety of the fifteenth century, with its emphasis on elaborate community rituals and outward forms of observance, had proven unable to function as a minority faith and was quickly dying in the early years of Elizabeth's reign. It was thus left to a group of clerics from the exile community at Louvain to infuse a new, activist spirit into English Catholicism in the 1570s when they inaugurated an English mission to revive Catholicism during what they hoped would be a brief interim of Protestant rule. The mission enjoyed an extraordinarily active phase in the later sixteenth century as clerics rode through England trying desperately to reconcile souls from schism and draw the English laity back into union with Rome; they encouraged forms of ritual practice and symbolic acts of separation from Protestant society that would increasingly convert Catholicism into a separatist sect. After the accession of James I, however, clerics and laity alike realised that they were fighting for a lost cause, and the mission was obliged to become dependant upon the English gentry for finances and a supply of men for the priesthood. Thus the 'age of the gentry' in English Catholicism began as a direct result of the vigour infused into the movement by foreign-trained missionaries.[13]

In a review essay of 1978, Christopher Haigh drew attention to a variety of problems in Bossy's work, his most important critiques centring on disenfranchisement as an engine of community-formation. Haigh pointed to the 'common experience of proscription, the sharing of a common legal status, [and] the need for cooperation against anti-Catholic activity' as factors which contributed to 'community ... cohesion,' and he thus asked to what extent 'Catholics acted as a political unit'.[14] These criticisms very cleverly suggested pushing Bossy's thesis further, to understand not only how the Catholic community fit into the religious landscape of England, but how post-Reformation Catholics operated as a counter-cultural force in English society. In subsequent articles, however, Haigh abandoned these issues and instead organised his critique of the Bossy thesis around the theme of 'continuity', arguing that Catholicism after the Elizabethan settlement owed much more to what had gone before than Bossy allowed.[15] By 'continuity,' Haigh meant a number of things. He emphasised 'organic continuity' in the personal experiences of individuals such as Cecily Stonor whose lives spanned the Marian and Elizabethan years. He employed the concept to refer to the traditional, continuous, and quasi-Catholic religious practices of rural laypeople, sometimes referred to as 'habits' or as collective 'local norms.' He stressed the continuing service of Catholic clerical personnel from Mary's reign during the important transitional years of the 1560s and 1570s. All of these arguments for 'continuity', which emerged naturally from Haigh's revisionist work on the Reformation, suggested that Bossy's emphasis on foreign-trained missionaries was unwarranted: it was Protestants rather than Catholics who needed to missionise in sixteenth century England. On the structure and substance of gentry Catholicism Haigh more or less agreed with Bossy, but he argued that, because Bossy's gentry constituted such a small minority of the English Catholic social body, the Elizabethan Catholic mission had to be regarded as a failure. To preserve their fledgling enterprise, the missionaries had focused their efforts solely on gentry households at the expense of the rural poor, consequently neglecting 'whole regions and social groups'. Far from saving English Catholicism, then, the missionaries were largely responsible for the failure of traditional English conservatism to reassert itself after 1569.

Both Haigh's and Bossy's positions can be criticised on semantic grounds, in the sense that both define 'Catholics' in such a way as to fit their argument. For Bossy the great mass of theologically unsophisticated semi- or reluctantly conforming churchgoers were very nearly Protestant, while for Haigh, with their ability to 'counterfeit' the mass out of bits and pieces in the *Book of Common Prayer*, they were very nearly Catholic. Similarly, Haigh saw continuities because of his largely devotional perspective: worshippers could create continuities by maintaining core Catholic beliefs and practices even if outward circumstances changed. Bossy, on the other hand, came at the issue from a sociological perspective, seeing change arising from the ways in which *communities* interacted; for Bossy, outwardly similar individual practices could not compare to fundamental differences in how conforming and non-conforming communities experienced the sacred.

Perhaps the greatest disappointment of the debate, however, was that there was so little attention given to the politicised nature of Catholicism after proscription; neither Haigh nor Bossy considered that different Catholics might have differed radically in how they perceived their relationship to the Reformation or that these disagreements might have been mediated through political rather than strictly spiritual debates. In particular, neither scholar considered that the relationships of individual Catholics to both their community and their heritage might have been influenced by their relationships to the Protestant regime. Hence a whole variety of issues that speak directly to the 'continuity' question were never discussed. What, for instance, were the effects of developing English anti-popery in shaping the identity of post-Reformation English Catholics? How did changing ecclesiastical politics affect the fortunes of English Catholics, and how did Catholics respond to the successive regimes of Archbishops Parker, Grindal, Whitgift, Bancroft, Abbot, and Laud? The 'continuity' debate thus emerges as something of a *question mal posée*. What might have been an increasingly broad discussion of the relationship of the evolving Catholic community to the rest of English society instead became an increasingly narrow discussion of that community's withdrawal.

III

The historiography of post-Reformation Catholicism has been rather mixed in the years since the debate over 'the fall of a church or the rise of a sect'. This has certainly not been due to any shortage of excellent studies since the 1970s, but rather has resulted from the very narrow series of issues that emerged from the ashes of the Haigh–Bossy debate. The terms of that debate focused attention so thoroughly on questions of social isolation and community-formation that it had little to offer the dominant debates of Stuart historiography: the political cultures of court and country, the place of puritanism in English culture, the causes of the Civil War, and so on. Hence 'mainstream' historians of Stuart England have felt little need to pay attention to Catholic history, while Catholic historians have more often than not been shooting in the dark, hoping that new paradigms would emerge from their sources on their own.

One of the most important exceptions is clearly Caroline Hibbard's *Charles I and the Popish Plot*.[16] Hibbard's book focused on the political activism of

Catholics at the Caroline court and the significance of their position for Protestant perceptions of popish corruption prior to the outbreak of the Civil War. Hibbard found that by ingratiating themselves with both the King and the French Catholic Queen, Catholics such as the papal agent George Con and the laymen Sir Kenelm Digby and Wat Montagu were able to exploit their position at court. They successfully advocated positions in foreign policy and organised contributions to the King's expedition against the Scots. With such findings, she was able to prove that Catholics played a vital role in the development of religious and political hostilities in the years before the war, and that contemporary fears among Protestants of a popish plot were not entirely misplaced.

These were weighty conclusions indeed, and her book was one of the few recent histories of Stuart Catholicism to make a significant impact in the larger field. Hibbard's narrative also contained some obvious points of difference from the interpretations offered by Bossy and Haigh. First, although the powerful lay protagonists in Hibbard's account could easily be accommodated into Christopher Haigh's version of 'elitist' Catholicism, Haigh's conception of the English mission as a pastoral enterprise was decidedly incompatible with Hibbard's depiction of the papal agent, George Con, who made little secret of his desire to convert the King and bring England back into union with Rome. Hibbard also explicitly criticised the Bossy thesis on the grounds that it was 'apolitical and Anglocentric'. Drawing a distinction between 'court' and 'country' Catholicism, Hibbard objected not to Bossy's claim that the bulk of Catholics were politically quiescent, but rather to his neglect of the court connections and internationalist outlook of the missionaries. If historians were to understand the political character of Catholicism, Hibbard maintained, they should look to the exile diaspora abroad and to the networks that carried printed books and Catholic education, or in her term the 'Continental Counter-Reformation', back to England.

Hibbard's book was an enormous achievement, but her work focused on a narrow segment of the Catholic population and a very brief time span; she never asked where all of these Catholics with pretensions to political engagement were during the 1610s and 1620s, in the years before a Catholic Queen and an anti-puritan archbishop made them welcome at court. Indeed, we are left wondering how we move from Professor Bossy's claim that Catholics had more or less recognised their political death after the Gunpowder Plot to Professor Hibbard's account of characters such as Sir Kenelm Digby in the 1630s. Hibbard's choice of the 1630s and 1640s as a subject thus starkly demonstrates one of the discontinuities between Catholic and Protestant English historiography. Over the past fifteen years, the post-revisionist movement in Stuart scholarship has increasingly pointed to the 1620s as the key decade for understanding the breakdown of English religio-political stability.[7]

Work on the Spanish match and the forced loan in particular has demonstrated both the tensions that existed within the polity and the ways in which politics functioned outside the traditional boundaries of parliament, court, and county-community. Yet the 1620s are a virtual no man's land for Catholic scholarship; A. J. Loomie's work on English exiles in Spain in James's reign is almost the only significant work on the subject, and even this work is not really integrated with the larger scholarship of the period.[18]

Hibbard's willingness to stray so far from the ground prepared by Haigh and Bossy has been the exception rather than the rule; most recent studies, even the best of them, have avoided heading too boldly into new territory. Thus, even though an excellent beginning was made in the study of Catholic political thought by Thomas Clancy, the fine studies that followed by Peter Holmes and Arnold Pritchard only focused upon the Elizabethans. As a result, our knowledge of English Catholic controversy, divinity, and polemic drops off after 1615. In addition, for all practical considerations the work of both Clancy and Holmes treated Catholic 'political thought' as if it was a corpus of literature internally constituted. There was little consideration of how Catholic political thinkers fit into larger English debates, or of how Catholic political thought was integrated into the fabric of Catholic life.[19]

Only in the last few years have a series of studies begun to point the way out of this morass. First, Anthony Milton's *Catholic and Reformed* has provided a crucial correction to the legions of scholars who have written separate Catholic and Protestant histories of Stuart religion. Milton has explored the dialectical process through which Catholic and Protestant identities were constituted, suggesting that if we are to understand how each opposing side participated in the ideological struggle for the soul of the nation, then we must understand how each side contributed to the other's self-perception.[20] Second, Alison Shell's work has shown that there needs to be far more detailed consideration of genres of Catholic literature, including poetry, balladry, and drama, that might be analysed as 'political' texts.[21] Third, Alexandra Walsham's groundbreaking work on *Church Papists* has pushed our knowledge of the relationship between Protestant and Catholic polemic to new heights, as well as raising important questions about the actual religious habits of the English populace.[22] And lastly, the work of Michael Questier has provided a myriad of exciting new directions for Catholic scholarship, from his analysis of the relationship between Jacobean Catholics and Catholic-hunters to his detailed study of the complex religious and political motivations that guided converts to Rome between 1580 and 1625.[23] All of these studies do not, it should be stressed, constitute anything like a coherent set of arguments or debates; it is yet to be seen how all of these fascinating approaches will be played out, or what sorts of interventions may still be made by Christopher Haigh, Eamon Duffy, and other well-established leaders in the field.

IV

This brief and admittedly incomplete survey of English Catholic historio-graphy has raised a series of questions and issues that we now want to discuss in some detail. To begin with, one of the most important contributions and greatest empirical strengths of revisionist historians of the Reformation has been their analysis of religious practice at the parish level. Indeed, the work of these historians has left the impression that one can best examine Catholi-cism as a strictly parochial religion. Yet there are serious limitations to such an approach. The experience and practice of Catholicism in the daily lives of English men and women was never strictly confined to the religious life of the parish; they could and did build their own institutions quite outside its limits. It was one of John Bossy's great insights to note that under a Protestant regime, Catholicism took place in abandoned barns and gentry households rather than in settings like parish churches that were designed for the purpose. Under Elizabeth and James, Catholics also engaged in the public profession of their religion as they embarked on pilgrimages to sites like St Winifred's Well or Mount Grace, traded books and held discussions in fields, sang verses attacking the national Church, or delivered speeches at their executions. We therefore want to focus on Catholic expressions of what Patrick Collinson has, in the context of English puritanism, called 'voluntary religion'; indeed we would stress that common experiences of exclusion from the established Church led Catholics and puritans to evolve very similar modes of religious activity.[24]

Similarly, Haigh's contention that the English mission failed to maximise the size and distribution of the potential Catholic community was based upon his conception of the mission as primarily a pastoral endeavour, organised around the need to administer sacraments and provide a Roman liturgy to those who required their services. This focus on the mission as a purely pastoral enterprise, however, has recently been challenged by the work of Michael Questier and Peter Lake. As their scholarship has shown, the work of missionary clerics could be remarkably aggressive, with strategies not unlike those of the best puritan ministers. Not only did they act as public defenders of Rome in the face of the Protestant Church and state, but they often assumed an evangelical stance, attempting to win over converts in Catholic circles or in prisons. Thus, while the physical presence of priests was clearly important in the operation of the mission, it is also necessary to recognise that the mission included tasks that far exceeded the bounds of private chaplaincy.[25] In practice, the mission involved a broad and variegated programme of activities, including the provision of Roman sacraments and liturgy, the public defence of the Church of Rome at trials, in prisons, and at executions, the composition of controversial literature to engage the regime in debate, and the printing and distribution of Catholic books. Certainly the more than sixteen hundred English Catholic books produced between 1558 and 1640, discovered in the bibliographic researches of Allison and Rogers, suggest that 'the mission' entailed a significant propagandist effort, and Alexandra Walsham has recently reinforced this impression.[26] The greatest evidence of these books' influence, moreover, lies not in the list of titles but in the *Responsa* of the English College at Rome, where hundreds of young men described the beginnings of their conversion to the Roman Church at the hands of Stapleton's translation of Bede or Parson's *Christian Directory*.[27] All of this suggests that historians should perhaps dwell less on the 'success' or 'failure' of the mission to provide the sacraments to individual Catholics, and focus more on analysing the structures, institutions, and strategies it employed.

Another point of interest is the persistent claim in current writing on the English Catholic laity that they were 'politically quiescent.' This was in some ways one of the great paradoxes of Bossy's thesis: the 'first dissenters' were relatively apolitical. This point was perhaps the one area of implicit agreement between Bossy and Haigh, and their conclusions have been seamlessly integrated into subsequent accounts of county politics or studies of the provincial gentry. J. T. Cliffe, likewise, found the Catholic gentry in Yorkshire to be mostly concerned with protecting the religion of their households by paying recusancy fines in exchange for de facto toleration.[28] Even in her study of political Catholicism at the Caroline court, Caroline Hibbard judged that the political creatures who inhabited this cosmopolitan world were a different breed from Catholics in the provinces.

Arguments that posit the provincial Catholic gentry as dissociated from either the court or mission bases in London, however, rest upon a distinction between 'court' and 'country' and a view of the self-sufficient county community that are no longer tenable in light of recent writing on early Stuart England. Many revisionist accounts of seventeenth-century political history have questioned the simple division between court and country attitudes, while the work of post-revisionist scholars like Ann Hughes has done much to challenge claims that county communities had little communication with the capital or interest in political matters.[29] As these historians have demonstrated, the counties were not islands unto themselves; even provincials without direct access to public life took an interest in parliamentary proceedings, court scandals, foreign policy, and other matters of 'high politics'. In light of this research, the complete isolation of the Catholic gentry in a disconnected system of recusant households seems questionable. We would suggest that post-revisionist models of political action without the institutional focus of parliament during the 1630s can be extremely useful in considering how Catholics discussed political issues and broadcast their opinions while they were officially disenfranchised. If Walter Yonge of Devonshire and William

Davenport of Cheshire could receive news and information from the capital from printed accounts or manuscript newsletters and separates, should it surprise us that Sir John Southworth, Sir Thomas Tresham, or even more humble characters like Peter Mowle likewise received such items of interest from their friends and missionary contacts?[30]

Catholic engagement in politics also should not be a surprise since highly 'political' issues were at the heart of the English Reformation: between 1534 and 1640 there were constant debates over acceptable levels of civil and religious conformity and over the place of Catholics within the polity. The positions in these debates were far from stable, and strange bedfellows often emerged; puritans and Jesuits converged in their attacks on church papistry, while many Catholic secular priests and their lay followers wholeheartedly supported the government's attacks on Jesuits. Religious disputes could be loaded with political dynamite. The Appellant Controversy over the structure of the Catholic Church *in* England, for instance, like the Admonition Controversy over the structure of the Church *of* England, was as much about loyalty to the regime and the potentially destabilising effects of evangelism as it was about religious doctrine. Similarly, both Catholics and puritans in the last years of Elizabeth's reign engaged in that most characteristic early modern political activity, debate over the succession; yet most of their pamphlets aimed not to derail James's claim to the throne for religious reasons but to pressure him into political alliance with their co-religionists when he inevitably came to power.

These ideas call into question another current trend in Catholic historiography, as well as 'mainstream' English historiography: an emphasis on consensus, quietude, and ideological indifference. In the narrative of English Catholicism offered by Lucy Wooding, for instance, the Reformation itself might almost be dismissed as a misunderstanding rather than the greatest revolution experienced in early modern society.[31] Similarly, the work of Ian Green and Muriel McClendon has emphasised the quest for consensus (if not always its achievement) and common pietistic practices among nearly all English Christians.[32] In the sense that these narratives move us beyond the apologetic and martyrological accounts written by Catholic historians of the early twentieth century, they are extremely constructive. But by minimising the importance of religious differences in this period, these historians have missed the importance of polemic, an ironically productive arena of interaction between Protestant and Catholic communities. Early modern religion was not only about formal beliefs and practices, but also about the ways those beliefs and practices were *glossed*. Hence it was not unimportant that even so devout a Protestant as Archbishop Parker could be accused of 'popery' in the controversy over vestments in the 1560s; he and his opponents differed almost imperceptibly on doctrine, but the rift created in the Church of England was no less real for it. On a more popular level, some toleration for Catholicism clearly existed in every English community, but that toleration was always balanced on the head of a pin. When it collapsed, as in 1588, 1623, and 1642, it was not because of changes in people's beliefs but because of changes in the public discourse of confessional identity.

V

Another central issue that this volume will explore is the vexed question of defining Catholics and Catholicism. Typically, histories of Catholicism after the Elizabethan settlement have discussed Catholic identities within the narrow framework established by conformity records, describing people as conformists, recusants, and (more recently) church papists. But as Michael Questier's study of conversion has shown, historians should not rely too heavily upon ecclesiastical performance as a barometer of religious conviction, since 'some recusants did not see statutory conformity at the dictates of Protestant churchmen as a permanent break with their Catholic past, while for others it had a seriousness that went far beyond church papistry'.[33] Indeed, it would be useful for historians of Catholicism to follow the example of debates in recent years over the construction of Protestant identities during the crucial years of the later Reformation. As scholars such as Patrick Collinson and Peter Lake have argued, puritan identity was a composite of theological beliefs, ecclesiology, 'styles of piety', and even social habits, and never constituted bare subscription to a single doctrine. A similarly broad approach to the study of post-Reformation Catholicism in England would examine the religious identities of Catholics as they were shaped by a number of factors, including doctrinal beliefs, ecclesiastical allegiances, religious prejudices, and political positions.

Indeed, in the case of Catholicism political positions were especially significant, since defining who was a full member of the Catholic community was often at the very heart of intra-Catholic political debates. We now understand that large numbers of early modern English people straddled the confessional fence, receiving both Roman and Anglican sacraments, selecting portions of the *Book of Common Prayer* that most reflected their Catholic upbringing, and acknowledging the monarch as supreme head of the Church while at the same time wishing for that monarch to promulgate doctrine more like the pope's. Whether or not these fence-sitters were 'Catholic' was a question constantly canvassed from the break with Rome onwards, with opinions shifting as political fortunes changed. Even the same people could change their minds with changing political realities. Reginald Pole, for instance, blurred all distinctions between heresy and schism in his writings in the 1530s, declaring supporters of the royal supremacy to be not merely outside the fold of the visible Church but followers of Satan; in the very different circumstances of

1554, he congratulated Henrician 'schismatics' such as Stephen Gardiner for successfully resisting the tide of heresy.[34]

It should be no surprise, then, that historians have been unable to agree on how many Catholics there were in early modern England. We would suggest that the whole idea of counting Catholics itself makes little sense, being conditioned by the static categories of theological certainty rather than the fluid categories of political ambiguity. Even if instead of our limited and ambiguous sources we were suddenly granted a beatific vision of English religion, with each individual's personal beliefs visible 'not through a glass darkly but face to face', the question of how many Catholics there were in England would *still* be unanswerable; any boundary that we chose to draw would simply recreate the highly contested political position of one or more early modern partisans. In Henry VIII's reign, for instance, many Catholic traditionalists included on their lists of government heretics such noted conservatives as John Longland, Richard Rich, and Stephen Gardiner; what, besides their comparative political weakness and inability to impose their views upon their neighbours, makes us think they were wrong? In Elizabeth's reign, many conforming Catholics were given communion by Catholic priests despite being technically schismatic and by some accounts excommunicate; who shall we accept as the arbiter of the 'community' and for what reason? In Charles I's reign, moderate puritans could be accused by radical separatists of 'popery', while those same moderate puritans could be accused by Arminians and Roman Catholics of radical separatism; can we not see the Civil War itself as a political struggle through which such ambiguities were disputed? From this perspective, the Reformation was not only a dispute over ideas themselves but a process by which those ideas were peddled, resisted, accommodated, manipulated, and imposed.

We would thus suggest that re-contextualising Catholic experiences within the larger narrative of English history can add much-needed clarity to scholarly debates over the definition and boundaries of Catholicism. Historians currently have a multitude of terms with which to wrestle: 'papist', 'recusant', 'Romanist', 'church papist', 'conservative', 'traditionalist', 'unreformed', and so on. Many of these terms, however, do not refer to groups of people at all, but to tendencies that might be experienced by all manner of people whom we would only with great hesitation call 'Catholics'. Indeed, 'traditionalism' or 'conservatism' in religious matters, and even experimentation with Roman books or services, were part of the normal spectrum of English religious activity. As Michael Questier has shown, dabbling with Catholicism was as recognisable a feature of Elizabethan elite society as experimentation with illicit substances often is in the modern world. Rather than trying to identify people as 'traditionalists' or 'Romanists', then, we see it as much more productive to consider these labels as modifiers: someone might have traditionalist feelings towards the sacraments or express Romanist tendencies in ecclesiology. By taking this perspective, we would highlight the interactions between Catholics and Protestants and the remarkable permeability of Catholicism rather than the exclusiveness of confessional boundaries. This is not to say that boundaries were not important; Catholics spent much of their polemical energy trying to define and even isolate themselves as a community. Yet in practice Catholicism and Protestantism could both be remarkably fluid, expanding socially, culturally, and politically to fill any available space, and definitions risk freezing that fluidity.

In all of this, we would do well to heed Michael Questier's warning that 'it is a misreading to see the English Reformation just as a struggle between two tightly consolidated blocs, Roman and Protestant, facing each other across a deserted religious no-man's-land'.[35] We must be precise in our terminology not in order to herd people into separate and fixed ecclesiological pens, but in order to understand better their own nagging insecurities about the ambiguities of religious identity.

VI

Lastly, we want to highlight certain 'public' aspects of Catholicism. Scholars have tended to concentrate upon the private, devotional life of Catholics, shaping the way they approach the significant body of literary sources produced by Catholics in this period. Despite the importance of Louis Martz's thesis that seventeenth-century English metaphysical verse was influenced by the meditative strategies of Luis de Granado and Gaspar Loarte, most literary scholars have continued to analyse English Catholic literature as if it were private and inward-looking.[36] Yet on the Protestant side of the spectrum, the work of scholars such as David Norbrook and Nigel Smith has heightened our appreciation of the polemical and highly political aspects of Renaissance literature. These insights have only recently been applied to English Catholic literature, especially in the work of Alison Shell.[37] In her recent study, for instance, Shell has emphasised the public and polemical aspects of Catholic literature that attacked both the Protestant Church and the political regime.

Catholics were also just as adept as their Protestant neighbours at the 'performance' of political action in public settings, but there has thus far been little research into the ways in which Protestants and Catholics joined each other's debates and imitated each other's political genres. For instance, while the connections between Protestant and Catholic resistance theories are well known, it is much less well appreciated how interconnected were the processes of Protestant and Catholic martyrdom on the stage of political theatre; William Prynne's spectacularly public testing of boundaries and subsequent mutilation owed a great deal to the model of Edmund Campion, while Campion's script can itself be read as an inverted chapter out of John Foxe.[38] Similarly, it is well known that Protestants glossed and circulated Catholic texts from Augustine to Bellarmine, but virtually no one has noticed how busily English Catholics were glossing and circulating all manner of texts from treatises to broadsides, many of them ostensibly 'Protestant', reinterpreting the same texts through which we habitually reconstruct English history in unapologetically Catholic ways. It seems clear that we must examine these practices together, observing their mutual contributions to a common political culture.

In all of these cases, we would stress that Catholic self-identity brought with it a whole host of issues, most crucially the problem of reconciling (for those who sought reconciliation) Catholic religion with allegiance to the English crown, and we should not imagine that Catholics struggled with these issues in private. Not only did Protestant polemicists have their own 'solutions' to offer, but many Protestants – including not only radical puritans but also the likes of Edmund Grindal and even William Laud – faced structurally similar problems themselves. The logic of the royal supremacy, with its odd displacement of theological doctrine into parliamentary debates and privy council meetings, meant that people of virtually all religious stripes had the shared experience of being at one time or another beleaguered minorities subject to state-sponsored persecution. Thus many of the centrally contested issues of early modern English culture fundamentally transcended the confessional divide: the necessity of religious conformity versus respect for individual conscience; the desire for confessional alliances in foreign policy versus the realities of state interests; and the political authorities' relentless manipulation of religious doctrine versus the practising Christian's need for doctrinal stability. All of these issues were canvassed in public settings by Protestants and Catholics alike, and it is only now being realised how closely interconnected their arguments were.

The issue of the public face of Catholicism is also important when considering the relationship between 'official' Catholicism (whether preached or printed) and the 'unofficial' Catholicism that was actually received and practised by the Catholic 'public'. One common approach to this issue is to posit that the brand of religion peddled by English Catholic missionaries was antithetical to the 'traditional' religion of the people. We would prefer, however, to utilise the work of both historians of English Protestantism and historians of continental Catholicism who have cast doubt on any such stark distinctions between 'popular' and 'elite' religion after the Reformation. The work of Tessa Watt, Ethan Shagan, and Adam Fox, for instance, has shown that we should not be too sceptical of the abilities of illiterate and semi-literate people to hear, discuss, and provide their own interpretations of extremely complex issues of theology, ecclesiology, court politics, and so on.[39] At the same time, the essays in Tim Harris's important collections *Popular Culture in*

England, c. 1500–1850 and *The Politics of the Excluded* challenge the assumption that either 'popular' or 'elite' culture can be separated in any meaningful sense from English culture as a whole.[40] On the continental side, works by historians such as Keith Luria, Philip Hoffman, and Henry Kamen have all suggested a far more complex picture of the interaction between elite, clericalist Counter-Reformation Catholicism and the traditional Catholicism of the people.[41] While in some circumstances there was significant friction between these contrasting religious styles, in nearly all cases communities evolved composite forms that combined their own ideas and practices with the views of the ecclesiastical elites.

All of this public religiosity belies that the idea that English Catholicism can be studied as a purely private exercise in conscientious devotion. The Reformation and Counter-Reformation were complex processes of revolution, resistance, collaboration, and reaction; any Catholic who withdrew from public life and elected not to engage in these processes was necessarily making as bold a public statement of his or her religio-political views as the most ardent revolutionary.

VII

It is our fundamental contention that all scholars of early modern England, whether specialising in religion, politics, social history, gender history, or whatever branch of scholarly endeavour, have a great deal to learn from the subject of English Catholicism.[42] By the same token, English Catholic historians cannot produce meaningful interventions in the larger flow of English historiography without being more aware of that historiography and how their own work might relate to it. The goal of this project is thus to take advantage of the wide variety of talented scholars with an interest in Catholicism, and to use that interest to re-contextualise English Catholicism within the scholarly world of mainstream English historiography. By combining the efforts of historians of Catholicism and historians of Protestant ecclesiastical history, we hope to reach out to both communities and produce a more meaningful dialogue. The various scholars assembled in this book have all separately reached the conclusion that the English Catholic community was defined as much by its interactions with the rest of English society as by its refusals to engage in such interactions. At the same time, we have all discovered ways in which Protestant England, in its political, religious, and social structures, was influenced by or constructed itself in reference to its Catholic population. By broadcasting these discoveries and showing something of the rich texture of Catholic experience in early modern England, we hope that this book will go some way towards banishing an unfortunate and unproductive barrier within early modern English historiography.

NOTES

1 For the 'continuity of Catholicism', see Christopher Haigh, 'The Continuity of Catholicism in the English Reformation', in Christopher Haigh (ed.), *The English Reformation Revised* (Cambridge, 1987).

2 See Anthony Milton, *Catholic and Reformed: The Roman and Protestant Churches in English Protestant Thought, 1600-1640* (Cambridge, 1995); Peter Lake with Michael Questier, *The Antichrist's Lewd Hat: Protestants, Papists and Players in Post-Reformation England* (New Haven, 2002).

3 The latter subject is under investigation by Margaret Sena, for instance in her 'William Blundell and the Networks of Catholic Dissent in Post-Reformation England', in Alexandra Shepard and Phil Withington (eds), *Communities in Early Modern England* (Manchester, 2000).

4 A. G. Dickens, *The English Reformation* (London, 1964).

5 See, for instance, Christopher Haigh, *Reformation and Resistance in Tudor Lancashire* (London, 1975); Margaret Bowker, *The Henrician Reformation: The Diocese of Lincoln under John Longland 1521–1547* (Cambridge, 1981); J. J. Scarisbrick, *The Reformation and the English People* (Oxford, 1984).

6 Christopher Haigh, *English Reformations: Religion, Politics, and Society under the Tudors* (Oxford, 1993); Eamon Duffy, *The Stripping of the Altars: Traditional Religion in England 1400-1580* (New Haven, 1992).

7 For attempts to move forward from these interpretations, see for instance Peter Marshall, *Beliefs and the Dead in Reformation England* (Oxford, 2002); Peter Marshall and Alec Ryrie (eds), *The Beginnings of English Protestantism* (Cambridge, 2002); Ethan Shagan, *Popular Politics and the English Reformation* (Cambridge, 2003).

8 See, for instance, Nicholas Tyacke, *Anti-Calvinists: The Rise of English Arminianism, c.1590–1640* (Oxford, 1987); Conrad Russell, *The Causes of the English Civil War* (Oxford, 1990).

9 Diarmaid MacCulloch, *Thomas Cranmer: A Life* (New Haven, 1996); Margaret Spufford (ed.), *The World of Rural Dissenters, 1520–1725* (Cambridge, 1995).

10 Haigh, *English Reformations*.

11 See, for instance, Richard Cust, *The Forced Loan and English Politics, 1626–1628* (Oxford, 1987); Thomas Cogswell, *The Blessed Revolution: English Politics and the Coming of War, 1621–1624* (Cambridge, 1989); Alastair Bellany, *The Politics of Court Scandal in Early Modern England: News Culture and the Overbury Affair, 1603–1660* (Cambridge, 2002).

12 Michael Bush, *The Pilgrimage of Grace: A Study of the Rebel Armies of October 1536* (Manchester, 1996); see also Shagan, *Popular Politics and the English Reformation*, ch. 3.

13 John Bossy, *The English Catholic Community, 1570-1850* (London, 1975).

14 Christopher Haigh, 'The Fall of a Church or the Rise of a Sect? Post-Reformation Catholicism in England', *HJ*, 21 (1978), 181–6.

15 Haigh, 'The Continuity of Catholicism in the English Reformation'; Christopher Haigh, 'The Church of England, the Catholics, and the People', in Christopher Haigh (ed.), *The Reign of Elizabeth I* (Basingstoke, 1984); Christopher Haigh, 'From Monopoly to Minority: Catholicism in Early Modern England', *TRHS*, 5th series, 31 (1981), 129–47.

16 Caroline Hibbard, *Charles I and the Popish Plot* (Chapel Hill, 1983).

17 See Cust, *The Forced Loan*; Cogswell, *The Blessed Revolution*; Richard Cust and Ann Hughes (eds), *Conflict in Early Stuart England: Studies in Religion and Politics, 1603–1642* (London, 1989).

18 A. J. Loomie, *Spain and the Jacobean Catholics*, 2 vols (London, 1973–8).

19 Thomas H. Clancy, *Papist Pamphleteers: The Allen-Persons Party and the Political Thought of the Counter-Reformation in England, 1572–1615* (Chicago, 1964); Peter Holmes, *Resistance and Compromise: The Political Thought of the Elizabethan Catholics* (Cambridge, 1982); Arnold Pritchard, *Catholic Loyalism in Elizabethan England* (Chapel Hill, 1979).

20 Milton, *Catholic and Reformed*.

21 Alison Shell, *Catholicism, Controversy, and the English Literary Imagination, 1558–1660* (Cambridge, 1999).

22 Alexandra Walsham, *Church Papists: Catholicism, Conformity, and Confessional Polemic in Early Modern England* (Woodbridge, 1993).

23 See particularly, among his many works on these subjects, Michael Questier, *Conversion, Politics, and Religion in England, 1580-1625* (Cambridge, 1996); Peter Lake and Michael Questier, 'Puritans, Papists, and the "Public Sphere" in Early Modern England: The Edmund Campion Affair in Context', *The Journal of Modern History*, 72 (2000), 587–627; Michael Questier, 'The Politics of Religious Conformity and the Accession of James I', *HJ*, 41 (1998), 14–30; Michael Questier, 'Practical Antipapistry during the Reign of Elizabeth I', *JBS*, 36 (1997), 371–96.

24 Patrick Collinson, *The Religion of Protestants: The Church in English Society 1559–1625* (Oxford, 1982), ch. 6.

25 Peter Lake and Michael Questier, 'Agency, Appropriation and Rhetoric Under the Gallows: Puritans, Romanists and the State in Early Modern England', *PP*, 153 (1996), 64–107; Peter Lake and Michael Questier, 'Prisons, Priests and People', in Nicholas Tyacke (ed.), *England's Long Reformation 1500-1800* (London, 1998).

26 ARCR; Alexandra Walsham, '"Domme Preachers?" Post-Reformation English Catholicism and the Culture of Print', *PP*, 168 (2000): 72–123.

27 See Alison Shell's chapter in this volume.

28 J. T. Cliffe, *The Yorkshire Gentry from the Reformation to the Civil War* (London, 1969).

29 Conrad Russell, *Parliaments and English Politics, 1621–1629* (Oxford, 1979); Ann Hughes, *Politics, Society, and Civil War in Warwickshire, 1620-1660* (Cambridge, 1987).

30 This paragraph was largely written by Margaret Sena, and these ideas continue to be expanded in her important work on early modern Catholic manuscript networks.

31 Lucy Wooding, *Rethinking Catholicism in Reformation England* (Oxford, 2000).

32 Ian Green, *The Christian's ABC: Catechisms and Catechizing in England c.1530–1740* (Oxford, 1996); Muriel McClendon, *The Quiet Reformation: Magistrates and the Emergence of Protestantism in Tudor Norwich* (Stanford, 1999).

33 Questier, *Conversion, Politics, and Religion in England*, p. 117.

34 See chapter 3 by Ethan Shagan in this volume.

35 Questier, *Conversion, Politics, and Religion in England*, p. 9.

36 Louis Martz, *The Poetry of Meditation: A Study in English Religious Literature of the Seventeenth Century* (New Haven, 1954).

37 David Norbrook, *Poetry and Politics in the English Renaissance* (London, 1984); Nigel Smith, *Literature and Revolution in England, 1640–1660* (New Haven, 1994); Shell, *Catholicism, Controversy, and the English Literary Imagination.*

38 On the subject of martyrdom, these connections have now been masterfully explored in Brad Gregory, *Salvation at Stake: Christian Martyrdom in Early Modern Europe* (Cambridge, Mass., 1999). But Gregory focuses on actual martyrdom rather than paying as much attention as we would suggest to the rhetoric of martyrdom and its political uses.

39 Tessa Watt, *Cheap Print and Popular Piety, 1550-1640* (Cambridge, 1991); Shagan, *Popular Politics and the English Reformation*; Adam Fox, *Oral and Literate Culture in England, 1500-1700* (Oxford, 2000).

40 Tim Harris (ed.), *Popular Culture in England, c.1500-1850* (New York, 1995); Tim Harris (ed.), *The Politics of the Excluded, c.1500-1850* (Basingstoke, 2001).

41 Philip Hoffman, *Church and Community in the Diocese of Lyon, 1500-1789* (New Haven, 1984); Keith Luria, *Territories of Grace: Cultural Change in the Seventeenth-Century Diocese of Grenoble* (Berkeley, 1991); Henry Kamen, *The Phoenix and the Flame: Catalonia and the Counter-Reformation* (New Haven, 1993).

42 On gender history, see Frances Dolan, *Whores of Babylon: Catholicism, Gender, and Seventeenth-Century Print Culture* (Ithaca, 1999).

Chapter 2

Is the Pope Catholic?
Henry VIII and the semantics of schism

Peter Marshall

The question of whether Henry VIII remained a Catholic after his break with Rome, and of whether the religious settlement he subsequently imposed represented 'Catholicism without the Pope', has long been a staple of historical and theological controversy. Henry's first modern biographer, A. F. Pollard, was insistent that the king 'never wavered in his adhesion to the cardinal points of the Catholic faith', a judgement endorsed in the 1930s by the French historian Gustave Constant, and in the 1940s by the Anglo-Catholic Henry Maynard Smith.[1] Yet at the same time, in a work of careful historical theology, E. C. Messenger took his fellow Catholic Constant to task for attempting to 'whitewash' Henry, solemnly pronouncing of the English Church that after 1535 'we must decline to give it the title of "Catholic", or to speak of its bishops as "Catholic bishops"'.[2] An equally emphatic judgement was reached by the priest-historian Philip Hughes, author of an undervalued three-volume account of the Reformation in England. Hughes syllogistically disposed of Henry's claims to be a Catholic ruler: Catholics are defined 'at all times' as those recognising the authority of the Church whose supreme earthly ruler is the Pope – a test Henry quite clearly fails.[3] Henry's most significant twentieth-century biographer, J. J. Scarisbrick, leaned in the same direction, writing that '"Catholicism without the Pope" will not do ... there can be no doubt that the Henrician Church took long strides towards the Reformers'.[4] Into the 1990s, scholars remained divided over whether 'Henrician Catholicism' should be regarded as a tautology or an oxymoron. L. F. Solt argued that in 'substantive matters of heresy, theology, and the cure of souls' the Henrician settlement could indeed be considered 'Catholicism without the Pope', a view shared, with caveats, by Glyn Redworth.[5] In a general survey of 1993 Richard Rex described 'Catholicism without the Pope' as a 'slick label' doing little justice to the idiosyncratic nature of Henry's religious settlement. Yet he accepts that the Henrician Church presented a fundamentally conservative doctrinal face, the creation of a king whose conscience 'had been formed, and largely remained, within the Catholic tradition'.[6] Any such concession is stoutly repudiated by the American scholar Paul O'Grady: 'a *mélange* of incoherent prejudices is very far from a firm Catholic theology, anti-papal or not'. Henry VIII was not a Catholic because 'he adamantly refused to define, or allow to be defined, the corporate nature of a visible, teaching Church'.[7] In the face of such entrenched positions, some historians have attempted a bold outflanking manoeuvre: the revival of a historio-graphical tradition regarding the Henrician Reformation as predominantly humanist or 'Erasmian' in character, and involving (at an official level at least) a more or less coherent blending of Catholic and reforming influences.[8]

Was Henry then a Catholic, and was Henricianism Catholicism? It seems to be a matter of perception and definition. But there is a danger here, whichever side of the argument one is inclined to support – the temptation to 'reify' or 'essentialise', to approach the Henrician religious scene via a notional and arguably ahistorical conception of Catholic 'orthodoxy': so many points deducted for dissolving monasteries, others awarded for retaining the mass. In fairness, much modern scholarship on the early English Reforma-tion has been keen to avoid anachronism and confessional rigidity, anxious to recognise the fluidity of religious positions and the problematic nature of religious labels. Few scholars writing today would commit N. S. Tjernagel's solecism, and refer to 'the leading Roman Catholic conservatives' among Henry's advisors in the 1540s, or to Henry's own 'personal faith in Roman Catholic theology'.[9] Indeed, it is questionable whether it is at all helpful to call Henry a 'Roman Catholic' even before he broke with Rome. As Diarmaid MacCulloch has observed, 'this familiar term makes no sense before the Reformation ... when everyone consciously or unconsciously formed part of the same Catholic church structure'.[10] Historians have become accustomed to recognising that, before the Council of Trent, Catholic belief was hardly rigidly codified, and also that 'evangelical' is a more apt designation than 'Protestant' for much early sixteenth-century heterodoxy.[11] But well-intentioned attempts to exclude anachronism can run the risk of readmitting it by the back door. In an influential study of Henrician humanism, Maria Dowling announced that, 'because such terms are anachronistic', she would not describe any of the subjects of Henry VIII as either 'Catholics' or 'Protestants' and, in a magisterial biography of Archbishop Cranmer, MacCulloch has likewise dispensed with the descriptive label 'Catholic', for fear of 'lapsing into anachronism and partisanship'.[12] There is no doubt that 'Protestant' is an anachronistic construction. A neologism of the late 1520s, it seeped into English usage during the early 1530s as a description of the German princes in opposition to Charles V.[13] It does not seem to have been applied to the domestic scene in Henry VIII's reign, or even much in Edward VI's. At the latter's coronation procession in 1547, a place was allotted to 'the Protestants', meaning the ambassadors of the German reforming Princes.[14] 'Catholic', by contrast, is a term which permeates the religious discourse of the age. It is, as we shall see, a highly problematic, even a protean word. But it is precisely for that reason that we are obliged to confront it: historical understanding is not served by banishing categories of classification employed by contemporaries because they might turn out to be partisan or imprecise. The following discussion therefore tracks occurrences of the word 'Catholic' (adjective, noun, occasionally adverb) across the textual landscape of Henrician England. The purpose, it must be stressed, is not to pronounce on whether Henry was *really* a Catholic, or whether the experience of 1534–47 was emphatically one of 'Catholicism without the Pope'. It is rather to observe contemporaries asking themselves these very questions and, by listening carefully to the modalities and inflections of their replies, to attempt to come to a more nuanced under-standing of the ways in which their religious identities were formed and tested. The catchpenny question in the chapter title is not a merely rhetorical one.

I

'Catholic' – word and concept – was woven deeply into the liturgical and doctrinal fabric of pre-Reformation England. At every mass, the priest offered the sacrifice on behalf of the Holy Catholic Church ('pro ecclesia tua sancta catholica'), and in the creed, belief was affirmed in 'unam sanctam catholicam et apostolicam ecclesiam'.[15] In a sermon of 1521, Bishop John Fisher remarked that the Church was called in the creed 'catholica, that is to saye unyversall ... bycause it is not lymyt to any certayne nacyon, but it is comen to all nacyons'.[16] But alongside its descriptive application to a supranational institutional Church, 'Catholic' carried for contemporaries a set of more emotive, normative meanings. Pre-eminently, it characterised orthodox Christian belief, what the Brigittine monk William Bonde termed 'the catholicall or generall fayth of the chirche', commending those 'that in a true herte catholycally byleveth the same'.[17] A devotional treatise on the Eucharist might be addressed 'to all good catholyke persones'.[18] In an early sixteenth-century translation of the French romance, *Melusine*, the eponymous lady protests that 'my byleve is as a catholyque byleve oughte to be', and requires her beloved to swear 'upon all the sacraments and othes that a man very catholoque and of good feith may doo'.[19]

Such descriptors point to negative as much as to positive attributes, for to be a 'Catholic man' meant as much as anything else not to be a heretic, to be like the early fifteenth-century regent of Scotland, the Duke of Albany, described by the chronicler Andrew Wyntoun as 'a constant Catholike, all Lollard he hatyd and heretike'.[20] In a famous sermon of 1511, John Colet warned that heretics might seem to be 'catholyke and faithfull men', and in Archbishop Warham's anti-Lollard sweep through Kent that same year, sentences specified deviation from 'the universal, catholic and apostolic church'.[21] One side of the linguistic coin was thus a token of devotional commitment, the other an instrument of ideological control. Almost inevitably, the latter emphasis was accentuated when new heretical currents flowed into England from abroad through the 1520s. In 1529 Convocation condemned works by Tyndale, Frith, and others as 'contraria fidei catholicae', and an anti-heresy proclamation of the same year boasted that the King's 'noble realm of England hath of long time continued in the true Catholic faith of Christ's religion'. A second proclamation of June 1530 condemned imported books intending 'to pervert and withdraw the people from the Catholic and true faith of Christ'.[22] Recanting heretics, such as William Goderidge in 1529, were made to promise 'to defend the Catholic faith of holy church'.[23] In June 1531, under episcopal suspicion, Nicholas Shaxton swore to uphold all 'articles and points as the Catholic Church of Rome believeth, holdeth, or maintaineth at this time'.[24]

Yet this explicit identification of the Catholic Church with the Roman Church begged the very question which a number of religious radicals were beginning to pose. At his execution in August 1531, Thomas Bilney denied that he had ever said he did not believe in the Catholic Church. But he admitted that at one time he had inadvisedly said that 'I believe not ecclesiam catholicam as it is now used'.[25] Suggestions that the real Catholic Church was something other than the institutional Church in communion with Rome infuriated the defenders of orthodoxy. In his sermon against Luther of 1521, John Fisher remarked that it was characteristic of heretics down the ages to 'repute themeself and theyr adherentes only to be of the chirche catholyke'.[26] Germaine Gardiner attacked Frith for portraying 'the holy Catholic Church of Christ' as a 'universal church of the elect', rather than as 'the known church' and 'the governors of the same'.[27] The theme was a major preoccupation of the polemical writings of England's best-known anti-Lutheran propagandist, Thomas More. 'Catholic' was for More a blunt-edged rhetorical weapon, a simple antonym of heretic. The 'trew catholyke folke' and the 'false heretykes' frequently stand in sharp juxtaposition.[28] But More's concern with the articulation of an explicitly Catholic identity went beyond mere name-calling. He argued that Luther's propensity to draw distinctions between the Church of the pope and the true Catholic Church would 'reduce the Catholic Church of Christ to two or three heretics buzzing in a corner'. Tyndale was admonished to submit himself to the judgement of 'the hole catholyke chyrche, not the chyrch of onely electys whyche no man can knowe, but unto the catholyke knowen chyrche'.[29] This phrase, 'the known Catholic Church', reverberates through More's massive *Confutation of Tyndale's Answer*.[30] Perhaps the most epigrammatic definition is to be found at the very outset of More's polemical career, in the *Responsio ad Lutherum* of 1523, where it is stated that the 'common and perceptible multitude of men professing the name and faith of Christ is the Catholic Church by whose teaching the scripture is determined and the faith is learned and recognised with certainty'.[31]

Subsequently, More accepted the challenge to prove that 'these wordes of the crede, *sanctam ecclesiam catholicam*, be understanden of the knowen catholyque chyrche', and he referred the reader to St Augustine's emphasis on the *universality* of the true Catholic Church, 'spred abrode thorowe out the hole worlde'.[32] Augustine's *obiter dictum*, that he would not have believed the Gospel, had not the authority of the Catholic Church moved him to, was a particular favourite of More's, cited at least thirty times in his writings.[33] For Augustine, More insisted, the adjective was in no sense detachable from the noun:

> evyn the very name he sayth of catholyke, that is to say universall, gave toward the gettyng of his credence the catholyke chyrche great authoryte, whych name of universall the same chyrche alone among so many heresyes hadde so obtayned, that where as every secte of heretykes wold fayne be taken for catholykes, yet yf a straunger shold come among them and aske where were any catholyke chyrche that he myghte go to, there were none heretyke that durst for shame bryng hym to any chyrch or any house of theyrs.[34]

More's persuasive rhetoric encased a paradox. The Catholic Church and its Catholic faith were represented in inclusionary terms, stressing their knowability and universality. But at same time, as continual referencing of past schisms and patristic disputes made clear, division, distinction, and exclusion were built into his definitions of what it was to be a Catholic: 'the generall catholyke churche is nat the nombre of all that embrace the name of Christ'. Heretics such as Luther, Zwingli, Wyclif and Tyndale 'wylfully leave and forsake the catholyke church and the catholyke faythe therof'.[35]

II

Even as More drew his line in the sand, seismic events were reshaping the ground beneath his feet. As England's links with the papacy were progressively severed in the early 1530s, the question of what it meant to be a Catholic man was reformulated in a new and pressing form. Could one be a Catholic without the pope, in spite of the pope? In a letter of February 1532, the Duke of Norfolk expressed satisfaction with the way he had hectored the papal ambassador; he had, he remarked, 'lyke a trew catholyke man discharged my conscience'.[36] Yet very different connotations of this powerful phrase were evoked a few weeks later when Thomas More met with George Throckmorton, an opponent of the government's legislative programme, in a little chamber in the parliament house. More told Throckmorton that he was 'very glad to hear the good report that goeth of you and that ye be so good a catholic man as ye be', and urged him to 'continue in the same way that ye began and be not afraid to say your conscience'.[37] In commending Throckmorton as a 'good catholic man', More might plausibly have claimed to be uttering a polite commonplace. In a work written that same year, More argued that it was appropriate for every member of the universal church to be called Catholic, something one could perceive 'by the very comon maner of every mannes talking, wherin every man sayth of an heretike, This man is no catholike man. And of him in whom they perceive by his faithful communicacion or his good verteouse christen workes, a good zele to the catholike fayth and doctrine, theie say, This is a good catholike man.'[38] But there is little doubt that More and Throckmorton's mutual recognition as Catholic men bespoke a coded commitment to oppose further moves against the papacy. The Lollards who referred to each other as 'known men' were perhaps not alone in England at this time in feeling a sense of a bonded secret identity.[39]

In the *Confutation*, More looked back to a time of persecution by Arians and Donatists, heretics who had grown so 'stronge and mighty that they had gotten into their secte the strength of greate princes of christendome'. But one thing marked them out as false believers: 'this word catholike ... made the difference betwene the true church and theirs'. Indeed, if any virtuous man of the Catholic Church met with another Christian, 'lest he might happe unware to meddle with ani heretike', he would demand of him first, 'arte thou a catholyque man?'[40] A thousand years later, the right to describe themselves as Catholic men was claimed as a badge of allegiance by irreconcilable opponents of the royal supremacy. In April 1540 the government got wind of a conspiracy in Calais centred around one of Lord Lisle's chaplains, Gregory Botolph. A witness deposed that Botolph had described Cardinal Pole as 'a good Catholyke man as ever I reasoned with', and had reported the pope's lamenting the condition of 'the good catholic men whiche be in ynglande'. Another witness was specifically asked by the commissioners 'yf ye hard hym not saie that Pole was a catholyke man?'[41]

Oppositionist rhetoric might lay claim to an exclusive Catholic identity openly as well as surreptitiously. After his condemnation for treason in July 1535, Thomas More put aside coded exhortations and oblique historical analogy to declare that 'this realm, being but one member and small part of the Church, might not make a particular law disagreeable with the general law of Christ's universal Catholic Church'. At his execution, More urged the onlookers 'to bear witness with him that he should now there suffer death in and for the faith of the Holy Catholic Church'.[42] Two weeks earlier, John Fisher had 'come hither to die for the faith of Christ's holy Catholic Church', and similar appeals to the authority of the Catholic Church seem to have been made at the execution of the three Carthusian priors and the Brigittine Richard Reynolds on 4 May 1535.[43] Writing to the Dominicans of Newcastle in early 1536 to explain why he had fled abroad, Prior Richard Marshall included among his grounds the teaching of the Catholic Church.[44] The same reasoning motivated a more famous exile, Reginald Pole, whose actions were justified 'afore God, and the Catholic Church'.[45] The most dangerous of Henry's internal opponents, the rebel leader Robert Aske, claimed that all men murmured against the Act of Supremacy, 'a mean of division from the unity of Catholic Church'.[46]

Whether or not Aske's view was as widely shared as he claimed, correspondence to and from the continent in the mid-1530s often evinced a sense that the English Church had ceased to be Catholic, that 'Catholics' in England were by definition the opponents of royal policy. Writing to the king in January 1532, Clement VII suggested that 'Catholics will grieve and heretics rejoice to hear that he has repudiated hys queen'.[47] A month later, the imperial ambassador Eustace Chapuys optimistically reported that the most part of Henry's subjects were 'good Catholics', whose refusal to live under an interdict might yet compel Henry to accept a papal sentence in his marital case.[48] That, of course, proved not to be the case, and by 1535 Catherine was writing to her imperial nephew urging him 'to bear in mind our holy Catholic Faith, and the peril in which this realm is standing for want of it'.[49] Shortly after Catherine's death the following year, Chapuys reported that her confessor, Jorge de Athequa, had tried to flee the country, 'finding that he could not live here as a Catholic'. In a letter to Charles V's counsellor Granvelle of around the same time, Chapuys included a bitterly ironic reference to Cranmer, 'this notable and good Catholic archbishop of Canterbury'.[50] Letters from the Emperor's proctor at Rome, Pedro Ortiz, reported that Fisher and More died 'for the Catholic faith'; that Catherine on her deathbed prayed God 'to bring back the Kingdom to the Catholic faith'; that Henry's excommunication was for 'his great sins against the Catholic faith'.[51] English travellers abroad in these years were sometimes left in no doubt that their hosts did not view them as fellow-Catholics. From Bilboa in June 1540, Roger Basyng lamented that the locals believed 'the busshop of rome and his cardynalles be Ecclesiam Catholicam, and he that denyeth this, they say is an heretycke and worthy to be brunte'.[52]

III

At home and abroad, then, the charge that the *Ecclesia Anglicana* had lost its claim to be part of the Catholic Church demanded refutation. As an irrevocable break with the papacy was being formalised in 1533–34, a number of opportunities were taken to reaffirm the Catholic identity of the English Church. The 1533 Act in Restraint of Appeals laid down that the clergy were to continue to administer sacraments in spite of any interdict from Rome 'as catholic and Christian men ought to do'.[53] The declarations accepting the royal supremacy imposed on religious houses and cathedral chapters from mid-1534 obliged signatories to preach the Word of God in a Catholic and orthodox way ('catholice et orthodoxe').[54] Similarly, an inhibition issued by Cranmer and other bishops in April of that year, requiring preachers to obtain new licences, instructed them not to teach anything that might 'bring in doubt and opinion the catholic and received doctrine of Christ's church'. A subsequent 'order taken for preaching, and bidding of the beads' required preachers to pray for 'the catholic church of this realm' and for the King, 'next unto God the only and supreme head of this catholic church of England'.[55] The clearest of all signals was contained in the 1534 Dispensations Act, which insisted that neither the King nor his subjects had any intention 'to decline or vary from the congregation of Christ's Church in any things concerning the very articles of the Catholic faith of Christendom'.[56] The politically astute among Henry's subjects quickly learned the style, whether the Cistercian monks of Coggeshall in 1536, complaining that their abbot had maintained the Bishop of Rome, in derogation of his duty to 'the supreme hede of the catholike chyrche of this realme', or the antiquary John Leland, in a dedication to the King rejoicing to see the 'craftely coloured doctrine of a rowte of the Romaine bishopes totally expelled oute of this your moste catholique realme'.[57]

'Catholic' was too valuable a piece of ideological currency to be lightly given away. Moreover, the political here was the personal, for if Henry was not '*the* Catholic King' (a title bagged by his Spanish erstwhile in-laws), he was in no doubt that he was *a* Catholic king, a motif which continued to shape the king's public and private persona. Thus, the proclamation against anabaptists and sacramentaries of November 1538 noted that 'his highness, like a godly and Catholic prince, abhorreth and detesteth the same sects'.[58] Other rulers might be chided for their insufficiencies on this score. In 1532 Henry let the Emperor understand that it would be 'not at all Catholic' if his manoeuvring for the kingdom of Hungary were to endanger Christendom. Requesting the hand-over of English exiles from the Netherlands in 1546, Henry sententiously reminded the governor that it was the 'part of a Christian ruler' to guard against 'the menace to the Catholic Faith through permitting heretics to spread their wicked opinions'.[59]

In May 1539, the evangelically-inclined Dean of Exeter, Simon Heynes, effused that Henry was 'cownted in all the world a christen catholik prince'.[60] That this was evidently not the case is suggested by the instructions the King himself drafted for Ralph Sadler on his departure to Scotland in February 1540, emphasising the importance of ensuring that James V was not deceived by 'persuasion of untrue and fayned tales', and was not to think of him 'otherwise than of every christen and catholique prince as he is in dede'.[61]

Even where Henry's status as a Catholic prince was recognised, it could be used to exhort as much as to flatter. In the early 1530s, more in hope than expectation, Thomas More was still praising Henry's 'moste catholyque purpose and entent' on the basis of his authorship of the *Assertio septem sacramentorum*.[62] Chapuys meanwhile was telling Henry he 'could not believe that so virtuous, wise, and Catholic a prince' would abandon Queen Catherine. When Henry replied that it was Charles who had shown him it was not always necessary to obey the pope, by appealing to a future council, Chapuys urged him to 'act like a good Catholic, to follow the same path and appeal to the Council'.[63]

Chapuy's reports of the mid-1530s suggest how the Catholic prince topos was being deployed for distinctly different purposes among Henry's leading servants. In May 1533 Edward Foxe informed the ambassador that since the King had been moved by the Holy Spirit to find that he could not keep Catherine as his wife, 'like a Catholic prince, he had separated from her'. Yet when news of Clement VII's final illness came the following year, Chapuys reported Norfolk and Exeter saying of Henry 'that like a Catholic prince, he would make no difficulty in obeying the new Pope'. At around the same time, Chapuys held a clandestine meeting with Lord Hussey, who expressed dismay that the Emperor, 'as a Catholic prince and chief of other princes', was not doing more to remedy matters in England.[64] Through 1535–36 the phrase became a verbal ping-pong ball in the diplomatic game-playing between Chapuys and Thomas Cromwell, each making sure to describe his own master as 'a virtuous and Catholic prince' while neglecting to extend the appellation to the other's.[65]

Henry's claim to be a just as much of a Catholic prince in 1535 as he had been in 1521 was thus a diplomatic resource as well as a piece of royal self-fashioning. It was a claim, moreover, with a considerable degree of theological ballast, for, in parallel with the divorce campaign and anti-papal propaganda of the 1530s, a new and distinctive ecclesiology was being forged for the Henrician Church, one in which assertions of an authentically 'Catholic' identity played an important part. An early and pithy statement was provided by an official tract of 1534, insisting that 'the Pope is neither the catholyke holy church of Christe, nor yet the head of the same', but merely 'a member thereof ... if he be a true Christen man'. Supporters of the pope who adduced 'this text *Credo sanctam ecclesiam catholicam*' spoke nothing to the purpose.[66] In a sermon preached and printed in the summer of 1535, Simon Matthewe invited his audience to commend to God 'the catholike church of christendom, in especial this churche of Englande'. He went on to clarify the relationship between the two. The Church was 'one misticall body, having dyvers membres deputed to dyverse offices'. Diversity of regions and countries did not make for diversity of Churches, but the 'unitie of fayth maketh all regions one church'.

This unity depended on the knowledge of Christ, so that many thousands are saved 'whiche never harde of Peter, nor yet of the bishop of Rome'. The Church of Rome was co-equal with all 'other churches in the worlde, both France, Britayne, Affrica, Persis', its bishop of no less or greater authority than 'at a poore citie in Italy called Eugubiu[m], or at Constantinople'.[67]

Very similar arguments were produced by a more significant Henrician theorist, the humanist Thomas Starkey. Starkey drew a distinction between political and spiritual unity; the former was no more than an agreement to enact and obey laws in common, while the latter was 'a certayne consente of spirite and mynde' established in His flock by Christ. This remained unbroken 'though there be never so moch diversitie of worldly policie', and it did not require papal headship. For having rejected papal claims, the Greeks were 'most uniustly noted, not to be as members of Christes universall and catholyke body'. The 'Indians' under 'Preter John, their kynge and heed' had been true professors for a thousand years without recognising papal authority, and it was entirely appropriate, Starkey thought, that the Armenian patriarch was termed *Catholicos* 'as he that was a trewe professour and maynteyner of the catholyke faythe'. Papal authority was at best a thing indifferent, taking its power from the consent of men 'and so som christian nations may it receyve and mayteyne, and some hit reiecte ... withoute anye breche of the christian unitie, by schism or heresie'.[68]

It should be evident therefore that supporters of the royal supremacy could recite without any qualms of conscience the creed's affirmation of 'the holy catholic Church'. Here, in fact, the regime could draw on the moral and intellectual authority of Erasmus, whose exposition of the creed was translated in 1533 by Cromwell's client, William Marshall, at the request of Thomas Boleyn.[69] Four tokens were provided by which the Catholic Church might be known, none of which were offensive to Henrician sensibilities: the authority of ancient councils, and that of canonised interpreters of scripture, the 'bredthe or largeness' of the Church, and the purity of life to be found within it. Erasmus also noted that the word 'ecclesia' had a double signification; on the one hand 'the prevy or secrete society and felowshyp of them that are predestinate to eternall lyfe', but also the totality of all who had received baptism.[70] This duality of meaning, which, as we have seen, was anathema to Thomas More, lay as a potential fault-line in the emergent landscape of Henrician ecclesiology. In his own exposition of the creed, in the official primer of 1535, Marshall distinctly emphasised the former sense, defining the Church as 'the congregation and comunyon of holy men, that is of righteous and faythfull men on the earth'.[71] The *Bishops' Book* of 1537 recognised that in scripture the word Church 'is taken sometime generally for the whole congregation of them that be christened and profess Christ's gospel: and sometime it is taken for the catholic congregation, or number of them only which be chosen, called, and ordained to reign with Christ in everlasting life', and a similar statement was supplied by the group of English and German theologians meeting in London in 1538.[72]

Interest in the Catholic Church as a congregation of the elect was, however, absent from the more conservative *King's Book* of 1543, and in the main the official formularies of Henry's reign were, like Matthew or Starkey, concerned with the nature of the Catholic Church as a visible institution. The *Bishops' Book* laid down that the Church was 'catholic' because 'it cannot be coarcted or restrained within the limits or bonds of any one town, city, province, region, or country; but ... is dispersed and spread universally throughout all the whole world'. It was composed of 'particular churches', between whom there was 'no difference in superiority, preeminence, or authority'. Therefore 'the church of Rome is not, nor cannot worthily be called the catholic church, but only a particular member thereof, and cannot challenge or vindicate of right, and by the word of God, to be head of this universal church'. Since (*à la* Starkey) the unity of the Church was 'a mere spiritual unity', particular churches might differ in outward rites and ceremonies without damaging the unity of the Catholic Church, and none of them 'ought to be reputed as a member divided or precided from the same, for any such cause of diversity or difference'.[73] The definition of the Catholic Church in the *King's Book* (approved by Convocation 'Pro Catholicis et Religiosis'[74]) followed that of 1537 in most respects, though with a still stronger condemnation of the 'hypocrisy and usurpation of the see and court of Rome'. The theme was elaborated that 'the church of Rome, being but a several church, challenging that name of *catholic* above all other, doeth great wrong to all other churches'; it had no more exclusive right to the name than 'the church of France, Spain, England, or Portugal, which be justly called catholic churches, in that they do profess, consent, and agree in one unity of true faith with other catholic churches'.[75]

Official determination to have this new doctrine understood was graphically displayed in May 1538 when an Observant friar, John Forest, was burned as a heretic for having maintained that 'the Holie Catholike Church was the Church of Rome, and that we ought to beleeve out of the same'.[76] In 1536 another suspected papalist, the Vicar of Croydon, Rowland Phillips, showed considerably greater circumspection when it was demanded of him 'whom he meant by the Catholic Church when he said that the Catholic Church shall never err in things that be necessary for Salvation?' He replied that he meant 'the universall multitude of Christian people, as well laymen as clergy, subjects as rulers'.[77]

IV

The precision of Phillips's reply, specifying clergy *and* laity, is significant, as this type of inclusionary language was a recurrent feature of the propaganda of the 1530s. Its characteristic note was struck by the Appeals Act of 1533, which defined the English Church as a 'body politic, compact of all sorts and degrees of people, divided in terms, and by names of spiritualty and temporalty'.[78] The polemical possibilities were explored in a tract by Thomas Swynnerton of the following year, significantly entitled *A Mustre of Scismatyke Bysshoppes of Rome*. Though the papists taught that the only way to discern the true word of God was by the spiritualty, lay people too were members of the 'the hole catholyke churche of god', whom the Holy Spirit would instruct in everything necessary for their salvation.[79] The common lawyer Christopher St German was much less of a theological radical than Swynnerton, but he too made use of the topos, accusing the clergy of 'meanynge only by that worde church, prestes: for all Catholyke people make the Churche, which is the spirituall mother, so that preestes be but onely a parte of it'.[80] The same point was made in a draft treatise prepared under conciliar auspices in 1539: 'the catholyque churche is a communion and congregation of all the ... hole clergye and realme considering the christen lay persons aswell as the clergye'.[81] This seems like tilting at a straw man, as it is unlikely that any papalist taught that the Catholic Church comprised the clergy only. Indeed, Thomas More had chastised Tyndale and Barnes for misrepresentation on this very point.[82] Nonetheless, the topos was clearly central to the articulation of a Henrician Catholic identity, one which saw itself as more authentically Catholic than a clericalist Roman model. One of the arguments put forward by a 1538 treatise on General Councils was that councils summoned by popes had displayed a flawed ecclesiology: princes and kings had been required to obey the councils, but neither they nor other laity had any voice there, the bishops, priests and religious supposing that they alone comprised the unerring universal Church. This, however, was a great error: 'the universall church is the congregation of all faithefull people'.[83]

The regime's recurrent interest in the idea of the General Council, a body represented in Henrician propaganda as quintessentially Catholic, was another important strand in the argument that 'Catholicism under the pope' was exclusionary and sectarian. By appealing to a General Council over the divorce, Henry was said in 1534 to have acted 'like a true Christened and catholike prince'.[84] In 1536, Thomas Starkey wrote that the usurped authority of the pope dispensed with 'the good and catholyke grounds and canonyke, propowned by generall counselles'.[85] In a letter to his former associate Reginald Pole, Starkey insisted that the pope had no power to dispense with 'laws made in General Councels, Catholic Laws and Universal grounds'.[86] The message that it was the pope who was the real schismatic was one Pole was hearing from other ex-friends simultaneously. When Cuthbert Tunstall wrote to condemn the wrong-headedness of Pole's *De Unitate Ecclesiae* he insisted that the king's purpose was not 'to separate himself from the Catholic Church, but to reduce his Church of England out of all captivity to foreign powers', a measure entirely compatible with the teaching of the eight General Councils.[87]

By the late 1530s the convocation of an actual council was the last thing Henry wanted to see, but official propaganda continued to affirm the ideal, while protesting against any council that might be summoned under papal auspices.[88] The treatise of 1538 made reference throughout to 'catholike general councilles' and argued that their function was to 'declare the trewe catholyke fayth, accordynge to the rules and grounds of scripture'. But at the present day, 'a free catholique generall councill' could only be convoked by kings and princes.[89] The *King's Book* insisted that the Bishop of Rome has no universal authority 'of any ancient catholic council'.[90]

In view of the papacy's subversion of Catholic General Councils, and its clericalist, sectional view of the composition of the Catholic Church, it might seem that supporters of the pope did not deserve to be called Catholics at all, and indeed the Henrician regime had another more appropriate name for them – papists. Versions of this epithet had been familiar in England a decade before the Break with Rome. Fisher's sermon against Luther of 1521 complained of his derisive use of 'papistas, papastros, and papanos', and More responded to Luther on behalf of those 'whom you call papists' ('quos tu papistas vocas').[91] The first anglicisation of the term, however, seems to be in the *Articles Devised by the Holle Consent of the Kynges Most Honourable Counsayle* (1533), where the superiority of a General Council over the pope was vindicated against 'the sayings or preachings of any papists'.[92] Much wider currency was provided the following year with the publication of *A Litel Treatise agenste the Mutterynge of Some Papistes in Corners*, and thereafter the expression became an enduring staple of religious discourse. Cromwell's remembrances in 1534 included a prompt 'to apprehend any Papists' who preached in favour of the Bishop of Rome, and his circular letter to JPs in May 1537 urged destruction of 'the privy maintainers of that papistical faction'.[93] A number of dignitaries, including the judge John Oliver, Lord Lisle, and Sir Thomas Denys, wrote to Cromwell in the late 1530s to clear themselves of 'the mortal, deadly shame of a papist'. Denys showed he understood the potency of the label by remarking 'I do reckon a papist and a traitor to be one thing'.[94]

But from the moment of its coining, the term's circulation as a unit of rhetorical currency was remarkably wide, denoting more than formal adherence to the papal primacy. In November 1534, for example, Stephen Vaughan wrote to his patron, Thomas Cromwell, attacking the new Bishop of Coventry and Lichfield, Rowland Lee, as 'a papist, and idolator and a fleshy priest'.[95]

More humble correspondents of Cromwell's also regularly attacked local enemies as 'papists' and maintainers of 'papistical custom' without feeling the need for much precision in the accusation.[96] Moreover, the regime itself found the capaciousness of the expression a useful propaganda tool. The surrender deeds of religious houses, for example, sometimes forswore 'papisticall ceremonies' such as the wearing of mendicant habits, while, in a further circular to JPs of December 1538, Cromwell characterised those spreading false rumours of taxes as 'miserable and papisticall superstitious wretches'.[97] No less than the term Catholic itself, 'papist' and 'papistry' proved highly susceptible to semantic slippage, and by the 1540s were regularly used by evangelical reformers not to vindicate the Henrician settlement, but to condemn practices and individuals who continued to enjoy official sanction. In the syllogistic reasoning of William Turner, Stephen Gardiner, Bishop of Winchester, was a papist: 'the Pope's doctrine is the Pope, and ye hold still the Pope's doctrine, ergo ye hold still the Pope.'[98] Gardiner recognised the rhetorical strategy of his opponents in representing transubstantiation as the doctrine of 'papistes': the term 'serveth for a token to them to prove the matter nought'.[99] Already in 1536, Thomas Starkey had lamented the outbreak of religious name-calling among Henry's subjects, 'pharisee or heretyke, papist or schismatike', and by 1545, the king himself was publicly echoing the complaint.[100] Starkey also bemoaned the tendency of religious factions to judge each other 'to be slypped from the trewe and catholike faithe', a frank admission that the term was open to rival appropriations and annexations.[101]

V

So far we have explored the significance of the word 'Catholic' as a contested trophy between opponents and supporters of the royal supremacy, the attempts of the latter to disengage the term from connotations of papal loyalism, and to effect its re-assimilation into approved discourse through the construction of a distinctively anti-papal set of ecclesiological descriptors for the Church of England. But a straightforwardly binary approach is hardly sufficient here. The next part of the chapter will describe the ways in which appeals to the 'Catholic' faith or Church acted as a cipher for distinctive agendas *within* the Henrician Church, and will suggest that the religious potency of this terminology, combined with its semantic plasticity, made it an almost inevitable focus of ideological confrontation.

The fact that so many of the official pronouncements and doctrinal formularies of the Henrician Church invoked 'Catholic' legitimation undoubtedly provided a kind of rhetorical space for religious conservatives, one in which they could simultaneously protest their loyalty to the regime while condemning whatever they saw as deviations from traditional orthopraxy. A good example is the letter Archbishop Edward Lee of York sent to Cromwell in February 1535, enclosing his profession to the supremacy. In language alarmingly reminiscent of Convocation's qualified acceptance of the supremacy in 1531 ('so far as the law of God allows'), Lee declared himself ready 'to folowe the pleasure and commandment of the kinge, so that our Lorde bee not offended, and the unitie of the faiethe, and of the Catholique chyrche saved'. But Lee did not wish it to be thought this was a grudging or partial acceptance – had not the Dispensations Act of 1534 contained a pledge to uphold the articles of the Catholic faith: 'for saveng wherof I well perceyve the kinges christen and catholique mynd in a statute the xxvth yere of the king in the xxi chapitr'.[102] Another conservative, Bishop William Rugge of Norwich, brought to task by Cromwell in April 1539 over the contents of his preaching, could protest that 'I have spokyne nothynge but that hath been conformyde to holy scripture, to the perpetuall consent of the catholyke churche'.[103]

Such protestations were by no means necessarily disingenuous, but one does not have to look very hard to find examples of distinctly partisan and exclusionary usage of the word Catholic by religious conservatives within the Henrician fold. In the early 1530s, a Bristol priest complained about the sermons of Hugh (soon to be Bishop) Latimer, saying that 'the good catholicke people in the seyde towne do abhorre all soche hys prechyng'.[104] In around 1539, another Bristol priest, Roger Edgeworth, argued that it was properly 'the exercise and labour of catholike clerkes' to interpret the Bible for the laity.[105] The passing of the Act of Six Articles was welcomed in some quarters as a party victory, one lay noble observing that 'never prince shewed him self so wise a man, so well lerned and so catholik as the kinge hath don in this parlyment'.[106] Another conservative observer in the early months of 1539 anticipated with excitement that 'the faith catholyc shalbe harde, for som that lately did prech luters herysess do now reform theymself and in thyr sarmones have revoked herises'.[107] A ballad rejoicing at the fall of Cromwell in 1540 crowed: 'Thou dyd not remembre, false heretyke, / One God, one fayth, and one kynge catholyke, / For thou hast bene so long a scysmatyke'.[108]

A similarly 'us and them' flavour adheres to evidence collected at the time of the attempted putsch against Cranmer in 1543, the so-called 'Prebendaries' Plot'. John Myllys reported the view that Cranmer was remiss in punishing the conservative preachers Edmund Shether and Robert Serles, 'which two hath the more part of the people ... to testify of their Catholic preaching'. Myllys had himself heard Shether, and judged that 'he preached all catholic and godly'. According to another of the conservative prebendaries, William Hunt, when the priest John Willoughby presented evidence to the council of heretical preaching in Kent, 'the Council well allowed him of that presentation', saying that he was (that evocative phrase again) 'a good Catholic man'.[109] That Cranmer's arch-rival Gardiner had come to regard 'Catholic' as an exclusive party badge seems clear from remarks in a work of 1546. Rejecting claims by his enemies that he operated in a devious and conspiratorial way, Gardiner denied that he had even 'kepte one scholer at Cambrydge or Oxford syns I was bisshop to be brought up in the catholyque opinion, whiche is also myne'. He admitted that his chaplain had dropped Robert Barnes from the preaching rota for Paul's Cross in Lent 1540 to make way for Gardiner himself, judging it 'better to disapoynt Barnes on the morowe then some other catholyque man'.[110]

The Catholic label served Henrician conservatives, however, not merely as a monogram of self-identification (in this they resembled their ideological cousins, unreconciled papalists). It was also a rallying call against doctrinal deviation. In an attack on Barnes in 1540, John Standish praised the king's readiness 'to pourge and clense this his catholyke regyon from all heresy and schismes', while, in a Paul's Cross sermon of 1545, Cuthbert Scott urged his listeners 'to maynteyne the trewe catholike fayth of christe'.[111] Religious conservatives in a position of authority could employ the term in a prescriptive as well as a persuasive context. In his visitation injunctions of 1542, Bishop Edmund Bonner insisted that every preacher in London was to declare the Gospel 'not after his own mind, but after the mind of some Catholic doctor'.[112]

As in the pre-Reformation period, the term's most overt application as a mechanism for controlling thought and behaviour is seen in recantation sermons, particularly those preached in Bonner's diocese of London. On 18 December 1541, the reformers Alexander Seton and William Tolwyn were made to recant at Paul's Cross. Seton promised hereafter 'to cleve unto the trouthe and catholyke determynacyons of our holy mother the church'. Tolwyn admitted to being suspected of heresy 'agaynst the catholyke fayth', and of failing to perform laudable ceremonies 'of this catholyke churche of Englande'. He undertook henceforth 'to lyve as a catholyke man ought'.[113] Robert Ward's abjuration included the admission that he ought to have sought 'good aduyse and catholique doctrine of other', and Edward Crome in 1546 was reported to have 'exhorted all men to embrace auncientnes of catholike doctrine, and forsake new fanggelnes'.[114] In the same year Nicholas Shaxton confessed how he had fallen into sacramentarianism, but by the learning of the bishops of London and Worcester and other doctors had been 'broughte from my said erroure and heresye unto the true catholyck faith'. He was now fully persuaded, 'specyalle by the unyforme consent of the whoole chatholyke churche in that Artycle evyn from the Apostells tyme unto this our age'.[115]

The close identification of the Catholic faith with the doctrine of transubstantiation was no accident, but a considered strategy, as a small batch of treatises on the eucharist published in the last year of Henry's reign reveals. Stephen Gardiner, in his *Detection of the Devils Sophistrie*, asserted that Satan was striving to lead people from 'the true catholique byleefe in this most holye sacramente'. He translated Damascene's *De orthodoxa fide* as 'of the right catholyque fayth', and argued that Christ's words of institution were 'the foundation of our faith in their right catholyque understanding'.[116] William Peryn's *Thre Godly and Notable Sermons* began by noting that the 'malignitie of thys present tyme' was a spur to the sincere Christian 'to bende and force hym selfe in the defence of the fayth catholycke'. Peryn himself claimed to be writing at the importunate request 'of certayne catholyque parsons, my frendes'. In dedicating the treatise to Bonner, Peryn hoped that it might find favour 'wyth the catholyke people', a group clearly not envisaged as the totality of the baptised. The doctrine of transubstantiation was repeatedly inscribed as a 'catholyke veritie', testified to by numerous 'auncient catholyke wryters'. Opponents of the doctrine, from Berengarius to Wyclif, were lumped together as 'the hateful enemyes of the evangelical and catholyke faythe' (a linkage for modern scholars to ponder).[117] In Peryn's theology, the body of Christ is simultaneously the symbol and the instrument of Catholic orthodoxy, the eucharistic sacrifice serving to 'gether together in to one syncere fayth catholyke, all christiane people ... and inclose them strongly within thy churche catholyke'. The treatise drew to a close in suitably epigrammatic fashion: 'Hec est fides catholica'.[118] A third text of 1546, Richard Smyth's *Assertion and Defence of the Sacramente of the Aulter*, was likewise saturated with tendentious references to 'the catholike church', 'catholyque faith', 'catholyke exposition', 'catholyke opinion', 'catholike custom and usage', 'catholyque writers'.[119] Like Peryn, Smyth saw the eucharist both as the doctrinal test for 'Catholics' and as a means for their incorporation: whoever denied the real presence 'is without doubte no membre of Christes churche, for Christes church is a catholyque and an universall congregation of faithful people and a body gathered togither in one christen faith'.[120]

VI

How did evangelicals react in the face of these attempts to disqualify them from any share in a Catholic identity? In some quarters, particularly by the 1540s, there was a sense of frustration with the propensity of conservatives to equate the term with their own party (and an implicit recognition of their success in doing so). In prison in 1543, for example, Robert Wisdom wrote sarcastically of the 'Holy Fathers and priests of our Mother the holy Catholick Chirche, which have procured the forbidding of the Scripture among the People'.[121] The manoeuvres designed to bring down Cranmer in the same year were ascribed by his secretary Ralph Morice to 'the pope-catholic clergy of Kent'.[122] An anonymous evangelical tract of the mid-1540s, complaining that royal injunctions concerning the clergy were ignored outside the capital, noted bitterly that 'whoso is most necgligent remisse and slak in dooing them, he is most catholyque'.[123] A similar charge was made by John Bale in 1544, attacking a 'hereticall, trayterous, and blasphemous' oration by the leading conservative preacher Hugh Weston, one that 'was iudged a good matter and a verye catholyck sermon'.[124] The conservatives' unrepentant self-ascription as the Catholics clearly rankled with Bale, for in the previous year he had devoted considerable attention to it in the course of a commentary on the abjuration of William Tolwyn. 'Catholic', Bale reminded his readers, was a 'terme the scripture hath not'. Yet it was a singularly appropriate description for 'the faythe of ther churche':

> For catholyk is as moche to saye, as unyversall or admyttynge all. For in ded they allowe all maner of faythes, that faythe only excepted which they owght to allowe most of all. No Iewyshe ceremonye refuse they, nor yet heythen superstycyon. So longe as the gospell is not trewlye preached, ther faythe is good ynowgh. For it is catholyck.

Tolwyn's promise to live as a Catholic man meant 'to Remayne from hence forth a false periured chrystiane, a double sworne papyst, a newe professed traytoure'. If Bonner were to look in the scriptures, he would find that 'every where are they contrarye to the catholyke faythe of your churche'. Yet the clergy of London diocese seemed to set more store by the *Enchiridion* of Johann Eck: 'everye Ser Iohan must have yt that can rede, to make hym therwith a christen curate, a good ghostlye father, and a catholyck member of holye churche'.[125]

Bale's disgust with traditional religion, and in the terms in which it was conventionally described are quite evident. But in the main reformers were not prepared to pass the title deeds to the Catholic faith and the Catholic Church into the hands of their doctrinal opponents. In 1540 the evangelical layman Richard Tracy applauded Henry's efforts to maintain the unity Christ had commanded to be 'kepte in the catholyke church', and, in a tract praising the King for leading his realm out of darkness and superstition, John Pylbarough rejoiced that it was now upon Christ that 'our catholyke congrega- tion immediately is firmely settled'.[126] Thomas Becon condemned anabaptism as 'contrary to the rule of the catholyke fayth', and William Turner wrote of 'the hole Catholike Chirche whiche is Christis spouse'.[127] In 1544, George Joye included among the consolations available to sufferers of persecution the 'great felowship emonge the faithfull congregacions of whom mencion is made emonge the articles of our faithe. We belevinge them to be the holy catholyke chirche'.[128]

As this last reference suggests, an impulse to contest the very nature of the Catholic Church remained close to reformers' hearts. Miles Coverdale argued that Standish had fundamentally misunderstood St Augustine's dictum about not believing the Gospel until the Catholic Church moved him to, inferring from it that the authority of the Church was somehow greater than that of scripture. The point was rather that Augustine would believe no doctrine other than the Gospel, which was maintained by 'the whole consent and auctorite of the catholike or universall church'. This was a slightly expanded translation, for as Coverdale pointed out, behind Augustine's Latin lay the Greek καθολικός, 'as much to say as universalis'. The Catholic Church was thus properly defined as 'the universall congregacion and multitude of them that beleve in Christ', and Coverdale repeatedly made reference to the 'catholike or universall church', a linkage clearly designed to detach the word semantically from its traditionalist associations.[129] Less sophisticated, but concerned to make essentially the same point, was a ballad in defence of Cromwell penned by William Gray in 1540, maintaining that the gospellers were 'I am sure more catholyck, then are your popysshe sorte / Beynge the membres of chryst, and him selfe the hed of the same / Neyther heretyckes nor papistes, but men of honest fame'.[130]

Such reflections may on occasion have provided a casuistical lifeline for persecuted evangelicals. If recantation sermons required an affirmation of the Catholic faith, but those who recited them had a completely different conception of that faith from those who wrote them, then they might prove an uncertain instrument for fastening consciences.[131] It seems likely that Thomas Cromwell exploited the interstices of meaning in his scaffold speech of July 1540, using words which might seem conventionally penitential in tone, but which were rich with the potential for ambiguity: 'I intend this day to dye gods seruant, and beleiue in the holy Catholique fayth. I beleiue in ye lawes ordained by ye catholique church, and in ye holy sacrament without any grudge.'[132]

The issue comes most clearly into focus with the persecution of the Lincolnshire gentlewoman Anne Askew in March 1546. Bonner drew up a recantation for her to sign, affirming belief in transubstantiation, and concluding: 'I do believe in this, and in all other sacraments of holy church, in all points according to the old catholic faith of the same'. Yet when this was passed to Askew, she wrote only, 'I Anne Askew do believe all manner things contained in the faith of the catholic church'. At this, Bonner 'flung into his chamber in a great fury', and was only persuaded out again by Dr Weston, who suggested that Anne had written 'catholic church' because she did not understand the expression 'holy church'. Yet it seems likely she knew exactly what she was doing. The exchanges provided her contemporary biographer, John Bale, with a chance to score points off his old adversary Bonner on a familiar topic:

> This word 'catholic' was not wont to offend them. How becometh it then now a name so odious? Peradventure, through this only occasion: they knew not till now of late years (for it come of the Greek) the true signification thereof; as that it is so much to say in the English as the universal, or whole. But now they perceive that it includeth the laity so well as them, no longer do they esteem it. Other cause can I none conjecture, why they should more contemn it than afore.[133]

Shortly before her burning in July 1546, Askew penned an appeal to the king, protesting that concerning the eucharist she believed as much as Christ 'willed me to follow and believe, and so much as the catholic church of him doth teach'. Even after her racking by Richard Rich and Thomas Wriothesley, she refused to sign the recantation with which she was presented, though in the end she subscribed with the following formula: 'I, Anne Askewe, do believe this, if God's word do agree to the same, and the true catholic church'.[134] Anne's fellow-martyr, John Lascelles, boasted to George Blagge in Newgate after his condemnation: 'My Lord Bishop would have me confess the Roman church to be the Catholic church, but that I cannot, for it is not true'.[135]

VII

This chapter has concerned itself solely with the reign of Henry VIII, though it is worth noting briefly that long after 1547 'Catholic' remained just as freighted a term of religious controversy. When in 1550 Cranmer published *A Defence of the True and Catholic Doctrine of the Sacrament*, Gardiner countered with *An Explication and Assertion of the True Catholic Faith, Touching the Most Blessed Sacrament*, marvelling that Cranmer could call his teaching Catholic when in the whole history of the church only some half dozen taught such doctrine.[136] After 1553, the Marian authorities made a concerted attempt to assert sole copyright to the epithet. Wayland's primer of 1555 was the first to be given the title *An Uniforme and Catholyke Primer*, and the articles put to heretics almost invariably laid a strong emphasis on the *Catholic* faith, in a way designed to make explicit that this was the exclusive property of the regime's supporters.[137] Yet at the examinations of John Rogers and John Philpot, for example, what precisely should be understood by 'the Catholic Church' was a highly contested issue.[138] The London martyr John Warne defined the Holy Catholic Church as 'a holy number of Adam's posterity, elected, gathered, washed, and purified by the blood of the Lamb'.[139] John Hooper counterposed 'god's most true and catholic religion' (set forth by Edward VI) with 'their papistical religion', spoke of the controversy between 'us catholics and Roman innovators' ('inter nos catholicos et Neotericos Romanos'), and judged that the Roman Catholic Church had as much to do with the Holy Catholic Church as Belial did with Christ.[140] At the Westminster Disputation of April 1559, the Marian Bishop Oglethorpe insisted, 'we are of the Catholic Church, and in possession of the truth', while the returned exile Robert Horne solemnly protested that his party 'stood to the doctrine of the Catholic Church, although they understood not by the Catholic Church the Romish Church'.[141] This pattern of rhetorical appropriations was to remain, *mutatis mutandis*, a permanent feature of the English religious scene. A Cambridge undergraduate in the early 1980s who admitted to being a Catholic was liable to be asked if he meant English or Roman.[142]

This survey has by no means been exhaustive, but sufficiently recurring and interlocking patterns have emerged to allow some concluding observations. It is evident that in the reign of Henry VIII, Catholicism (if we allow that slightly anachronistic formulation) was an unstable category, a polemical construction, a matter of ascription rather than description, a contested discourse. Yet these rather glib phrases do not convey much sense of the pain felt by contemporaries at the splintering of previously shared attitudes and values. As Reginald Pole wrote ruefully to Tunstall after Henry's break with Rome, and Pole's break with Henry, had driven a wedge between them: 'we are brought to such case, worse than Babylon, that no man understands another in his own tongue. What one calls captivity, another calls liberty; [what] one says is against the King, another calls with the King.'[143]

Yet amid the fragmentation, that venerable token of a common faith – 'Catholic' – continued to function as a theological lingua franca. For the Henrician schism it represented a pledge of continuity and supplied a major source of ideological legitimacy, but only in so far as it could be comprehensively annexed from the remaining adherents of Rome, a task which was never successfully accomplished. At the same time, the near universal recognition of one 'Holy Catholic Church' allowed both proponents and opponents of further Reformation a 'semantic space' in which to operate with a modicum of safety. All sides recognised the potency of the term, and it helped to bind them in discourse with each other, even as it focused and accentuated their theological differences. The semantic history of this one word (and similar explorations could be made for a number of others) serves as a reminder that formations of religious identity in the sixteenth century were fundamentally dialectical processes. In this area, the word and the thing, the signifier and the signified, cannot be considered separately from each other – after all, in English usage 'denomination' means a name for purposes of classification, as well as 'religious sect'. Religious identities are created, not independently of, but through, language. Historians delude themselves if they suppose that the language can be stripped away like old wallpaper to expose a free-standing reality underneath. In addressing the history either of 'Catholics' or of a 'Protestant Nation' we should, in the idiom of medieval scholasticism, adopt a nominalist rather than realist approach. Words matter, and it undoubtedly has something important to tell us about the culture of mid-sixteenth-century England that a word whose etymology denotes universality and inclusivity should come to feature so prominently in the pathology of religious division.

NOTES

For references and advice received in the course of preparing this chapter, I am very grateful to Steve Hindle, Ethan Shagan, and especially Alec Ryrie.

1 A. F. Pollard, *Henry VIII* (London, 1902), p. 310; G. Constant, *The Reformation in England: I. The English Schism*, trans. R. E. Scantlebury (New York, 1934), pp. 430–5; H. M. Smith, *Henry VIII and the Reformation* (London, 1948), pp. 167, 452.

2 E. C. Messenger, *The Reformation, the Mass and the Priesthood*, 2 vols (London, 1936–37), I: vi, 240.

3 P. Hughes, *The Reformation in England*, 3 vols (London, 1950–54), I: 197, 217, 278, 360.

4 J. J. Scarisbrick, *Henry VIII* (London, 1968), p. 399.

5 L. F. Solt, *Church and State in Early Modern England 1509–1640* (Oxford, 1990), p. 41; G. Redworth, *In Defence of the Church Catholic: The Life of Stephen Gardiner* (Oxford, 1990), pp. 48–9.

6 R. Rex, *Henry VIII and the English Reformation* (Basingstoke, 1993), pp. 171–3.

7 P. O'Grady, *Henry VIII and the Conforming Catholics* (Collegeville, Minn., 1990), p. 10.

8 See J. K. McConica, *English Humanists and Reformation Politics under Henry VIII and Edward VI* (Oxford, 1965), esp. ch. 6; G. W. Bernard, 'The Making of Religious Policy, 1533–1546: Henry VIII and the Search for the Middle Way', *HJ*, 41 (1998); G. W. Bernard, 'The Piety of Henry VIII', in N. S. Amos, A. Pettegree, and H. van Nierop (eds), *The Education of a Christian Society: Humanism and Reformation in Britain and the Netherlands* (Aldershot, 1999); Lucy Wooding, *Rethinking Catholicism in Reformation England* (Oxford, 2000), ch. 2.

9 N. S. Tjernagel, *Henry VIII and the Lutherans* (St Louis, 1965), p. 212.

10 Diarmaid MacCulloch, *Reformation: Europe's House Divided 1490-1700* (London, 2003), p. 38.

11 Redworth, *Church Catholic*, pp. 48–9; G. Walker, *Persuasive Fictions: Faction, Faith and Political Culture in the Reign of Henry VIII* (Aldershot, 1996), pp. 136–7; Peter Marshall and Alec Ryrie (eds), *The Beginnings of English Protestantism* (Cambridge, 2002), pp. 5–7.

12 M. Dowling, *Humanism in the Age of Henry VIII* (London, 1986), 'Note and Acknowledgements'; Diarmaid MacCulloch, *Thomas Cranmer: A Life* (New Haven, 1996), p. 3. A similar demur was made in the 1950s by L. B. Smith, *Tudor Prelates and Politics 1536–1558* (Princeton, 1953), p. 132.

13 See, for example, PRO SP 1/202, fo. 193r; ; *LP*, xix (1). 302, 558; xx (1). 1226.

14 Diarmaid MacCulloch, *Tudor Church Militant: Edward VI and the Protestant Reformation* (1999), p. 2; MacCulloch, *Reformation*, p. xx.

15 J. W. Legg (ed.), *The Sarum Missal* (Oxford, 1916), pp. 221, 211. The equivalents of 'Catholic' in Latin and the major West European languages are fairly exact ones.

16 John Fisher, *The English Works*, ed. J. E. Mayor, EETS, extra ser. 27 (London, 1876), p. 343.

17 William Bonde, *The Pylgrymage of Perfeccyon* (London, 1531), pp. 186, 197.

18 Friar Garard, *The Interpretacyon and Sygnyfycacyon of the Masse* (London, 1532), fo. 1r.

19 A. K. Donald (ed.), *Melusine*, EETS, extra ser. 68 (London, 1895), pp. 31–2.

20 J. A. F. Thomson, *The Later Lollards 1414–1520* (Oxford, 1965), p. 202n.

21 J. H. Lupton, *Life of John Colet*, 2nd edn (London, 1909), p. 298; N. Tanner, 'Penances Imposed on Kentish Lollards by Archbishop Warham 1511–12', in M. Aston and C. Richmond (eds), *Lollardy and the Gentry in the Later Middle Ages* (Stroud, 1997), pp. 245–9.

22 G. Bray (ed.), *The Anglican Canons 1529–1947*, Church of England Record Society, 6 (London, 1998), p. 24; P. Hughes and J. F. Larkin (eds), *Tudor Royal Proclamations*, 3 vols (New Haven, 1964–69), 1: 181, 183, 194.

23 John Foxe, *Acts and Monuments*, ed. S. R. Cattley and G. Townsend, 8 vols (London, 1837–41), 5: 27.

24 Hughes, *Reformation in England*, 1: 206.

25 Foxe, *Acts and Monuments*, 4: app. III.

26 Fisher, *English Works*, pp. 342–3.

27 Cited in J. C. Warner, *Henry VIII's Divorce: Literature and the Politics of the Printing Press* (Woodbridge, 1998), p. 136.

28 Thomas More, *The Apology*, ed. J. B. Trapp (New Haven, 1979), pp. 9, 11, 29, 32, 41, 45, 46, 49, 155, 158, 160; Thomas More, *A Dialogue Concerning Heresies*, ed. T. M. C. Lawler et al. (New Haven, 1981), pp. 33, 361, 406, 409; Thomas More, *The Confutation of Tyndale's Answer*, ed. L. A. Schuster et al. (New Haven, 1973), pp. 29–30, 38–9, 57, 470, 625, 649, 658, 727, 789, 954; Thomas More, *The Answer to a Poisoned Book*, ed. S. Foley and C. H. Miller (New Haven, 1985), p. 3; Thomas More, *The Debellation of Salem and Bizance*, ed. J. Guy et al. (New Haven, 1987), pp. 15, 25; Thomas More, *Treatise on the Passion*, ed. G. Haupt (New Haven, 1976), p. 171; Thomas More, *Letter to Bugenhagen. Supplication of Souls. Letter against Frith*, ed. F. Manley et al. (New Haven, 1990), p. 236.

29 Thomas More, *Responsio ad Lutherum*, ed. J. M. Headley (New Haven, 1969), p. 119; More, *Confutation*, p. 62.

30 Ibid., pp. 134, 147, 275, 379, 390, 398, 561, 564, 574–6, 598, 603, 649, 655–6, 662, 668–9, 673, 675, 678, 682, 712, 724, 727, 734, 740, 801, 835, 839, 841–2, 909, 912, 914, 939, 942, 951, 975, 980–1, 993 ff.

31 More, *Responsio*, p. 201.

32 More, *Confutation*, pp. 975–6.

33 More, *Apology*, pp. 316–17n.

34 More, *Confutation*, p. 735.

35 Ibid., p. 562.

36 PRO, SP 1/69, fo. 121r.

37 J. Guy, *The Public Career of Sir Thomas More* (New Haven, 1980), pp. 198–9, 211.

38 More, *Confutation*, pp. 1025–6.

39 For the significance of this phrase, see A. Hudson, *The Premature Reformation: Wycliffe Texts and Lollard History* (Oxford, 1988), pp. 57, 143.

40 More, *Confutation*, p. 1027.

41 PRO, SP 1/158, fos. 180r, 181r, 208r.

42 William Roper, 'The Life of Sir Thomas More', in R. S. Sylvester and D. P. Harding (eds), *Two Early Tudor Lives* (New Haven, 1962), pp. 248, 254.

43 Hughes, *Reformation in England*, 1: 280; L. E. Whatmore, *The Carthusians under King Henry the Eighth* (Salzburg, 1983), pp. 73–4, 83; J. Strype, *Ecclesiastical Memorials*, 3 vols (London, 1721), 1: i. 197.

44 Geoffrey Elton, *Policy and Police: The Enforcement of the Reformation in the Age of Thomas Cromwell* (Cambridge, 1972), p. 18.

45 Strype, *Ecclesiastical Memorials*, 1: ii. 222.

46 *LP*, xii (1). 901 (p. 407).

47 *LP*, v. 750.

48 *LP*, vi. 142

49 *LP*, viii. 514.

50 *LP*, x. 429, 283.

51 *LP*, viii. 786; *LP*, x. 427, 82. Granvelle similarly saw Fisher and More as 'these two good Catholics and martyrs': *LP*, ix. 449.

52 PRO, SP 1/160, fo. 152r. On this theme, see Peter Marshall, 'The Other Black Legend: The Henrician Reformation and the Spanish People', *EHR*, 116 (2001).

53 H. Gee and W. J. Hardy (eds), *Documents Illustrative of English Church History* (London, 1896), p. 191.

54 Elton, *Policy and Police*, p. 228 ; BL Cotton MS Cleo. E iv, fo. 14v.

55 Thomas Cranmer, *Miscellaneous Writings*, ed. J. E. Cox (Cambridge, 1846), pp. 283, 460.

56 Gee and Hardy (eds), *Documents*, p. 225.

57 PRO, SP 1/103, fo. 212r; L. Toulmin Smith (ed.) *The Itinerary of John Leland* (London, 5 vols, 1964), 1: xxxviii.

58 Hughes and Larkin, *Tudor Royal Proclamations*, 1: 272.

59 *LP*, v. 850; *LP*, xxi (1). 1098.

60 BL Cotton MS Cleo. E v, fo. 60v.

61 BL Cotton MS Calig. B i, fos. 59v, 62v–63r.

62 More, *Confutation*, p. 28; More, *Letter to Bugenhagen. Supplication of Souls. Letter against Frith*, pp. 10, 162, 233.

63 *LP*, vi. 351.

64 *LP*, vi. 465; vii. 1257, 1206.

65 *LP*, viii. 556, 666; x. 351.

66 N. Pocock (ed.), *Records of the Reformation: The Divorce 1527–1533*, 2 vols (London, 1870), 2: 543, 546.

67 Simon Matthewe, *A Sermon Made in the Cathedrall Churche of Caynt Paul at London* (1535), sigs. A5v–8v, C4v.

68 Thomas Starkey, *An Exhortation to the People, Instructynge Them to Unitie and Obedience* (1536), fos. 64v–69r, 60v–61r.

69 McConica, *English Humanists*, pp. 136–7.

70 Desiderius Erasmus, *A Playne and Godly Exposition or Declaration of the Comune Crede* (1533), sigs. D1r–v, N7v–8v, O1v–2r.

71 *A Prymer in Englyshe, with Certeyn Prayers and Godly Meditations* (London, 1535), sig. C8r.

72 C. Lloyd (ed.), *Formularies of Faith Put Forth by Authority in the Reign of Henry VIII* (Oxford, 1825), p. 75; Cranmer, *Miscellaneous Writings*, pp. 473–4; Tjernagel, *Henry VIII and the Lutherans*, pp. 290–2.

73 Lloyd, *Formularies*, pp. 52–7.

74 Strype, *Ecclesiastical Memorials*, 1: i. 378.

75 Lloyd, *Formularies*, pp. 246–8. It seems nonetheless to have been common in the 1540s for English diplomats to label the contending parties in Germany 'the catholykes' and 'the protestantes': PRO SP 1/161, fos. 26r–v; PRO SP 1/202, fo. 193r; *LP*, xix (1). 302, 558; xx (1). 1226.

76 C. Wriothesley, *A Chronicle of England*, 2 vols, Camden Society, new ser., 11 and 20 (London, 1875–77), 1: 79. The episode is examined in detail in P. Marshall, 'Papist as Heretic: The Burning of John Forest, 1538', *HJ*, 41 (1998), 351–74.

77 S. Brigden, *London and the Reformation* (Oxford, 1989), pp. 261–2.

78 Gee and Hardy (eds), *Documents*, p. 187.

79 Thomas Swynnerton, *A Mustre of Scismatyke Bysshoppes of Rome* (London, 1534), sig. F2r.

80 Christopher St German (?), *A Treatise Concernynge Divers of the Constitucyons Provynciall and Legantines* (London, ?1535), sig. A8v.

81 PRO, SP 1/143, fo. 200r.

82 More, *Confutation*, pp. 600, 614, 831.

83 *A Treatise Concernynge Generall Councilles, the Byshoppes of Rome, and the Clergy* (London, 1538), sigs. C5r–v. The treatise is attributed to Alexander Alesius by P. A. Sawada, 'Two Anonymous Tudor Treatises on the General Council', *JEH*, 12 (1961), 197–214, though there are circumstantial and stylistic reasons for suspecting it to be the work of St German – a suggestion I owe to Richard Rex.

84 Pocock (ed.), *Records of the Reformation*, 2: 546.

85 Starkey, *Exhortation*, fo. 66r.

86 Strype, *Ecclesiastical Memorials*, 2: ii. 188.

87 *LP*, xi. 72.

88 See Marshall, 'Burning of John Forest', pp. 359–61.

89 *Treatise Concernynge Generall Councilles*, sigs. A2v, A3r, C4v, C7v, C8v, D3r–v.

90 Lloyd, *Formularies*, p. 283.

91 Fisher, *English Works*, pp. 344–5; More, *Responsio*, pp. 224–5.

92 Pocock, *Records of the Reformation*, 2: 526–7. The term was also used in 1533 in George Joye's *The Souper of the Lorde*: R. Rex (ed.), *A Reformation Rhetoric. Thomas Swynnerton's The Tropes and Figures of Scripture* (Cambridge, 1999), p. 164.

93 *LP*, vii. 177, 420; Elton, *Policy and Police*, p. 253.

94 Dowling, *Humanism in the Age of Henry VIII*, p. 47; *LP*, viii. 607; *LP*, xiii (1). 120.

95 Hughes, *Reformation in England*, 1: 266n.

96 Elton, *Policy and Police*, pp. 20, 250; *LP*, ix. 747; *LP*, viii. 297; *LP*, xiii (2). 658.

97 *LP*, xiii (2). 501, 1171.

98 Cited in Smith, *Tudor Prelates and Politics*, p. 161.

99 S. Gardiner, *A Detection of the Devils Sophistrie* (London, 1546), fo. 8v.

100 Starkey, *Exhortation*, fo. 27v; E. Hall, *Hall's Chronicle*, ed. H. Ellis (London, 1809), pp. 864–5.

101 Starkey, *Exhortation*, fo. 31r.

102 PRO SP 1/190, fo. 172r.

103 PRO SP 1/150, fo. 182r.

104 BL Cotton MS Cleo. E v, fo. 394v.

105 Roger Edgeworth, *Sermons very fruitfull, godly and learned*, ed. J. Wilson (Cambridge, 1993), p. 141.

106 BL Cotton MS Cleo. E v, fo. 138r.

107 PRO SP 1/143, fo. 121r.

108 E. Dormer, *Gray of Reading: A Sixteenth-century Controversialist and Ballad Writer* (Reading, 1923), p. 77.

109 *LP*, xviii (2). 546 (pp. 365, 368).

110 Stephen Gardiner, *A Declaration of Such True Articles as G. Joye Hath Gone About to Confute* (London, 1546), fos. 7r–8v.

111 John Standish, *A Lytle Treatise Composed by Johan Standyshe against the Protestation of R. Barnes* (London, 1540), sig. A2r; W. Chedsay and C. Scott, *Two Notable Sermones Lately Preached at Pauls crosse* (London, 1545), sig. F2v.

112 W. H. Frere and W. M. Kennedy (eds), *Visitation Articles and Injunctions of the Period of the Reformation*, 3 vols (London, 1910), 2: 89.

113 Alexander Seton, *The Declaration Made at Poules Cross* (London, 1542), sigs. A3r, B2v–3r; Brigden, *London*, pp. 335–7.

114 London Guildhall MS 9531/12, fo. 62v; H. Ellis (ed.), *Original Letters illustrative of English History*, 2nd ser., 4 vols (London, 1827), 2: 177.

115 Foxe, *Acts and Monuments*, 5: app. xvii.

116 Gardiner, *Detection*, fos. 5r, 32r–v, 54v.

117 William Peryn, *Thre Godly and Notable Sermons of the Moost Honorable and Blessed Sacrament of the Aulter* (London, 1546), sigs. *2r–v, *4r, B6r, D3r, D8v, G6v, H1r, H2r, H6r, M5v.

118 Ibid., sigs. *8r, N8r.

119 Richard Smyth, *The Assertion and Defence of the Sacramente of the Aulter* (London, 1546), fos. 6r, 7r, 11v, 12r, 14r–v, 26r, 57v, 63v, 69r, 77r, 78r, 79v, 83r, 93r, 94r, 109v, 121r, 140r, 194r, 195r, 205r, 214r, 220r, 223v, 236r, 247r, 253v, 256v, 258v.

120 Ibid., fo. 57v.

121 Strype, *Ecclesiastical Memorials*, 1: ii. 316. The act which restricted access to scripture claimed to be in agreement with 'the true doctryne of the catholike and apostolicall church': A. Luders et al. (eds), *Statutes of the Realm*, 11 vols (London, 1830–52), 3: 894.

122 *LP*, xviii (2). p. li.

123 BL Royal MS 17 B xxxv, fo. 8v.

124 John Bale, *The Epistel Exhortatorye of an Inglyshe Chrystian* (Antwerp, 1544), fo. 30v.

125 John Bale, *Yet a Course at the Romyshe Foxe* (Antwerp, 1543), fos. 16v, 30v–33v, 54v.

126 Richard Tracy, *The Profe and Declaration of Thys Proposition: Fayth only Iustifieth* (London, 1540), sig. A2v; John Pylbarough, *A Commemoration of the Inestimable Graces and Benefites of God* (London, 1540), sig. B1r.

127 Thomas Becon, *A New Yeares Gyfte More Precious than Golde* (London, 1543), sig. D6r; William Turner, *The Rescuynge of the Romishe Fox* (Bonn, 1545), sig. B4r.

128 George Joye, *A Present Consolacion for the Sufferers of Persecucion* (Antwerp, 1544), sig. E5r.

129 Miles Coverdale, *A Confutacyon of That Treatise, Which One John Standish Made* (Zurich, 1541), sigs. K6r–L1r, L6v.

130 William Gray, *The returne of M. Smythes Envoy* (London, 1540).

131 Susan Wabuda has demonstrated how Edward Crome and other evangelicals were sometimes able to subvert the intentions of their persecutors on these occasions: S Wabuda, 'Equivocation and Recantation During the English Reformation: The "Subtle Shadows" of Dr Edward Crome', *JEH*, 44 (1993), 224–42.

132 Bodleian Library, Fol. Δ 624, p. 462.

133 John Bale, *Select Works*, ed. H. Christmas (Cambridge, 1849), pp. 175–8.

134 Ibid., pp. 217, 230.

135 D. Wilson, *A Tudor Tapestry: Men, Women and Society in Reformation England* (London, 1972), p. 229.

136 J. A. Muller, *Stephen Gardiner and the Tudor Reaction* (London, 1926), p. 209.

137 See Foxe, *Acts and Monuments*, 6–8 passim.

138 Ibid., 6: 593 ff.; 7: 669–75.

139 Ibid., 6: 83.

140 John Hooper, *Later Writings*, ed. C. Nevinson (Cambridge, 1852), pp. 375–6, 401, 532. For further instances of Marian martyrs insisting that theirs was the true Catholic Church, see Patrick Collinson, 'Night Schools, Conventicles and Churches: Continuities and Discontinuities in Early Protestant Ecclesiology', in Marshall and Ryrie (eds), *Beginnings of English Protestantism*, pp. 231, 233–4.

141 Messenger, *The Reformation, the Mass and the Priesthood*, 2: 227–8.

142 An experience of my elder brother's. Cf. MacCulloch, *Reformation*, p. xix: '"Catholic" is clearly a word which a lot of people want to possess.'

143 W. Schenk, *Reginald Pole: Cardinal of England* (London, 1950), p. 74.

Chapter 3

———◆———

Confronting compromise:
the schism and its legacy in
midTudor England

Ethan Shagan

I n the final, deeply moving pages of *The Stripping of the Altars*, discussing
how many 'decent, timid men and women' compromised aspects of their
Catholicism in order to protect their core beliefs, Eamon Duffy noted that
inevitably 'the price for such accommodation ... was the death of the past that
it sought to preserve'.[1] This observation seems beyond dispute, but like all
really incisive historical models it raises as many questions as it answers. It
not only leads us to wonder how and why some English people chose to
compromise with the Reformation while others did not, but it also leaves us
wondering exactly which aspects of the Catholic past really died. After all,
Christopher Haigh has provided a cogent model of Catholic 'continuity' in
which only an outward superstructure died, and Catholics who clung to their
core beliefs remained viable heirs to medieval devotion until they were abandoned by the post-Tridentine Church. What does it mean, then, to say that
English Catholics paid a terrible price for their accommodation? Did they
themselves realise the price they were paying, and would they have thought it
too high had they known?

In this article, I want to explore these questions and suggest that English
Catholics themselves disagreed significantly over both what this price was and
whether it was worth paying. Thus I want to build on the best aspects of both
Duffy's and Haigh's interpretations, on the one hand accepting that the
Reformation destroyed something that could never be rebuilt, but on the other
hand accepting that many Catholics who lived through that process believed
that it did not reach to the vital core of their religious identity. In order to
bridge the gap between these two views, I want to look at a subject that has
never been explored in depth for the mid-Tudor period: the ways that Catholic
compromisers were regarded by their contemporaries, especially their puta-
tive co-religionists. To put it mildly, reactions were mixed. After all, no matter
how attractive these 'decent, timid men and women' are to our romantic

sensibilities, it is not necessarily the case that all contemporaries saw virtue in the moral 'grey zone' of compromise. Moreover, many instances of Catholic compromise with the Reformation shaded uneasily into collaboration with the heretical regime, in the process tainting the whole idea that 'traditionalist' ends could justify 'newfangled' means. Thus while many people did indeed consider themselves conventionally pious Catholics despite their concessions to the Tudor regime, this is only half of the story at best, since many other Catholics spent their energies harassing and intimidating them. These more intransigent men and women, too, have a history that spans the sixteenth century. They, too, claimed to be the legitimate heirs of the Catholic past, and we must ask why they came to believe that anyone who accommodated the Tudor government could not maintain 'continuity' with the Church of St Thomas Becket.

In the following pages, then, I want to foreground the conflict between these conflicting visions of English Catholicism in the era before 1558. I will argue that the spiritual accommodations of the Reformation era were not polemically neutral attempts to preserve self-evidently 'core' beliefs, but rather were part of a deeply contested debate over what constituted that core. If we want to search for the 'continuity' of Catholicism in the English Reformation, then, we might do well to avoid privileging one voice in these contemporary debates about what exactly Catholicism *was*. Indeed, if we notice that these conflicts in the years before 1558 bear a striking resemblance to *later* Catholic controversies, we might even recognise that the debate itself, rather than any one position within it, is what most vividly demonstrates the sustained vitality of English Catholicism.

I

I want to begin in Henry VIII's reign, because it was in that highly volatile and utterly perplexing climate that the greatest range of Catholic responses to religious demands was possible. It was in the ecclesiastical chaos of the 1530s – while Henry VIII still maintained that he was a devout Catholic, and the full theological consequences of his polices were far from clear – that so many traditionalists began the series of compromises and accommodations that would eventually constitute so much of the English Reformation. To see the range of Catholic responses, at least among the clergy who hoped to provide good examples for their flocks, we need look no further than the issue which the king and Thomas Cromwell chose as the first real test of their newly asserted authority over the Church. In 1535, the government ordered that the name of the pope be obliterated from all liturgical books where it appeared; in modern discourse, Henry VIII tried to *disappear* the pope.

At least in the aggregate, the government enjoyed considerable success in this unprecedented programme, as can be seen from the countless surviving service books where the word *papa* has been excised. Many complied with the order immediately, following bishops like Stephen Gardiner and John Longland who provided theological cover for conservative priests who wished to maintain their conservative credentials while obeying their rightful King. Gardiner in fact provided two helpful but potentially contradictory arguments for the clergy to comply. First was the argument from obedience for which he is best known: the King had ordered service books to be defaced, and the Bible required obedience to him in all things without 'one syllable of exception' unless obedience to God was compromised. Second, and more interesting, was an argument from experience and justice. The people of England had 'bid the bishop of Rome farewell' because it was only natural to 'turn such a chaplain out of the doors' who had been 'hired or prayed to minister divine service, [yet] hath not showed himself faithful and diligent in his office'.[2] This latter argument is a cogent reminder that in the 1530s the break with Rome was not intended as revolution but as reform, and as such it naturally appealed to some portion of the conservative population.

Inevitably, however, there were also intransigent Romanists who refused to comply with the order and left their books unaltered. At Harwich in Essex, for instance, the parson ignored numerous pleas from his parishioners to erase the pope's name and was eventually denounced by them to the authorities.[3] At Dymchurch in Kent, the parson was arrested for failing to erase the pope's name from both his own books and the books of the parish.[4] Given the inefficiencies of Tudor government, such disobedience, if hidden from potential local informants, could remain secret for years; as late as June 1551, for instance, a Norfolk priest called Richard Ussher was accused of using a missal containing 'diverse false, profane rubrics and papistical writings'.[5] Here, then, was a strict nonconformist position that we can imagine evolving over the Tudor century into what we call recusancy. It denied the legitimacy of the King's authority in spiritual matters, and it implicitly defined the headship of the Church as a spiritual matter despite the insistence of conformists like Stephen Gardiner that it was no such thing.

If straight compliance and straight refusal were the only two positions available, we might believe that the Reformation acted in rather simple fashion to separate 'ultramontane' Catholics from those willing to accept 'Catholicism without the pope'. But on the contrary, there were a wide variety of other positions canvassed that challenged this simple dichotomy. Some priests, for instance, attempted to square the circle by effacing the name of the pope from their books in incomplete or easily reversible ways. At Stanton Lacy in Shropshire, for instance, the vicar in some places in his service books left the word *papa* unerased and in other places covered the word 'with small pieces of paper' that could later be removed to reveal the pope's name 'as fair as ever it was and as legible'.[6] Christopher Michell, a Yorkshire parson, used the same trick, covering the word *papa* with small pieces of wax paper.[7] A Welsh priest put a single line of his pen through the word *papa*, thus arguably complying with the letter of the order but clearly violating its spirit by leaving the word legible.[8] These half measures, like the manœuvres of so many 'church papists' in Queen Elizabeth's reign, presented the government with a challenge only insofar as it chose to notice; the charade of bare compliance masked what was clearly ambivalence at best, but on the other hand, only compliance was officially required.

Other priests constructed complex casuistical positions in which they could erase the name of the pope yet at the same time uphold papal authority in front of their parishioners. For instance, William Cobbe, Vicar of St Peter's in Thanet, preached to his congregation in 1536, 'Many men, because this name pope is taken away, have therefore a scrupulous conscience. But as for the taking away of his name it is no matter, for he never wrote himself *"papa"* but *"sumus pontifex"*, and as for his authority he hath not lost an inch thereof, I warrant you.'[9] A similar strategy was adopted several years later by Thomas Bennett, a Somerset priest who was prosecuted in King's Bench for telling his parishioners, 'You shall not call the bishop of Rome pope, but ye shall call him the high bishop.'[10] Here was a much more fundamental challenge to the government's rather strained attempts to separate ecclesiological conformity from theological belief. These priests supported the pope's authority and believed they had a positive obligation to instruct their flocks to believe the same. Yet at the same time, they attempted to construct their position within a loyalist paradigm. This was, *mutatis mutandis*, the tactical godfather of Edmund Campion's 'brag': absolute obedience masterfully combined with absolute defiance.

Most astonishingly, we can also find Catholic priests who rejected any form of obedience, and indeed even passive disobedience, as complicity with heresy. In 1538, for instance, John Lyle, curate of the parish of Wrynkton in Somerset, was repeatedly warned by his parishioners to 'correct and amend his books according to the King's injunctions'. When they investigated they found not only the word *papa* unerased and 'Thomas Beckett's name with his whole legends and stories ... still uncorrected', but also 'these words *"rege nostro"* and this letter "R" blotted out'.[11] In other words, Lyle had defaced the name of the King rather than the name of the pope! This same radical inversion of royal commands was practised by the Cornish priest Andrew Furlong, who had a Bible in his possession whose first three or four leaves were 'cancelled and blotted out in such manner as no man could read the same, but known by the sight of another Bible, which matter so cancelled was in effect the high praise of the king's majesty as supreme head of the Church of England, with other things to his high honour and praise in faith and virtue'.[12]

Here, then, we can see the complete range of Catholic responses to a characteristically ambiguous royal command. For many priests, it seems, erasing the pope's name could be glossed as a spiritual irrelevancy or, at worst, as an onerous task. To these priests, the order was little more than a dispute over jurisdiction which was, for all the King's bluster, presumably as temporary as the excommunication of King John. For those of a slightly different frame of mind, however, the order to erase the name of the pope could be seen as an attempt by the Crown to alter the liturgy of the universal Church and thus as the thin end of a very dangerous wedge. To these priests, conformity was tantamount to heresy, and they were to define themselves as enemies of Henry VIII's policies, if not always enemies of the King himself.

The Catholicism of Henry VIII's reign, then, encompassed far more than the apolitical humanism that has recently been attributed to it; it inculcated in the people of England a series of starkly contradictory views of exactly what the Reformation was and where their responsibilities lay.[13] The question, then, is how did these people get along as the Reformation progressed and the government's demands became more and more radical? If we were to imagine them all sitting down for supper together in the blissful reprieve of Queen Mary's reign, what would they have had to say to one another?

II

One could answer this question rather simply, of course, and suggest that they would have understood that sometimes strategic allies adopt diverse or even contradictory tactics against a common enemy. Indeed, this has been the implicit assumption of historians who have stressed the relief that greeted Queen Mary's accession. Yet this rosy view does not take into account the very messy and politically contentious circumstances in which these various strategies were implemented on the ground. After all, those who chose obedience of one sort or another found themselves in countless situations where their co-religionists were not their allies at all. Sometimes the compromisers found themselves duty-bound to denounce nonconformists to the authorities. Sometimes patronage or financial reward flowed to the compromisers rather than the nonconformists because of their willingness to embrace the status quo. Sometimes the compromisers found that their conformity could be an effective weapon in litigation or in local politics against their more intransigent neighbours. None of this made the compromisers any less Catholic, but it helped shape a polemical context in which Catholics would be bitterly divided.

The first place I want to explore these divisions is the 1549 rebellions and their lingering aftermath. These rebellions, both eastern and western, were the catalyst for a great deal of retrospective conflict and recrimination that has hitherto gone unnoticed, or at least has not been analysed in detail.[14] In the west, where the rebellion was unambiguously Catholic, its perpetrators were horrified that so many of their co-religionists had chosen loyalty over faith. In the east, where the rebellions had an evangelical tint, things were more complicated. Some people were offended that their neighbours had involved themselves in the rebellion, but, more interestingly for our purposes, there was also dispute within the traditionalist community itself: some people were angry about how their conformist neighbours had allocated the community's resources while doing their supposed duty to the Crown.

One interesting case of this latter scenario comes from the village of Calcott, Cambridgeshire. In 1549, Robert Peck, clerk of the peace and an inhabitant of Calcott, was responsible for outfitting four armed men from his community to join royal forces suppressing Kett's Rebellion in Norwich. This task proved difficult, however, because Calcott was a village with 'only nine households' and could not afford to supply so many men. The result was that, on Peck's advice, the villagers sold a silver chalice worth four marks and used the proceeds to pay for soldiers. This would seem to be an example of a very common strategy in Edward's reign: suspecting that they would soon have to yield church goods to the crown, many communities sold them first to meet other financial obligations.[15] Yet regardless of its conservative motives, the transaction proved controversial – selling a chalice was hardly an ideology-free act, especially in a small parish that probably did not own another chalice to replace it – and at the beginning of Mary's reign Peck's enemies had occasion to punish him. During the Jane Grey *coup d'état* in the summer of 1553, the lord of the manor of Calcott mustered his tenants to support Jane, with Robert Peck as his lieutenant. After the *coup* was defeated and Queen Mary was safely on the throne, the villagers of Calcott shopped Peck to the regime not only for supporting Jane Grey, but also for allegedly *embezzling the proceeds from the chalice sale four years earlier.* His neighbours demanded that Peck provide the community with the money to buy a new chalice. This was a perfect example of the sort of retroactive revenge that could be taken against local men who had collaborated in Edward's reign. It reveals that the sale of the chalice, while seemingly a simple financial expedient, had in fact profoundly divided this small community.[16]

In the context of the western rebellions, sympathisers with the rebels were appalled that seemingly good Catholics had dared to oppose the men and women who fought for the Church. As far away as Winchester, conservatives plotted to march on Salisbury with a banner of the five wounds of Christ, not to join the rebellion *per se* but rather to attack the 'villains which began against the western men.'[17] In the west country itself, retrospective conflict arose from the fact that, during the suppression of the rebellion, Lord Russell had issued a proclamation that if his soldiers captured any 'captains and stirrers' of the rebellion, those soldiers 'should take their goods and chattels as goods forfeited and confiscate to their own proper use'. This quasi-legalised plunder helped Russell secure collaboration from soldiers with divided loyalties, but it was a recipe for later conflict. A government soldier named William Lowre, for instance, had 'apprehended one John Bealbury, a priest and notable rebel', and took from him goods worth £8. In the very different political environment of Mary's reign, however, the estate of the now-deceased priest John Bealbury sued Lowre in Chancery for the recovery of Bealbury's goods, presumably intending to use them to refurbish the parish church. This dispute grew so heated that the Marian Lord Chancellor was warned that it threatened to revive 'many controversies, now being quieted, touching the said commotion'.[18]

Another example comes from the town of Langton, and this case is parti-cularly interesting because the Edwardian loyalists scrounging for spoils were not members of Lord Russell's army but *local* opponents of the rebels. The parson of Langton named John Brown was killed during the rebellion, at which point his goods were confiscated by three men named Stephen Foolde, Richard Predom, and Robert Brayleghe. The last of these men is identified as a 'clerk,' so in all probability they were not soldiers. They claimed that they took Brown's possessions 'under colour of a gift ... to them made by the Lord Russell,' presumably in thanks for their loyalty during the uprising, and probably in thanks for killing the parson. These would-be plunderers un-doubtedly believed their confiscations to be safe since the object of their plunder was dead, but, unfortunately for them, not all of Parson Brown's friends died with him. In the changed political context of Mary's reign, one of those friends, John Taylor, claimed that he had purchased from the deceased parson a large quantity of household goods, including a feather bed, a gown, and three ale barrels, amounting to more than £6. Yet these goods had remained temporarily in Parson Brown's possession and had thus been confiscated by his enemies during the 1549 rebellion. Needless to say, this claim by Taylor that it was actually his goods rather than the parson's goods which had been plundered is extremely far-fetched; it is far more likely that Taylor found a convenient excuse to financially crush the men who were responsible for the death of his friend and parish priest.[19]

I want to stress that I have chosen these particular cases because there were no allegations that any of the people involved were Protestants, even though all of these cases come from the Marian courts, where superfluous allegations of heresy were commonplace and extremely useful if litigants thought that they would hold water. What we are looking at, then, are battles within a single, theoretically unified Christian community rather than battles over doctrine. Yet while these were not debates over religion per se, they were nonetheless unquestionably *Reformation* debates, concerned with the crucial question of how far Catholics might accept and profit from the policies of an heretical regime.

As these examples suggest, a certain amount of friction between Catholics was economic. Yet it would be wrong to suppose that just because the context of disputes was financial, therefore the *motivation* was financial; certainly in the case of Robert Peck of Calcott, the financial question was only one part of a broader issue involving both religious loyalty and community consent, and this seems to have been the case elsewhere as well. So, for instance, in the parish of Wadhurst in Sussex there was a plot of woodland that in the fifteenth century had been bequeathed to help the parish church. During Edward's reign, of course, the Chantries Act should have resulted in the forfeiture of this land to the crown, but it was concealed by its executor, one John Crotehole, who illegally leased the land to his son-in-law. This would seem to be a case of resistance to the Reformation, but in fact it was an act of private greed rather than public service, and Crotehole merely took advantage of the regime's opposition to the cult of the dead to expropriate the land. Hence at the beginning of Mary's reign, as soon as they could act with impunity, the community struck back; the new churchwardens of Wadhurst raided the land with axes in hand, cutting down dozens of trees and hauling them off for the use of the parish.[20] Clearly financial issues were involved here, but it is equally clear that the raiders acted on behalf of community values against someone whose actions seemed every bit as sacrilegious as the predations of the regime.

Another case which deserves more detailed attention concerns the rectory and parsonage of Addenburgh in Nottinghamshire, which in Henry VIII's reign had come into the King's hands as a result of the dissolution of the monasteries, and which soon afterwards were leased to the gentleman William Bowles.[21] Some time in the years that followed, Bowles became involved in a bitter lawsuit with one Richard Whaley, a powerful gentleman and officer of Edward VI's Court of Augmentations who was notorious for enriching himself through the dissolution of monasteries and chantries. As a precaution against losing the Addenburgh parsonage in this lawsuit, Bowles attempted a quasi-legal but very common manœuvre. He granted a *conditional* lease of the property to his son Bonaventure. If Whaley won his lawsuit against Bowles, then Bowles's son would receive the parsonage to keep it in the family; if Whaley lost his lawsuit, then the grant would be nullified and Bowles would keep the property himself. In the event, the lawsuit was settled out of court and Bowles retained possession of the parsonage. But as was so often the case, the end of the lawsuit did not end the property dispute. Several years later, a client of Whaley's named George Petit claimed that he had been legally granted the parsonage by Bonaventure Bowles, and thus that he was its lawful owner. And early in Queen Mary's reign, Petit and his men entered the parsonage on the basis of this claim and not only took over the property but also stole or spoiled what was now allegedly £200 worth of goods belonging to the parsonage.

So to summarise, we seem to have here a very common story from the English Reformation. There was a dispute over the property rights to a parsonage. One claimant to those rights had apparently left the church's goods intact and was traditionalist enough to name his son Bonaventure; the other claimant was the local client to a notorious spoiler of church goods and supporter of the Edwardian government. It is never suggested in the dispute that any of these men were Protestants, even though Bowles certainly could have scored significant points in the case by making that allegation. Rather, this is a case where those who had collaborated with and profited from the spoliations of the Reformation squared off against those who had resisted those spoliations, all against the backdrop of Queen Mary's attempts to restore traditional religion.

So what was the result? On 24 May 1557, according to the testimony of George Petit, William Bowles gathered a crowd of eighty craftsmen, labourers, and other villagers and forcibly seized the property. Eighty men may seem like a lot, but this was not a case where the allegation of riot was a mere artifact of court procedure; in this case even the defendants admitted that there was a large, violent disturbance. According to William Bowles himself, he came to the parsonage with about five of his servants, intending to use them to help cart away his goods. However, when he arrived Petit's servants appeared with 'bows, arrows, guns, and crossbows' and repeatedly shot at them to force them off the property. And this is where the story gets really interesting. According to the defendant Bowles, just by coincidence that day was also the occasion of the annual Rogationtide procession in the parish church, and just at that moment 'a great multitude of people being gathered together to go in procession according to the use and custom happened then to be near the said parsonage, and by reason of this unwanted noise the people assembled themselves together about the same parsonage'. According to the defence, in other words, the crowd that gathered was not a rampaging mob but rather a devout processional. Yet even Bowles' own witnesses sheepishly admitted that, for reasons they could not adequately explain, some of the villagers marching in this church processional just happened to have brought with them swords, daggers, staves, and bows and arrows, and they apparently used those weapons to help William Bowles retake the parsonage.

What I want to suggest from this story, then, is that it gives us a hint of the sort of conflict that was common in Mary Tudor's reign. It was without question an example of 'Reformation' conflict: it concerned ecclesiastical property that had been confiscated by the government, and it took on an almost quintessential Counter-Reformation form as an instance of ritual violence that developed out of a church processional. Yet the people against whom violence was directed were not Protestants, and hence the event appears neither in Foxe's *Book of Martyrs* nor in any other history of the period written over the last four centuries. What was at issue in Addenburgh was not theology, nor even property per se, but rather a very basic dispute over how to interpret the events of the previous twenty-five years. People disagreed violently about the legitimacy of recent government actions, as well as the moral status of people who had benefited from those actions; hence when some members of the community tried to press a legal claim to Church property which depended upon the legitimacy of government spoil, other members of the community responded with knives and swords.

IV

If we leave popular politics behind and instead look at the views of elite Catholic nonconformists in Edward VI's reign, we find much the same sort of frustration at the politic or rapacious actions of their co-religionists. One notable Catholic lament, for instance, was *The Complaint of Grace*, penned by John Redman, former master of Trinity College, Cambridge, shortly before his death in 1551.[22] In the *Complaint*, an allegorised figure of Grace tells the story of human history since the creation of Adam, with the present era described as unparalleled in its sinfulness: 'As the age of the apostles and martyrs surmounted all other in virtue and godliness, so neither the age of the universal flood, nor of the tower of Babel, nor of Amalek and all the giants, nor of all wicked kings of Israel, nor of all the bloodthirsty and idolatrous tyrants, is worthy to be compared to thee in greatness of iniquity.' Redman located the source of this modern iniquity in England's government and the unwillingness of English subjects to oppose its wickedness. All through history, Grace claimed, she had strengthened men's hearts against the ungodly laws of wicked magistrates. Shortly after Christ's ascension, for instance, Grace told his disciples 'not to be afraid of any power, carnal or spiritual, visible or invisible, but with all confidence and courage defy the world and the prince thereof, and fight valiantly in the battle of God against the old serpent'.[23] In modern times, however, compromise had afflicted the people, especially priests who, 'forgetting the battle of God whereunto they were taken and appointed to fight against the world, began to take truce with the world, and so to lose the service of God and the wages promised for the same'.[24] Redman made it clear that greed was the root of spiritual infidelity and compromise, and he presented the figure of Avarice as Grace's allegorical nemesis: 'O filthy Avarice, how hast thou infected and poisoned all vocations, offices, all states and degrees? Thou hast extinguished the lamps of clergy, thou hast disdained the honour of [the] nobility, thou hast corrupted all the mean and inferior sort of the commonalty. Law, justice, conscience, honesty, fidelity, [and] mercy are all through thy violence trodden under foot.'[25]

Richard Smith likewise saw greed as the source of England's disastrous compromises with heresy, and he identified priests as particular offenders. In his *Brief Treatyse Settynge Forth Divers Truthes* (1547), Smith derided priests who condemned their flocks to damnation through their willingness to pursue career advancement at the expense of true religion. It had recently become commonplace, he suggested, for ambitious priests to 'make friends for the obtaining of [benefices]' and to 'give money very largely for them, for benefices are now common merchandise'. This was clearly to suggest that the 'friends' priests made to advance their career were the office-holders in Thomas Cranmer's Church. If instead of this corruption priests obtained advancement through 'learning and virtue,' then 'heresies and errors should very little prevail'. Smith thus condemned priests for their collaboration with the government, finding an apt proof text in his loose rendition of Romans 1:32: 'Not only they that do such things are worthy of death, but they also which do consent to the doers.'[26]

This sort of recrimination within the clerical community can also be seen in an open letter written in 1550 from one former monk to another, condemning his decision to marry. He addressed the fallen cleric as 'Lucifer' – once the light-bringer, now a rebel against God – and asked him rhetorically 'How art thou fallen from heaven to earth, how is gold changed to muck?' While we might guess that the married priest was a Protestant, in fact his erstwhile friend thought otherwise; instead he saw the priest's marriage as yet another example of how compromise with the world had undermined English Catholicism. In the writer's mind, it was his former brother's 'dissimulation' and lust that was to blame, rather than any spiritual conversion: 'How can you say, "I have fought a good fight" when ye resist and fight not against tempta-tion but utterly offer yourself to be overcome? ... How preposterous an order is it to be chaste in your youth and wanton in your old age?' In the mind of the letter-writer, the priest had completely abdicated his responsibility to die before abandoning his clerical vows: 'It seemeth a just cause for a priest to offer himself to martyrdom to withstand that a virgin consecrate be not given to marriage.'[27]

Perhaps the most interesting of the Edwardian Catholic laments, however, is a virtually unknown poem that survives only in one much later copy, preserved in the Harleian Manuscripts and bearing the title, 'The Ballad of Little John Nobody, who (under that Name) Libels the Reformation under King Edward VI'.[28] The ballad describes a conversation between the narrator, who defends the Reformation, and a character called 'Little John Nobody, that durst not speak.' John Nobody is a deeply conflicted figure; on the one hand he viciously satires the religious policies of Edward VI's government, but on the other hand he claims to be a loyal subject and denies that he would ever meddle in the affairs of government or Church. Thus, while the character of John Nobody castigates Protestant innovations, the ballad employs a devastating irony by putting these words into the mouth of a compromiser who watches with detached frustration rather than wholehearted resistance while the world falls apart around him.

At the beginning of the ballad, the Protestant narrator finds John Nobody sitting by himself, writing a song 'of trifles' to the effect that 'few were fast in the faith'. Here, then, we have an immediate complaint against Catholic compromisers. But when the Protestant narrator defends Edwardian religion, angrily asking whether John Nobody 'wanted wit, or some had done him wrong,' John responds merely that he is 'John Nobody, that durst not speak'. John, then, is more or less what he despises: a Catholic who will not put himself in jeopardy.

Of course, when the narrator asks John what exactly he had in mind when he said that few were 'fast' in their faith, John is more than happy to respond with a series of brutal and often hilarious attacks on the Reformation. For instance, John mocks peasants who debate the scriptures:

> These gay gallants, that will construe the gospel,
> As Solomon the sage, with semblance full sad,
> To discuss divinity, they naught adread.
> More mete it were for them to milk kine at a flake.[29]

Another verse attacks Thomas Cranmer's *Book of Common Prayer*, with its strange new English services:

> For our Reverend has set forth an order,
> Our service to be said in our seigneur's tongue.
> As Solomon the sage set forth the scripture,
> Our suffrages and service with many a sweet song,
> With homilies and godly books us among,
> That we, no stiff stubborn stomachs, we should freak.
> But wretches never worse to do poor men wrong:
> But that I, Little John Nobody, dare not speak.[30]

Here we can see some of the author's frustration at a population with 'no stiff stubborn stomachs' whose laxity made them susceptible, and indeed complicit, in the growth of heresy. Yet nonetheless, John Nobody himself did not dare to oppose the regime openly, and hence in the last stanza he is removed from the real world into the world of allegory:

> Thus in no place, this Nobody in no time I met,
> Where no man then naught was, nor nothing did appear,
> Though the sound of a synagogue for sorrow I sweat,
> That Hercules through the catch did cause me to hear.

Then I drew me down into a dale, where as the dumb deer
Did shiver for a shower; But I shunted from a freak.
For I would no wight in this world wist who I were,
But Little John Nobody, that dare not once speak.[31]

Hence the narrator is converted to the opinions of John Nobody and goes to reside with the 'dumb deer,' in other words the non-speakers like John himself. But these non-speakers are at the same time effectively removed from reality, with John Nobody disappearing literally into no man's land; Catholic resistance might succeed in a pastoral dale, we are told, but not in England, where the sounds of the 'synagogue' drown out any voice that might try vainly to protest.

V

Why should these mid-Tudor Catholic writers have been so sceptical that compromisers with the Reformation had maintained their core religiosity while trying to navigate difficult circumstances? We can find part of the answer in the Catholic restoration of Queen Mary's reign, when many Catholics found, to their dismay, that their co-religionists would not stop compromising with the world just because the old religion was once again ascendant. Nothing displayed this problem more starkly than the difficulties encountered by the Marian regime when it attempted to rebuild 'traditional' Catholicism in the radically desacralised landscape of the 1550s. Queen Mary and Reginald Pole firmly believed (anticipating the opinions of some revisionist historians) that much apparent acquiescence to the Tudor government's ecclesiastical predations had masked a powerful undercurrent of resentment against the state-sponsored Reformation. In other words, they believed that people who had profited from the dissolution of monasteries and chantries were pious traditionalists who looked forward to a time when churches, monasteries, and chantries could be restored to their former glory. Imagine their surprise, then, when large numbers of supposedly 'Catholic' subjects refused to return plundered wealth to the Marian Church.

Just as Henry VIII had created a vast bureaucracy to raid the Church, Queen Mary created new government agencies to restore it. At the core of this endeavour were the commissioners for church property, William Berners, Thomas Mildmay, and John Wiseman, who were given the crown's considerable investigatory apparatus to track down and re-appropriate plundered goods. They met with considerable resistance, however, and their surviving archive tells a story of frustration which in many ways mirrors the difficulties experienced by Henry VIII's and Edward VI's commissioners over the previous twenty years. In a letter to James Starkey in February 1555, for instance, the commissioners wrote that £159 in cash and 113 ounces of plate due to the crown from chantries and churches remained in private hands in Cheshire; accompanying this letter they sent a list of twenty-eight individuals who had failed to deliver their goods, along with twenty-eight privy seals to encourage compliance.[32] Two years later they investigated Margaret, Countess of Lennox, for having embezzled ten ounces of plate and 13s in goods from the chantry of Newsham in the parish of Wressle, in Yorkshire. She at first sent her servant to deny the charges, but finding that the commissioners were 'not satisfied in my said servant's answer', she was forced to write another letter reaffirming that she 'never had the value of one farthing'. Whether she was telling the truth or not, clearly *someone* had stolen the chantry's goods and refused to return them even under a Catholic regime.[33] In 1556, a privy seal was issued to one Richard Jones of Thornbury, Gloucestershire 'for the delivery ... of one cross of silver belonging to the late chantry of Our Lady in Thornbury'. When the commissioners investigated Jones's claims of innocence, they were told by numerous witnesses that Jones never had the cross, but rather it had been in the keeping of the churchwardens, 'which said cross among and with diverse other things ... before the time of the late inventory made, was embezzled and stolen away out of the said church'.[34]

Another list of presentments survives from Kent, where another set of government officials encountered similar difficulties retrieving embezzled items despite the government's oft-stated commitment to revive their religious usage. Thomas Bet of Elmstead, for instance, refused to yield eleven tapers 'which tapers did burn in the rood loft beside the chantry of Our Lady'. William Sanders of Woodnesborough would not return a 'church cow, wherewith the paschal was always maintained'. In Chilham, the parish failed for years to recover a stipend of £9 6s 8d that a former vicar, Sir Robert Pele, had granted to the clothworkers' guild in London for the health of his soul. Thomas Keys of Folkestone refused to yield 'a house of 12d a year out of a piece of land that should find a canopy light to burn before the sacrament'.[35]

Even in the conservative heart of Lancashire the Marian government could not count on compliance. In May 1555, for instance, the queen and her new husband issued a commission to investigate alleged thefts after they were 'credibly informed that there is diverse stocks of kine, chalices, jewels, plate, bells, ornaments, and such like which were given to the use and maintenance of the late chapel of Farnworth, being within the parish of Prescot in our county of Lancaster, remaining in diverse men's hands, which were never answered to us nor any our progenitors ... and some plate thereof is embezzled away'. They experienced these difficulties recovering the chapel's property even though they 'appointed [the chapel] to be a chapel of ease for the administration of sacraments and sacramentals' and ordered that the recovered goods be immediately given 'to the churchwardens of the said chapel' for 'the maintenance of God's service'.[36]

What must be understood about these confrontations is that for Catholics who had remained unequivocally committed to the pre-Reformation Church, such embezzlements were not merely avaricious but sowed the seeds of heresy. Let us consider the views of Cardinal Pole. In the 1530s, of course, Pole had argued that Henry VIII's break with Rome was not merely schismatic but heretical. This position, if carried to its logical conclusion, would have made it difficult for Pole to work with bishops such as Gardiner who had conformed with 'Henrician' religion and renounced their allegiance to the pope. But Pole was a politician as much as a churchman, and he recognised the need to moderate his views. Thus in a 1554 letter to Gardiner he extravagantly praised those 'valiant champions' who had refused 'to separate from the body of the Church', in other words the most intransigent Catholic nonconformists; but he also thanked God for such men as Gardiner who, 'though they fell into the first grave error' of separation from the Church, nonetheless maintained 'constancy and fortitude in defending the true and holy doctrine against the heretics'.[37] It was under this logic that the government allowed former con-formists such as Bonner and Gardiner merely to be reconciled from their 'schismatic' state rather than undergoing formal heresy proceedings as Latimer and Cranmer did. Pole, in other words, was not above compromise.

But even this expedient flexibility concerning the line between schism and heresy had its limits; once English subjects were reconciled to the Catholic Church, they were supposed to be *truly* reconciled to it. It made no sense, in Pole's view, to welcome prodigal sons back to the Church if they insisted upon keeping the fruits of their schism; this was equivalent to pardoning the sins of people who neither performed their penance nor felt contrition for their sins. When he was first charged in August 1553 with the task of reconciling England to Rome, Pole assumed that he would refuse absolution to any English subjects who would not return their formerly ecclesiastical lands. Then a year later, under tremendous pressure, Pole agreed to separate the issue of absolu-tion from the question of ecclesiastical property in all but the most extra-ordinary cases. Even this proved insufficient to placate the English landed classes, however, because they conceived of the whole negotiation process in reverse: they would accept no reunion with Rome until Rome agreed to accept their ownership of church lands. Thus under pressure from the Privy Council in December 1554, Pole agreed to accept the disposition of all Church lands, with no strings attached, prior to any reconciliation between England and Rome. But Pole did not accept this necessity without lashing out at the immorality of the Privy Council to their faces, comparing them to the legendary pagans who had stolen the gold of the temple at Toulouse, and reminding them that God had already showed his displeasure towards the architects of the spoliation: Cromwell, Somerset, and Northumberland. It was only thanks to the saintly intervention of Thomas More and John Fisher that

God had now given England a Christian Queen, and Pole bluntly reminded the Privy Councillors that those saints had given their lives to protest against a regime which they all had willingly followed.[38]

Pole and other Catholics of his complexion thus believed that the refusal to return ecclesiastical wealth represented a fundamental break from the Catholic past, conferring an irredeemable corruption on those who would not renounce their transgression and seek absolution. It was in this spirit that in June 1555 John Feckenham chose to address part of a sermon at St. Paul's to 'ye gentlemen and noblemen which in living here in this world be very politic and full of all manner of worldly provisions'. The wealthy men were told that they must make provision for the 'four last things' – death, judgment, heaven, and hell – which in their case meant fulfilling their responsibilities towards 'the maintenance of God's glory and honour'. In particular, the preacher scathingly asked whether their 'pretensed seeking of God's glory' was really enough:

> O ye that are wandering here in this world ... as people without counsel and void of wisdom and all foresight, is this a provision for the upholding of Christ's Catholic faith and religion here in this realm (by night and day prayer, by reading, preaching, and teaching, by liberal alms-giving and relieving the poor members of Christ) to overthrow monasteries, colleges, and hospitals, to spoil bishoprics and their cathedral churches, so craftily to cramp and fleece the universities by a covetous exchange of their lands? Is this your provision? ... O, would God you would once become wise, to perceive and understand that except ye shortly shall repent and do penance here in season for your great wickedness, here to confess and acknowledge the same, here to make satisfaction and to restore again, doubtless your provision for these last four things will be very slender and right naught worth.[39]

Even harsher rhetoric was used in a November 1553 sermon by James Brooks, master of Balliol College, Oxford. Citing St Cyprian and St Augustine, Brooks argued that anyone who 'doth separate himself from the Catholic Church, how commendably and how godly soever he thinketh himself to live, and it were no more but for this one heinous offence only, that he is separate from the unity of Christ, he shall not have life, *non habebit vitam* ... he shall be counted as dead'. Therefore the Church of England as a whole had been not merely damaged but *killed* by the apostasies of the Reformation, and the Holy Catholic Church might mourn for her: 'Lord, my daughter the Church of England (as touching the life of lively unity) she is even now (in a part) deceased and dead.'[40] Even given this pessimistic assessment, Brooks accepted that the Church in England might, despite its discontinuity with the past, be revived. But in practice this revival was endangered by an outpouring of sins, not least of which were the actions 'of certain of the laity, which hath what by hook, what by crook, wrung out of the hands of the clergy not only benefices and tithes but also the best part of the temporalities of bishoprics.

Hath they dealt (think you) charitably with them therein? No verily, unless you will call that charity which Julianus the Apostata once used with the Christians.' Indeed, England remained so corrupt in the aftermath of the Edwardian Reformation that even St Polycarpus, who had cried out to God, '*Deus Bone, in quae tempora me reservasti*', would be horrified at what he found. This included not only 'swearing, perjury, blasphemy, and usury', but also 'the pulling down of God's houses and hospitals; the defacing of churches in spoiling their goods and ornaments; the breaking down of altars; the throwing down of crosses; the casting out of images; the burning of tried holy relics'.[41] All of these sins might be overcome, and God had sent Queen Mary as his agent for the revival of the English Church, but that depended upon the restoration of 'all good order, all good living, all good believing, all godliness, and goodness'.[42]

The point is that the question of the return of ecclesiastical property – a question seemingly more related to worldly matters than the epic battles of the Reformation – transcended its apparent context and raised fundamental questions about Catholic identity and the success of the English Reformation. If England would not perform its penance, if its people did not recognise their sins, how could it be forgiven? If the compromisers of the Reformation continued to deny that their previous conformity had constituted a rupture in Christ's Church, in what sense could they truly be called members of that Church now?

VI

None of this is meant to suggest that we should accept at face value the laments of these mid-Tudor Catholics about the collapse of traditional religion. Like the laments of puritans two decades later, bemoaning the 'failure' of reform in the face of a superstitious commonalty, this Catholic perspective represents only one side of a long-running and multi-faceted contemporary debate over the meaning of the English Reformation. I would suggest, however, that the evidence presented here shows the inherent limitations of any historical model that chooses sides in this debate. To some men and women who lived through the English Reformation, it clearly seemed better to live to fight another day – and perhaps even accept some good that had grown from the Tudor reforms – rather than risk their lives for a lost cause. These men and women could argue persuasively in Mary's reign that they had done the right thing, remaining loyal to their king and waiting for God to strike him down. For others, however – men and women who looked just the same and shared the same faith – it seemed that a huge gulf had opened up between themselves and the pre-Reformation past. They looked at the compromisers with sadness, and sometimes with hatred, wondering what might have been.

Ethan Shagan

One conclusion that I would suggest from these observations is that 'English Catholic history' as a field – usually taken to begin in 1558, when 'Catholic history' can first be meaningfully separated from English religious history as a whole – might usefully learn a great deal from its Reformation antecedents. After all, the debates I have described here look eerily similar to the debates of the Appellant Controversy, when once again Catholics argued over the success or failure of the English Reformation. When the anti-Jesuit faction suggested that a viable Catholic Church still functioned in England at the turn of the seventeenth century despite the ravages of the Reformation, they were in essence choosing sides in a debate that stretched back generations. Likewise, the 'church papists' whom Alexandra Walsham has so usefully brought to our attention claimed continuity with one strand of loyalist Catholicism in the English Reformation. But it is worth remembering, as we consider their place in the patchwork quilt of Elizabethan religious identities, that many of their ostensible co-religionists had denounced such compromisers as the *enemies* of Catholicism since the 1530s. To state baldly that these 'Church Papists' were *real* Catholics, then, is to take one side in an ongoing sixteenth-century debate.

Another way to approach this issue is to think about what constituted Catholic 'resistance' in the Reformation. Historians who have examined Catholic 'resistance' have generally pointed to relatively minor actions, for instance burying saints' images rather than surrendering them, or saying mass in private after using the Edwardian service book in public. This is a perfectly reasonable approach, and no doubt the people who performed such actions believed sincerely that they were resisting the Reformation. But it is not without importance that many among their Catholic neighbours could interpret this sort of 'resistance' as unacceptable compromise. It was these more radical resisters who arose in 1536 and 1549, and it was their priests who erased the name of the king instead of the name of the pope from their service books in 1535. As this essay has shown, it is unhelpful for us to apply our own categories of what 'resistance' meant instead of listening to the debates of contemporaries. And crucially for our understanding of later English Catholic history, there were plenty of contemporaries in Edward VI's reign who would have far preferred an influx of foreign missionaries or soldiers to the underground survival of the mass.

What I want to suggest in conclusion, then, is that without paying more attention to the political divisions among Catholics – and I use 'political' here in a broad sense – Catholic history as a subject cannot be rescued from the notion that it is sectarian history rather than a useful and important part of English history. Through close attention to these divisions, we can begin to see how people with a shared theology could nonetheless participate in widely different communities in addition to their seemingly common 'Catholic community'. We can begin to see how the choice to identify with certain other Catholics because of their shared beliefs, or shared history, or shared circumstances, was not inevitable or unalterable; it was indeed a choice.

NOTES

1 Eamon Duffy, *The Stripping of the Altars: Traditional Religion in England 1400-1580* (New Haven, 1992), pp. 592–3.

2 Pierre Janelle (ed.), *Obedience in Church and State: Three Political Tracts* (New York, 1968), pp. 99 and 157.

3 PRO SP 1/99, fos. 200r–204v [*LP*, ix. 1059].

4 PRO SP 1/106, fo. 161r [*LP*, ix. 447].

5 PRO KB 9/1004, fo. 196r.

6 Geoffrey Elton, *Policy and Police: The Enforcement of the Reformation in the Age of Thomas Cromwell* (Cambridge, 1972), p. 131.

7 Elton, *Policy and Police*, p. 237.

8 Ibid.

9 PRO E 36/120, fo. 49r [*LP*, xi. 464].

10 PRO KB 9/978, fo. 34r.

11 PRO E 36/120, fo. 53r–v.

12 PRO SP 1/242, fo. 103r [*LP*, *Add.*, 1370].

13 See Lucy Wooding, *Rethinking Catholicism in Reformation England* (Oxford, 2000).

14 Historians such as Diarmaid MacCulloch, while not analysing these incidents for their own political significance, have used them very successfully to reconstruct events in the risings. See Diarmaid MacCulloch, 'Kett's Rebellion in Context', *PP*, 84 (1979), 36–59.

15 For many examples of this, see Ethan Shagan, *Popular Politics and the English Reformation* (Cambridge, 2003).

16 PRO C 1/1379, fos. 91r–92r and C 1/1385, fo. 37r.

17 PRO SP 10/8, fos. 74r–75v.

18 PRO C 1/1367, fo. 82r.

19 PRO C 1/1387, fo. 14r.

20 PRO C 1/1319, fos. 31–4.

21 PRO STAC 4/5/2.

22 John Redman, *A Compendious Treatise Called the Complaint of Grace* (London, 1556?).

23 Ibid., sigs. E7v.

24 Ibid., sigs. G1v, F6v–F7r, F7v, G3r.

25 Ibid., sigs. K7v–K8r.

26 Richard Smith, *A Brief Treatyse Settynge Forth Divers Truthes* (London, 1547), sigs. B7r–v.

27 BL Cotton MS Titus A. xxiv, fos. 211v–217r.

28 BL Harleian MS 372, fo. 114r–v.

29 Ibid. A 'flake' is a wooden frame, like a saw-horse. I would like to thank Bill Jordan for this esoteric definition.

30 Ibid. 'Freak' in this context means to change suddenly or capriciously.

31 Ibid. To 'sweat' in this context can mean either to undergo severe affliction or punishment, or to fume or rage. The word 'wight' is attested as an adjective meaning 'strong', but the usage as a noun here may be *sic* for 'wit.' The word that I have modernised as 'catch' is 'ceche' in the manuscript.

32 PRO E 117/13/83.

33 PRO E 117/14/119.

34 PRO E 117/14/31.

35 'Extracts from Original Documents Illustrating the Progress of the Reformation in Kent', ed. C. E. Woodruff, *Archaeologia Cantiana*, 31 (1915), 92–120, at pp. 109–10.

36 PRO DL 42/96, fo. 122r–v.

37 *The Letters of Stephen Gardiner*, ed. J. A. Muller (New York, 1933), pp. 489–90.

38 J. H. Crehan, 'The Return to Obedience: New Judgment of Cardinal Pole', *The Month*, new ser. 14 (October 1955), p. 226.

39 John Feckenham, *A Notable Sermon Made within S. Paules Church in London* (London, 1555), sigs. D1r–D3v. I have added parentheses to this quotation to aid comprehension.

40 James Brooks, *A Sermon Very Notable, Fruicteful, and Godlie* (London, 1554), sigs. C5v, C8v.

41 Ibid., sigs. G3r–v, H7v–H8r.

42 Ibid., sig. I7v.

Chapter 4

Elizabeth and the Catholics

Michael C. Questier

In a recent volume, *The Myth of Elizabeth*, capitalising on the interest in all things involving Elizabeth Tudor, a number of scholars reviewed fictions, both contemporary and more modern, about the Queen.[1] One curious, indeed distinctly bizarre, omission from the volume was any sense of the political myth-making potential concerning the Queen generated by the 'Catholic issue' in the post-Reformation period. Perhaps the editors thought that there was no myth about the relationship between Gloriana and her Catholic subjects, in the sense of a single historiographical falsehood or fantasy which, if only we could discover and expose it, would change our view of her, them, and perhaps the world. Admittedly we are unlikely now to discover any single piece of paper which radically re-writes our account of this particular aspect of her regime. It seems, after all, to have been her fashion to say little on such subjects as religion, at least by comparison with her successor, James Stuart, who enthusiastically and openly addressed questions of doctrine and ecclesiastical politics. But the inescapable fact is that many accounts of the relationship between Elizabeth and her Catholic subjects are still heavily built on 'myths' – not actual falsehoods, of course, but a species of generalisation that has tended to flourish in the absence of any considerable body of modern research on what remains a relatively unfashionable topic. Clearly this is something of which the editors of *The Myth of Elizabeth* were unaware. I want to suggest that by discussing and, I hope, by decoding some of these myths we can open up a crucial, though curiously under-discussed, political issue of the period. What follows is thus, essentially, a 'thought piece' on the subject, based principally on readings of a few well-known polemical texts – texts about the Queen, about Catholics, about the extent to which they might be considered 'loyal' to the last of the Tudors, and about how far their duty to remain loyal to the sovereign precluded them from critiquing aspects of her government which they disliked or thought unwise.

Let us consider briefly, therefore, two strands of mythic tenet about the Queen and the Catholics. The first is the 'loyalism' myth. English Catholics, we are often told, were (for the most part) 'loyal' to Elizabeth, whom they recognised as their legitimate sovereign, and they scorned foreign schemes to send her tumbling from her throne.[2] If the pope chose, as Pius V did in *Regnans in Excelsis* (1570), to declare her excommunicate, accursed, and deprived of her title, that was his business, not theirs. Their martyrologies denied that the Catholics who suffered the full extremity of the treason statutes were, or had ever been, in any sense disloyal or even 'political'. Catholic martyrs prayed for the Queen before death, disclaimed any wish to see her fall from power, and repudiated plots against her life. In one famous vignette, the priest Edmund Gennings, just before his execution in Gray's Inn Fields in late 1591, is described as being taunted by Richard Topcliffe – 'Gennings, Gennings, confess thy fault, thy popish treason, and the Queen by submission no doubt will grant thee pardon.' But Gennings replied, so we are told, 'I know not, Mr. Topcliffe, in what I have offended my dear anointed princess; for if I had offended her, or any other, in any thing, I would willingly ask her and all the world forgiveness', though he added that she might be offended at him without cause, for matter of religion only.[3] A few Catholics, such as Cardinal William Allen and the archetypal 'evil' Jesuit Robert Parsons, *did*, of course, express bitter political and personal hostility to Elizabeth. (Allen's *Admonition to the Nobility and People of England*, written with the 1588 Armada in mind, described Elizabeth as 'an incestuous bastard, begotten and born in sin, of an infamous courtesan'. She was 'an infamous ... accursed, excommunicate heretic, the very shame of her sex, and princely name; the chief spectacle of sin and abomination in this our age ... the only poison, calamity and destruction of our noble church and country'.[4]) But the average seminary priest was not trained to partake in such high matters, and confined himself to issues of doctrine, to 'religion' in other words.[5]

So, were Catholics in fact loyal to the Queen? In the sense that there was only one major 'Catholic' rebellion during her reign, they were. The Catholic gentry did not generally rise in arms against the regime at the drop of a hat, and clergy in the seminaries were not given training in bomb-making techniques. But, if this is the case, then it is difficult to explain exactly why the regime associated loyal, quiescent, largely gentrified Catholicism with the spectre of a rampant fifth column waiting only until they saw the Spaniards coming ashore to rise up in revolt – unless we assume that Elizabeth's government was run largely by reference to the (alleged) screaming insecurities of anti-popery discourse about the world-historical threat which Romish religion (the mystery of iniquity) represented to true religion and the realm of England.[6]

And yet there is a strand of historiographical opinion, also verging at times on the quasi-mythical, which says that actually a significant proportion of

Catholics were indeed traitors, and therefore that all Catholics could be regarded as potentially disloyal. Conyers Read argued that the regime was entirely justified in its suspicions of the seminary priests because they disseminated 'potentially traitorous doctrines'.[7] Michael Carrafiello contends that the strategy of the Jesuit mission to England of 1580 was always governed by political considerations, not pastoral ones. Its alleged pastoral concerns were never more than a front for the political ambitions of its leaders, and such ambitions were uniformly detrimental to the Queen's rule.[8] Here there is almost an equivalence with the line spun in government polemic, principally Lord Burghley's *Execution of Justice* of 1583, which said that the motive for English Catholics' dissent was treason but they made 'defence of their lewd and unlawful facts by untruths and by colouring and covering their deeds ... with pretences of some other causes,' namely the 'religion of Rome' and the authority of the pope.[9]

Inevitably, the extremes of this account of politicised Catholicism (the 'disloyalty' myth) spawned a critique of such assumed connections between Catholic faith and Catholic treasons (following, of course, contemporary Catholics' own refutations of the government's claims).[10] By distinguishing the bulk of the Catholic population from the plotters of the Elizabethan Catholic underworld it was possible to claim that the 'majority' of Catholics were indeed loyal to Elizabeth precisely because they were not like Anthony Babington. Their concerns must have been merely 'religious'.[11] Even the sceptical and caustic Hugh Trevor-Roper subscribed to something like this thesis when he argued that the 'lay' Catholics of England were out of sympathy with Jesuit intrigue.[12] And so the 'debate' tends to go rather uncritically round and round in circles. The 'loyalism' thesis has been heavily drawn on by the so-called 'revisionist' account of Elizabethan Catholicism, for instance in Christopher Haigh's claim that seminarists and Jesuits such as the saintly Edmund Campion were concerned simply with sustaining 'the faith of the Catholics of England' by preaching and administering the Catholic sacraments.[13] Here, contemporary Catholics' loyalist self-fashioning has been drafted into service to shore up suppositions about the natural vigour of popular religion in the average Elizabethan parish. When historians have tried to problematise and nuance the issue, as we see in Thomas McCoog's subtle questioning of the way in which the Jesuit mission of 1580 was carried out (arguing that there were real ambiguities about what was supposed to happen when Campion and Parsons got to England), somewhat less well-informed critics, such as Eric Carlson, apparently unaware of the importance of this debate about religion and politics, have written this off as reading matter primarily for other British Jesuits.[14]

This is perhaps not the place to embark upon a long consideration of contemporary understandings of the dividing line between politics and religion, nor to discuss what, for contemporaries, was treason and what was loyalty, although a more sophisticated cultural approach to the politics of religious identity in the period is already helping to make sense of the religious name-calling at which contemporaries were so adept.[15] Yet to leave it at this risks merely accepting contemporary polemical accounts of the Catholic issue which, if teased out to their full extent, do not really make sense. It is therefore worth asking again what it was that made Catholicism such a fraught political question for so many contemporary commentators. One way of doing this is to return to the relationship between the Queen and the Catholics. If we can establish some kind of fit between her attitude to them and what they said about her, we can start to define that relationship, and to say something about the structural positioning of Catholicism as a political issue during this period, even if we cannot say exactly what every identifiable Catholic thought about the political topics that interested them.

I

We have a number of pronouncements made by the Queen (though often reported by others) where she expressed her opinions about her Catholic subjects. They have formed the basis for the line that she was personally tolerant and did not support the proposals for really harsh measures against papists. Sir John Neale, for example, argued that it was the Queen who was the principal stumbling block in the way of the parliamentary anti-Catholic measures of the 1570s and early 1580s, for she was naturally moderate, high-minded, and statesmanlike.[16] It was sometimes put out by the regime that the execution of Catholic traitors where the full sentence was commuted to mere strangulation was an act of the Queen's clemency, that is, modifying the full penalty of the law for treason which stipulated disembowelling while still alive.[17] We are told that she strongly rejected characterisations of her as a persecutor. The French diplomat André Hurault recorded that, in a meeting with the Queen on Christmas Eve 1597, she denounced not just the Spaniards but also the wicked rumours spread on the Continent about the cruelty with which she treated her Catholic subjects.[18]

Significantly we find similar stories circulating among English Catholics about Elizabeth's habit of clemency towards females. For example, the Jesuit William Weston recounted that, when informed that recusant gentry were being carted off to prison, 'the queen was asked to make the same provision for women' but 'she is said to have answered: "You have had your way with the men. Would you have me shut the women up too – like nuns in a convent?"'[19] This line featured strongly in Catholic martyrology where it was claimed that Elizabeth was capable of individual acts of mercy. In the case of Robert Southwell, on a petition made by his father, she was alleged to have intervened to improve the conditions of his imprisonment.[20] Katherine Longley cites the reprieve of the leading recusant Mrs Wiseman in 1598, before whose intended execution the Queen heard how 'for so small a matter she should have been put to death' and 'rebuked the justices of cruelty'.[21]

But another Catholic tradition declared and commemorated Elizabeth's personal vindictiveness and brutality. This got its most public airing over the Mary Stuart case, though Elizabeth made haste to claim that she had been landed in it by her ministers. We know, however, of Elizabeth's apparent occasional personal hostility towards individual Catholics. In the well-known progress into East Anglia in 1578, we have what looks like the Queen, in tandem with her councillors, playing a complex 'good cop, bad cop' game with leading Catholic gentry. Various Catholic gentlemen's houses were visited by the Queen en route to Norwich, and some of them got more than the general stench and inconvenience which were associated with a visit from the royal train. At Euston in Suffolk the head of the Rookwood family was honoured by the Queen's presence, was allowed to kiss the Queen's hand and was thanked for allowing the Queen the use of his abode. Immediately the Earl of Sussex launched into a tirade against Rookwood for his Catholicism and told him to avoid the royal presence. A statue of the Virgin was then discovered during a search for a supposedly lost piece of plate, and the Queen presided over an impromptu auto-da-fé (for the statue).[22] There were claims that the executions of Campion and his friends drew Catholic muttering that Elizabeth was the cause.[23] The Jesuit Annual Letter of 1581 identified as the root of her insane malignity Elizabeth's alleged hatred of Catholicism.[24]

There is evidence that Elizabeth, caught off guard, apparently, by the revelations about the Babington plotters, did indeed think that hanging (alone) was too good for them and demanded that a more extreme punishment than the already existing penalties for treason be devised, though Burghley could not think of one.[25]

Stories about Elizabeth's personal animosity towards Catholics can be paralleled quite easily with stories of Catholics showing explicit hostility towards her. In the Catholic martyr accounts, the mask of martyrdom is occasionally allowed to slip – in the form of disdain for the Queen, even if only for the writer to emphasise the martyr's subsequent return to civility, charity, and temperance. Thus the narrative of the execution of the recusant gentleman Swithin Wells noted that, when provoked by Richard Topcliffe's taunting that papists 'follow the Pope and his Bulls; believe me, I think some bulls begot you all,' Wells retaliated, 'if we have bulls to our fathers, thou hast a cow to thy mother', making, as Arthur Marotti comments, 'a Catholic misogynistic swipe at Queen Elizabeth in her role as "Supreme Governor" of the English Church'.[26] (Wells, however, soon recovered his composure and instead prayed that Topcliffe might be converted.[27])

James Leyburn, a cousin of Anne Dacres (wife of Philip Howard, Earl of

Arundel), hated the queen unreservedly. According to Christopher Grene, 'touching the Queen, his opinion was that she was an usurper, and unlawful, a lascivious and very wicked person; in which opinion he was very resolute'. So vitriolic was his attitude to her that even some early seventeenth-century Catholic martyrologists balked at including him in the catalogues of their co-religionists who had perished for the faith.[28] In early May 1599 a series of examinations concerning a Hampshire gentleman, one Henry Carey, revealed that, when on board a ship called the 'Tobacco Pipe' at Bordeaux, he had been taunted by having two coins thrust in front of his face. One was a 'Spanish sixpence'. Carey proclaimed that he honoured it 'with his heart'. He was then shown an English coin with Elizabeth's face on it. Carey now declared that 'if he had her there he could find in his heart to be her hangman, and to hang her at the yard arm'.[29] In April 1604, just as the new regime was starting to tighten the screw against Catholic nonconformity again, it was reported by an informer that one of the 'banished priests' sent to the Continent by the new regime, the Jesuit Henry Floyd, had concealed in his prison chamber a paper which described the hatefulness of 'her sacred Majesty that dead is, and the State which governed under her'.[30] Sir Thomas Tresham discarded his former studiously loyal pose towards Elizabeth when in April 1605 he let fly in public with some notable abuse about the late Queen.[31]

These instances of intemperance were undoubtedly the tip of quite a threatening Catholic iceberg, the existence of which was hardly concealed from contemporaries. But, of course, such openly hostile expressions were probably not typical, just as they were undoubtedly unwise, and arguably politically naive. More often, one suspects, hostility to and outward profession of affection for the Queen were held together in a kind of tension. During the course of a progress in summer 1591, Elizabeth visited Cowdray, the palatial home of the first Viscount Montague. On the surface the occasion was marked by a display of loyalty to the Queen by the Catholic peer and her royal affection for him, although this was shortly before the regime launched a massive purge of the recusant body and its priests with the royal proclamation of October 1591 against seminary priests and Jesuits. A welcoming speech made by a 'porter' on the day of her arrival insisted that 'as for the owner of this house, mine honourable lord, his tongue is the key of his heart: and his heart the lock of his soul. Therefore what he speaks you may constantly believe: which is, that in duty and service to your Majesty, he would be second to none: in praying for your happiness, equal to any.' During her stay she was treated to further recitations by Montague's servants, attired as rustics, each stressing the love and loyalty which she could expect from Catholics in this part of the world. But the visit can be read, so Curtis Breight persuasively argues, as an occasion of considerable tension between the Queen and the Viscount, whose local power and influence the regime had sought to circumscribe and repress.[32]

II

Now it may be that perceived differences of opinion between Catholics over their demeanour towards Elizabeth, and in particular over what constituted loyalty, suited the regime quite well. In this way it could divide and rule. Perhaps moderate Catholics were sufficiently well regarded by the crown to make it worth their while recycling narratives about the Queen's compassion, while the extremists got what they deserved, even if their supporters complained vigorously in consequence. The well-known machinations of Bishop Richard Bancroft in sustaining and patronising the Appellant clergy indicated to contemporaries that the regime was seizing on an opportunity to damage the internal political coherence of the Catholic community by granting limited and temporary favour towards a few self-proclaimed 'loyalist' Catholic clergy. In July 1602 the newsletter writer known as 'Anthony Rivers' alleged that Elizabeth herself remembered how 'Walsingham thought to have set a faction amongst the cardinals, and afterwards to have nourished the like in the seminaries', and so she personally directed Sir Robert Cecil and Bishop Bancroft to stoke the fires of the Appellant dispute.[33]

It would be easy, then, to go for a middle-of-the-road position somewhere – to say, as does Read, that Elizabeth shaped 'her ecclesiastical policy' in order to obtain 'primarily ... a national church under the control of the crown'. This 'might serve also to conciliate the great mass of her subjects who still retained their affection for the old forms'. Only the war against Spain meant 'she was compelled by circumstances in some sort to assume the [Protestant] role assigned to her'.[34] Patrick Collinson notes a range of views, contemporary and modern, about Elizabeth – in which she figures as politique, conservative, Protestant, and atheist – and concludes merely that she had good political reasons for representing herself in more than one way to different opinion groups.[35] For Haigh, Elizabeth initially postured as the head of a reforming regime but was alarmed by resistance from leading peers and privy councillors. She decided therefore to pander to the religious conservatives. A number of compromises were arranged which fudged almost all the major issues – vestments, communion tables, the prayer book, and so on, so Catholics 'came to think that the Queen might be won over'.[36]

But which Catholics, exactly, were these? To note, as Haigh rightly does, that there were Catholics in Elizabeth's realm and court, and that she considered recourse to leading Catholics for support at the time of the Anjou Match,[37] is not to say what those Catholics thought of her, or how non-courtier Catholics regarded her, or how this led to the conflicting Catholic opinions which, as we have seen, were voiced during her reign about how she treated them. Of course, Elizabeth could personally tip the scales towards relative tolerance, for example in 1563 ordering that the full penalties of the recent anti-Catholic statute should not be enforced. 'But Elizabeth's tolerance was extremely limited', Haigh says, not through deliberate craft and guile, but because she may have been badly informed: 'she claimed, as in 1591, that Catholics were executed only for treason, not for "matter of religion" – but if she believed that, it was because she allowed herself to be deceived by officials who framed Catholics, and because the definition of treason had been extended to include actions which Catholics could hardly avoid.'[38] There is at least the potential for some confusion here. We are told that, after 1580 and the coming of the Jesuits, 'Elizabeth adjusted slowly to the new circumstances' and held out until 1582 when a proclamation declared priests and Jesuits to be traitors. But Edmund Campion and his friends had been executed in 1581. Was she responsible for or ignorant of that? 'The rhetoric of the free conscience was maintained', says Haigh, 'but Catholics were fined, imprisoned, and even executed for what had been winked at before.'[39] Here we have a picture of an originally tolerant Queen, losing patience after years of relative leniency, though Catholics basically stayed the same as they always had, celebrating the mass and not liking Protestant preaching. 'Perhaps', suggests Haigh, 'she vacillated between policy options, or followed all of them irresolutely, or muddled through by good luck.'[40]

Clearly, either Elizabeth was getting irredeemably irritable and confused by about 1580 (and Catholics were resigning themselves to the prospect of suffering in silence for the foreseeable future) or this picture stands in need of some revision. What the stories and rumours of clemency and cruelty, loyalty and hatred, alert us to is exactly how complex and nuanced the relationship was between Catholics and the Queen, a relationship in which loyalty was always to some degree, and sometimes extremely, conditional. The phrasing of this conditional loyalty towards Elizabeth was, for all its deliberate rhetorical and polemical obfuscation and double-speak, one of the principal Catholic styles of expression during this period, and one of the prime sites for Catholics to say, even in smoke-and-mirrors mode, what they actually thought their position in the Elizabethan polity was. Here also it was possible for them to interrogate the structure and purposes of that polity and pose a number of questions about the place of true religion within the commonwealth, and about whose religion, in that context, was more likely to be true and godly.

III

I want to look now at a few of the Elizabethan Catholic polemical tracts which asked these questions, namely the better-known 'evil counsellor' polemics written between the early 1570s and the early 1590s.[41] While some Catholic tracts of the period were couched in overtly humble submissive phraseology, and others utterly rejected Elizabeth's title and rule, this Elizabethan 'evil counsellor' manner of writing (commonplace, as we know, in much political critique, and prominent, for example, in the crisis of the Pilgrimage of Grace[42]) inhabited a type of middle ground where Elizabeth's alleged good parts are admitted but turned, or potentially turned, against her by reference to the political company she kept.[43] For in such company her good qualities became mere weakness. Her consequent failure to root out the corrupt influences around her threatened a colossal failure of leadership and the imminent collapse of good government, the law, national security, and godliness. Here, then, Catholics postured as supporters of the regime, but, in the circumstances, the regime might take the view that this was support the Queen could well do without.

One prime instance of this genre is the *Treatise of Treasons* (1572), generally attributed to the pen of John Leslie, Bishop of Ross. This tract alleged and excoriated an appalling mismanagement of the Elizabethan State by Sir William Cecil and Sir Nicholas Bacon ('those to whom above others your queen committed even from the beginning, the chief cure and charge of her affairs'). They were said to have manipulated Elizabeth for their own evil ends and, at the same time, imperilled the commonwealth.[44] Written in reply to a pamphlet (usually ascribed to Cecil) entitled *Salutem in Christo*, the immediate context of the tract was the northern rebellion and the continuing perceived political threat represented by Mary Stuart.

The rebellion had been a godsend for government apparatchiks such as Thomas Norton who used it to argue that at last the papists had shown themselves in their true colours: papistry could now safely be identified with treason.[45] Not a bit of it, claimed the writer of the *Treatise of Treasons*. The real traitors were at the heart of the administration, namely Cecil and Bacon. The pithy initial preamble describes how the first part of the work 'confutes the false accusations, and slanderous infamies, printed in certain nameless and infamous libels against the queen's majesty of Scotland [Mary Stuart], heir apparent to the crown of England', and against the recently executed 'Thomas duke of Norfolk ... and defends the honour and loyalty of the said princes'. The second part of the tract 'detects sundry deep and hidden treasons, of long time practised and daily contrived, against the honour, dignity, safety, and state of Queen Elizabeth, her royalty, her crown, and all the blood royal of England, by a few base and ingrate persons, that have been called to credit by her', and 'lays open also, the dangerous state, that the said queen and realm do stand in, if those confederates and their conspiracies be not prevented in time'.[46] The essence of their treason was 'the alteration of the succession of the crown ... by untimely extincting both those lines, in which it presently rests, and should first fall unto, by all laws of nature, nations' and by English law. Their secret agenda was 'to confirm and establish unto certain base persons ... the perpetual regiment of the same', for their purpose was to bring 'the crown immaturely to the ... House of Suffolk, unto which themselves are united, and their children incorporated'.

For this reason, the tract claimed, they frightened Elizabeth by inventing false fears of danger from Mary Stuart and Philip II, 'and persuaded [her] withal, that there was none assured pillar for her to lean unto against all events, but to keep her self free, to hold her self unmarried', until she should be too old to wed and procreate. This was nothing else but 'to kill her alive' and 'with her body to bury her memory: and with her corpse, to carry all her succession unto her sepulchre'. And 'like as by art they have provided, she shall have no children naturally, even so by statute they have prepared, she shall have no heir judicially'. Here they went against nature, for there is nothing so pernicious in nature as for someone to have no heir, as much for their own protection as for the passing of property. 'Who revenges the husband's murder, but the wife? Who the father's, but the child?'[47]

Mary was not Elizabeth's enemy at all. There was no evidence that she sought to take the crown from Elizabeth 'other than the joining of the arms of England and Scotland in certain scutcheons set up by her husband's the French king's commandment, at a triumph in France, more than thirteen years ago', which she was entitled to do anyway by blood.[48] In fact Mary and Elizabeth were jointly the injured parties. (One needed only to observe how their common enemies had interfered in Scotland, e.g. in aiding Arran's and Moray's rebellions against Mary, and in their subsequent dealing with and imprisonment of her, to see how this was true.) Their enemies' secret grand scheme was, therefore, to open up again the issues which had been rehearsed and apparently settled in the Wars of the Roses between Lancaster and York.[49]

In terms of the pure mechanics of the succession problem of the 1560s, particularly the late 1560s, the *Treatise of Treasons* bears more than a passing resemblance to Stephen Alford's recent exposition of the 1569 crisis where a perfectly acceptable dynastic solution (marriage between Norfolk and Mary) to the issue of who would succeed Elizabeth proved irreconcilable with the 'political' solution, sponsored by Cecil, to the larger 'British' problem of England's relationship with Scotland and Ireland, a solution which left no room for such a match.[50] The potential acceptability of the Norfolk scheme was signalled by the large amount of support it received at court, even while it was partially concealed from Elizabeth. As the *Treatise of Treasons* put it, 'the duke did not only (before any least attempt thereof) make all that were of the privy council acquainted with his intention, namely the earls of Arundel, Pembroke, Leicester, and the Secretary, besides many others of the nobility'.[51] In fact Norfolk was 'rather by them moved and invited to attempt the same, before he sought it by any least mean'.[52]

At one level the author of the *Treatise of Treasons* was conspiracy-theorising simply in order to protect the imprisoned Norfolk and Mary, both in extreme danger as the regime seemed to be preparing the ground for their judicial termination. But the tract was also a 'commonwealth' polemic, construing and evaluating the regime's policy-making within a series of either/or choices, the validity and rectitude of which can be construed ultimately by reference to Catholicism understood as an ideological system encompassing and protecting European peace and prosperity. The tract was set up in part as an analogy of the Graeco-Trojan wars and the fall of Troy through the infamous mechanism of the wooden horse. After the reign of Mary Tudor, with the country still solidly 'Catholic,' the Protestants, like the Greeks, got in by artifice and dissimulation; once inside the city of Troy, the Greek soldiers were released from the wooden horse by Sinon, whose lies (that the horse was dedicated to the goddess Pallas) had persuaded the Trojans to take it into the city in the first place. The Greeks/Protestants then wrought havoc and confusion.[53]

The new religion had been an ideological lever to prise apart the arrangements made to safeguard the succession and the security of the English State. The settlement of 1559 was a *coup d'état* by stealth, wherein the new 'lawless faction of Machiavellian libertines' recruited 'a rabble of unbridled persons' to execute the commands of 'those that have created and set up the Faction'.[54] The inevitable outcome was the undermining of the commonwealth, engagement in needless foreign war, the slaughter or confusion of ancient nobility and commoners alike, and a collapse of standards in public life. Here the evil counsellors' own lusts for power and wealth were connected with the perceived excesses and disasters in domestic and foreign policy which the *Treatise of Treasons*'s author identified. The northern insurgents were merely warning Elizabeth of the danger she was in.[55] Even the rebels' approaches to Spain were made only in order to re-establish good relations between the realm and Elizabeth's natural friend Philip II, who had been alienated by the malice and scheming of 'the faction' which had violated 'the long continued amity with the house of Spain', and had broken 'the ancient league with the house of Burgundy, by forcible taking of the king's money, by paying the same unto his own and other princes' rebels ... by furnishing of pirates, in infinite numbers, to rob him and his people'.[56] (Considering the recent drift of Elizabethan foreign policy, this was at least a credible line of argument.) The *Treatise of Treasons*'s author wanted to 'tie this bell about the cat's neck', and warn Elizabeth of the deceptions used against her and Mary.[57]

What we have in this 'metaphor' (as its author calls it), comparing ancient and modern history, is a sophisticated commentary on the relationship of English Catholicism to the Queen. The author accumulates and merges various aspects of what might be understood as 'Catholic' thought and practice, and makes them a politically coherent alternative to the policy lines being pursued by some of Elizabeth's leading advisers. This was not, therefore, just an apologia for Mary Stuart and the Duke of Norfolk, or the northern rebel peers themselves, the earls of Northumberland and Westmorland, who are, in fact, barely alluded to. The author does not say that Catholics are loyal to Elizabeth because they accept the philosophical essentials of non-resistance theory. Nor was their respect for her derived just from a secret belief that she was in fact some kind of Catholic, or at least moderate and compassionate towards her Catholic subjects, though the *Treatise of Treasons*'s author did mention the retention of the 'cross in her own chapel, the lights on the table there' and 'the decent attire of ministers' as all being good signs.[58] Instead the tract was predicated on the claim that Protestantism was a deeply dangerous political deviation from normal and traditional modes of making policy. Protestants had, for reasons of self-interest, deceived Elizabeth into investing in a national change of religion, from which had followed all the disastrous things which the *Treatise of Treasons* listed, disasters which were caused by listening to Protestants' 'evil counsel' but which Catholics had resolutely opposed.

But this assurance that all Catholics' concern was for the security of her own title and a lawful and peaceful succession was hardly an unconditional endorsement of her rule. Like Eve, she had been weak and had been tempted by a serpent – in her case 'to intrude and entangle her self in the ecclesiastical ministry'. The reptile had deceived her by telling her that if she reformed the ministry after a Protestant fashion 'all the princes her neighbours would follow her therein'.[59] Elizabeth had fallen into the sin of schism. The implication is that she must submit to Catholics' judgment as well as beg the pope's mercy in order to be saved, politically as well as spiritually.

The other really well-known tract in this 'evil counsellor' genre of Elizabethan Catholic polemic was the *Copie of a Leter, wryten by a Master of Arte of Cambridge* (1584), usually referred to as 'Leicester's Commonwealth', which, as Simon Adams remarks, uses 'many of the [same] basic arguments' as the *Treatise of Treasons*.[60] Here the anonymous writer/s[61] played up Elizabeth's clemency and natural capacity for good government, and then pointed out how odd it was that so many things had gone wrong on her watch. The cause was identified as the dominion acquired and exercised by the venomous, wife-murdering Earl of Leicester and his friends.

Of course, 'Leicester's Commonwealth' was a very different polemical piece from the *Treatise of Treasons*. As Adams, John Bossy and Peter Holmes have all argued, Robert Parsons was heavily involved in its production (his printer printed it), even if many of the stories about Leicester were clearly from within the Court circle which had sponsored the Anjou Match and had been severely irritated by its failure. (First and foremost among these people was Charles Arundell, though Adams suggests that Henry Howard's influence can be detected as well.) Adams notes that the work was first mooted at the time of the invasion project of 1582, and it appeared almost simultaneously with Allen's *True, Sincere and Modest Defence*.[62] Taking into account Parsons's deep implication in an assassination plot in 1583, Bossy has suggested that the loyalist rhetoric of the work is entirely 'phoney', merely a blind to fool the reader, and in no way reflecting the intentions of the writers.[63] Indeed, all this can be seen as entirely logical and consistent, since 'Leicester's Commonwealth' more or less assumes that the Queen is about to be assassinated and points to exactly the people who might be thought to be about to do it – namely Leicester's crew. So the tract can in fact be seen as preparing the ground for a Catholic-sponsored murder of the Queen, which killing could then be blamed on Leicester, and support could thus be rallied for the Scottish Queen.[64]

Yet the fact remains that, even if the tract anticipates regicide, it still resorts to and emulates the *Treatise of Treasons*'s rhetoric and indicates that the two mind sets (of potential compromiser and of out-and-out root-and-brancher) are not mutually exclusive. Even at this juncture in the mid-1580s it made political sense, although for very different reasons and in very different circumstances, to circulate the *Treatise*'s language, what we might call sabre-toothed loyalism, in order to make the Catholic case for Mary Stuart.

And while Dudley appears to be the sole scapegoat (William Camden later took up some of the accusations in 'Leicester's Commonwealth' in order to exculpate Elizabeth from charges of political mismanagement[65]), the tract represents a veiled but potentially lethal attack against Elizabeth. For the tract is also a succession tract, and it considers the claims of the various contenders for the crown. Praise for the Queen initially looks unstinting. How had the problem of the ravenous Dudley got so out of hand? It was because of her 'gracious and sweet disposition' towards the monster whose dorsal fin could be seen circling 'her noble person'.[66] Nevertheless, as in the *Treatise of Treasons*, the account of Elizabeth's supposed virtues is a barely concealed critique of her. Perceptions of the Queen's unstable political position (the book reminds the Queen that the Anjou Match would have been a good thing, and that Leicester and his friends had opposed it[67]) turn on precisely the mismatch between Leicester's vaulting ambition and the Queen's vulnerability. Leicester had 'possessed himself of all the strength, powers, and sinews of the realm', and aimed at nothing less than the crown.[68] Leicester's strategy was allegedly focused on his brother-in-law Henry Hastings, third earl of Huntingdon, who had a claim to the throne. If Leicester was planning 'to give the same push at the crown by the house of Huntingdon, against all the race and line of Henry VII in general, which his father gave before him by pretence of the House of Suffolk against the children of King Henry VIII in particular', all he had to do (as indeed he had done) was to surround Elizabeth with his own clients. Huntingdon was himself an 'open competitor of the sceptre'. The fact that Leicester had no title to the crown himself was irrelevant, for 'whether he mean the crown for himself or his friend [Huntingdon] it imports not much, seeing both ways it is evident that he means to have all at his own disposition'.[69]

As Dwight Peck comments, the tract 'attempts to stir the English reader's fear for his sovereign's life by emphasizing her immediate danger at the hands of her lord and subject'. The book stressed, however, that the entire line of Henry VII was thus threatened, and that, of course, included Mary Stuart. Mary and her son James were therefore also the first and best line of defence against the threat of a Leicestrian coup. As long as they remained alive, Elizabeth's death would profit him little or nothing.[70] Peter Lake notes how the tract hissed at Leicester for spreading rumours that James VI was a papist, likewise for the purpose of obstructing his path to the throne.[71]

There is an obvious similarity here to what the *Treatise of Treasons* had said when it attacked the 'faction' for deliberately keeping Elizabeth unmarried and childless, preparing her downfall for the benefit of the House of Suffolk. But again, while posturing as a natural bulwark against identified ill-willers to the Queen, the conjunction in 'Leicester's Commonwealth' of the earl's strength and Elizabeth's weakness, his ambition and her vulnerability, became a lethal critique whereby Elizabeth was rhetorically deprived of her power – virtually ordered to dismiss Leicester and his friends from their privileged positions or face the consequences.[72] Not to dismiss Leicester was to associate herself with his misdeeds, with his pillaging of the commonwealth. The identification of Leicester at the centre of a circle of committed puritans provided the means for alleging that Protestant religion had corrupted the essential mechanisms of good government, in particular due legal process. Leicester's power subverted the law, as was demonstrated by the instances of those who had sought royal justice against him and been undone, even though they had right on their side.[73] So, even if these allegedly heartfelt Catholic fears for the Queen's safety were pretty shallow and transparently false, 'evil counsellor' rhetoric and stories were still being used to recruit, in some sense, Elizabeth (though metaphorically kicking and screaming) to the Catholic 'cause,' on the basis of her own presumed interest in sustaining the succession from the first Tudor through to the Stuarts.

In the early 1590s a whole flurry of 'evil counsellor' tracts issued from continental presses in response to the 1591 royal proclamation.[74] Among them was Thomas Stapleton's *Apologia pro Rege Catholico Philippo*, which specifically warned Lord Burghley to consider what had happened to other 'evil counsellors' in English history. Robert Parsons's tract known as 'Philopater' attacked five councillors by name – Bacon, Hatton, Leicester, Walsingham, and Burghley – though, by this date, only Burghley was still alive. Victor Houliston notes how Parsons claimed that the queen was not responsible for the proclamation but only just 'stops short of arraigning Elizabeth as a tyrant'.[75] But, for our purposes, the reply to the proclamation which perhaps most closely resembles the 'evil counsellor' polemic of the 1570s and 1580s is Richard Verstegan's *A Declaration of the True Causes of the Great Troubles,*

Presupposed to Be Intended against the Realm of England. (It predated 'Philopater' by some months, and, with Verstegan's *Advertisement Written to a Secretarie*, was intended as pre-publication publicity for Parsons's larger work.[76]) It was popularly known as 'Burghley's Commonwealth,' and it recycled arguments about the stupidity of undermining the ancient nobility and the lunacy of engaging in war with Spain. Here the Lord Treasurer was once again the villain (though the deceased Leicester was vilified as well), pilloried for trying to distract the attention of the realm from its miseries and dangers by the spectacle of legal anti-popery, namely of the shameful executing of 'a few poor priests and Jesuits'. The tract commenced by casting its readers' minds back to the moment of Elizabeth's accession when she, 'a princess young and beautiful, and abundantly adorned with the gifts of nature, and princely education', had had the opportunity to live in peace with Spain and indeed the rest of Europe. But 'as the Serpent, being subtler than all the beasts of the field, did sometime seduce the first woman and queen of the world, to break the commandment of God', so now 'a sly Sycophant' suggested to 'this princess' that she should 'break the unity of God's Church' and launch into European war.[77]

Within this account of the settlement of 1559 and of her foreign policy, drawn virtually verbatim in places from the *Treatise of Treasons* (though naturally incorporating perceived disasters since 1572), Verstegan located and interpreted the more recent struggles of the Catholic community with the State. The Catholic clergy's attempt to reconvert the realm was not, therefore, a withdrawal of the Queen's subjects from their allegiance (as statute law alleged) but was in fact an attempt to bring her realm back to peace and order. Significantly, Verstegan, an intimate of Robert Parsons, was a leading English Catholic Hispanophile. He lambasted the Anjou Match which had been the great project of the Francophile Catholic court faction in the late 1570s and early 1580s.[78] And yet he could use the same 'evil counsellor' rhetoric as had been employed earlier by the pro-Stuart Catholic writers. At precisely the time that Verstegan wrote, the Catholic movement was beginning to fracture as various Catholics manoeuvred to present themselves to James in the best possible light. As is well known, a powerful Catholic lobby was gearing up to attack so-called 'Jesuited' co-religionists for their alleged Hispanomania and disloyalty to the Elizabethan regime. The Appellant clergy could, in the later 1590s, publicly allege that the Jesuits' disregard for the true Stuart succession should encourage James to reward his true supporters whose loyalty to Mary Stuart, and indeed to Elizabeth (even under the most extreme of provocations), showed that they were the Catholics who would most willingly and sincerely endorse both James and his theories of monarchical absolutism, despite their differences with him over matters of religion. And yet, in Verstegan's tract, we can see the (for want of a better word) 'Jesuit' wing of the

Catholic community adopting an 'evil counsellor' polemical style and alleging much the same kind of loyalism towards Elizabeth which the anti-Jesuits also professed.[79]

In this kind of political discourse, then, dis/loyalty is not really the issue, at least in the way that some of the 'mythic' accounts of Elizabeth and her Catholic subjects might lead us to expect. Clearly it does not amount to any principled unwillingness to rebel or even disinclination to assassinate the Queen; at the same time it does not directly excoriate the Queen's person. Instead, clasping Elizabeth to themselves in a somewhat uncomfortable embrace, these Catholic polemics use the Queen to advance whatever bit of the Catholic 'cause' they are currently pushing. In each case the evil counsellors are few in number, limited to one faction: Bacon and Cecil in the *Treatise of Treasons*; Leicester and his coterie in 'Leicester's Commonwealth'; Cecil (primarily) again in Verstegan's *Declaration* and other replies to the 1591 proclamation. The *Treatise of Treasons* explicitly emphasised: 'of these two men, I say, and of none other, am I to be understood in this treatise, when I use any term, that may seem to touch authority: because I mean none other authority, than of them two only'.[80] Adams notes that in 'Leicester's Commonwealth', Burghley, the principal target of the *Treatise of Treasons*, '(it is implied) was open to argument; the real advocate of persecution was Leicester, acting as patron of the puritans'. Burghley has to some extent been rehabilitated, by virtue of being Leicester's perceived enemy, and 'there is scarcely any reference to Sir Francis Walsingham'.[81] By claiming that the source of the evil is limited, the reader is led to understand that a reconciliation between the Queen and her Catholic vassals is a possibility – indeed a certainty if the wicked counsellors can be got rid of.

In some ways, this simply restates Holmes's well-known distinction between 'resistance' and 'compromise' modes of Catholic thought. For Holmes, 'Leicester's Commonwealth' displays 'elements of the old ideology of loyalism and non-resistance', but also expresses 'the new political ideas of resistance as well', as if the writers could not quite make up their minds, whereas Allen's *Admonition to the Nobility and People of England* was by contrast a full resistance work, 'a slightly hysterical commentary on the bull *Regnans in Excelsis*'.[82] We should make a mistake, though, if we see Allen's tract as no more than an expression of venomous pent-up hatred only partially concealed in the 'evil counsellor' tracts, blurted out in frustration after years of waiting for Elizabeth to marry, die, or just see sense. The difference in tone is indeed crucial. For while the topics are much the same – the ruin of the ancient nobility, the depredations by low-born courtiers, the spoil of the Church, failure to provide for the succession, and so on – Elizabeth is now described as the root cause rather than the victim of the evils narrated.[83]

IV

Now it is time to return to the questions and hypotheses, which we were considering at the beginning, about the structural relationship between the Queen and her Catholic subjects. Having looked at the 'evil counsellor' literature, we might still be wondering what the connection was between a few polemics produced by disappointed courtier-politicians and the wider English Catholic community. How could they be a key to the complexities and varied manifestations of Catholic dissent – partial and absolute recusancy (elite and popular), a separatist seminary-trained clergy, the occasional treasonous plot, contacts with foreign diplomats, squabbles among Catholic exiles, and specu-lation about the succession (which in the end went to a Calvinist)? In fact these 'evil counsellor' discourses are a crucial means of deciphering the politics of the English Catholic movement – in particular why that movement which was supposedly separatist was never quite separate, and why its 'exclusion' from many aspects of public and political life did not lead to its disappearance from view. For while we often imagine that the politics of Elizabethan Catholicism was characterised by an out-and-out furious determination to get rid of the 'incestuous bastard' Queen, and consequently failed, in reality the logic of the Queen's refusal to produce or name a successor meant there was always more to be gained for Catholics by constantly realigning themselves in order to seize the moment when such a successor should appear. So what we have in the 'evil counsellor' tracts is a means of interpreting whole swathes of Catholic political action – not just the attempt to infiltrate the regime in the late 1570s and early 1580s, but also the schism in the Catholic movement in the 1590s during the Appellant dispute – as the seriously divided wings of the Catholic movement struggled to position themselves for the actual succession to Elizabeth. In this controversy, we can see Catholics of very different political hues and inclinations, including those who had once argued the benefits of a swift ejection of the last Tudor, now trying harder than ever to argue Catholicism's potential for integration within a well-governed (even if not exclusively Catholic) commonwealth – in exactly the same way that the 'evil counsellor' polemic had done.

Thus, whether they liked her or loathed her, Elizabeth performed a crucial role for English Catholic opinion. Politically she represented for them a blank space, but not blank because unimportant; blank rather, because they reckoned it/she could be inflected and glossed by reference to certain key political topics, principally the succession. The writers of the 'evil counsellor' tracts evidently believed that what they wrote would have considerable resonance for contemporaries because what these Catholics were attacking, or demonising, was potentially real. Patrick Collinson has pointed out in his analysis of the Elizabethan 'monarchical republic' how seriously we should take the 'Mary

Stuart' problem, and how, for many Protestants, it was utterly crucial to have a credible Protestant successor to block her candidacy in the event of Elizabeth's death.[84] The unavoidable political issue was that Mary, even in her prison, was by many accounts the next heir. Those who would not accept her would inevitably have to look for someone else and exclude her. In this Elizabethan 'exclusion crisis,' it was vital to consider who Elizabeth's successor would actually be. For all the Earl of Huntingdon's reputed lack of ambition to advance his claim to the throne, Protestant contemporaries might wonder who was the better choice, one of the Grey family (utterly discredited anyway by the bastardisation of Catherine Grey's children by the Earl of Hertford) or, rather, 'Henry IX.' Huntingdon was, as 'Leicester's Commonwealth' insisted, *the* likely candidate for many Protestants, though the line taken there is that Huntingdon would be entirely Leicester's dupe, and the means by which Leicester would come to supreme power.

While it may not be a great revelation to say that many Catholics were interested in the succession issue during the course of Elizabeth's reign, it may be somewhat innovatory to claim, against the grain of much current historiography, that some important strands of later sixteenth-century Catholicism were structurally imbricated within Elizabethan political culture and had a stake in the Queen's future. What we have here is a rather different account of Elizabethan Catholicism from the one which circulates in most textbooks – where Catholicism is regarded as largely and deliberately separate from mainstream political issues. (It is certainly different from our double myth about dis/loyalty.) And, ironically, we have arrived at it by putting English Catholics in the context of their relationship with Elizabeth, a queen whom most of them probably never saw, and who was in many senses not 'their' queen at all. Recurring periods of political instability allowed the Catholic issue to be driven, coach-and-four style, through the apparently easy and natural phrasing of the anti-recusancy statutes which claimed to be proscribing essential aspects of Romish Catholicism as a self-evidently malign threat to the commonwealth. The 'evil counsellor' tracts reversed the logic of government conspiracy theorists, such as Norton and Burghley, and identified Catholics' interests as often identical to Elizabeth's.

Let us look briefly, then, at what happened after James's accession, in order to see how the conditional loyalism of the Catholic 'evil counsellor' writers rephrased itself now that the Catholic community had got the monarch, or at least the dynasty, which it had so frequently said it wanted. The vast majority of English Catholics overtly supported James's title. Both before and after March 1603 there was a well-organised and extensive Catholic petitioning campaign in order to capitalise on James's many expressions of goodwill to men of conscience, even if they were of a different religion from his own. Many Catholics now argued that their suffering under the late Queen had not been for their religion so much as for their support for James's mother, Mary Stuart, and by implication James himself. As John Watkins has brilliantly demonstrated, the transfer of sovereignty from Elizabeth to James was marked by an extensive polemical battle in which Protestants tried to represent James as the heir of Elizabeth while Catholics argued that he was first and foremost the heir of Mary Stuart, the assumed fact of whose 'martyrdom' conferred an additional, spiritual, legitimacy on him.[85]

Of course, as the various Catholic factions publicly paraded their loyalty to the new monarch, it made little sense for them to hark back to the times when they had been circumspect about the extent of their loyalism to the now dead Queen. As John Bossy has shown, some of those 'loyal' Catholics who were loudest in their denunciations of 'Jesuit' treasons themselves had quite a lot of monarchomach baggage to discard. Some of the Appellants had formerly had friends and patrons within the French Catholic Holy League.[86] However, the strains of 'evil counsellor' modes of Catholic political thought were still reverberating at James's accession, punctuating rather uncomfortably the more syrupy and straightforward loyal pleas for tolerance put out by the Catholic clergy. As Peter Lake shows in this volume, Ben Jonson's *Sejanus*, written in 1603 and published in 1605, a play about the tyranny which sets in when a weak and corrupt ruler (Tiberius) falls under the spell of even more corrupt and loathsome favourites (Sejanus and Macro), patently drew upon many of the archetypes and much of the rhetoric of Elizabethan Catholic critiques of official tyranny, cruelty, and corruption. Lake argues that Jonson, who had converted to Rome in 1598, was hauled in for questioning about this piece precisely because it was too reminiscent of the mode of critique adopted by *Leicester's Commonwealth*, even though it was not a straight Catholic diatribe, and was, in a real sense, an endorsement of 'some of the central orthodoxies of what we might term an emergent Jacobean (absolutist) political style'.[87]

In the event, James was unable to honour his many promises to Catholics (at least not in the sense that they expected him to). He rapidly found that he had to re-gloss what he had meant by tolerance. (He could not, as D. R. Woolf demonstrates, afford to ditch as much of the Elizabethan past as Catholics undoubtedly would have liked.[88]) When the penalties for Catholic noncon- formity started to be reimposed in 1604, the Jesuits began to contrast James unfavourably with Elizabeth. Henry Garnet wrote in October 1605 that the persecution was now worse than in 'Bess's time'.[89] The coterie of gentry who became infamous as the instigators of the powder treason were, apparently, finally goaded into action by James's apparent duplicity in failing to live up to his pre-accession tolerance rhetoric. Richard Blount SJ in April 1607 complained that he had heard that 'his majesty is gone this last day to Newmarket to hunt. As he passed by Tyburn, being a little past it, he returned back to the gibbet, rode under it, looked upon it and struck it with his rod, saying scoffingly, all you ... Jesuits and priests that have been hanged here pray for me'.[90] Here a leading Jesuit was saying that James was explicitly mocking and rejecting the complex political balance between loyalism and principled passive resistance which Catholics had laboured to sustain, and which was typified by the fortitude of the Elizabethan martyrs.

Yet, disappointed as many Catholics undoubtedly were, they did not simply withdraw from the political arena. Instead they concentrated on the continuous stream of James's pronouncements that he was prepared to favour those of a moderate disposition and punish only the extremists. Some kind of deal could still be worked out with the King: all that was necessary was to persuade him that the Catholic religion was no threat to his person, title, or dynasty. After the powder plot, Catholics engaged in a fierce debate with the regime over the 1606 oath of allegiance and the question of what constituted true loyalty. In fact, James's extremely equivocal attitude towards the pan-European 'Protestant Cause' made it possible for English Catholics to rebut the standard line in Protestant polemic that they were all fifth columnists and traitors. During the period of the Spanish Match negotiations, when James was under the gun from an anti-popish polemical critique of his dynastic policy, his Catholic subjects could credibly pose as his natural supporters.

So, even if James's accession did not quite usher in a golden era for the Catholic community, the political logic of the Elizabethan Catholic 'evil counsellor' tracts had at last started to work itself out. Ironically, that brand of 'evil counsel' discourse was a prequel to the much better known puritan critiques of court corruption during the reigns of James and Charles, an opposition which used many of the same methods and much of the same language as the Elizabethan Catholics had resorted to.[91] The Duke of Buckingham was attacked in precisely this vein after 1625 when the early Caroline war policy started to unravel. In Parliament in June 1628 Sir Robert Phelips proclaimed, 'it is not King Charles advising himself, but it is King Charles advised by disordered counsel that had occasioned' the King's unsatisfactory reply to the most recent Commons petition.[92] The same 'evil counsellor' notion obviously lies beneath the crescendo of accusations in the late 1620s and all through the 1630s that the stewardship of the Church of England was being undermined by papists at court, both open Roman Catholics and more covertly popish individuals, 'Arminians' and the like.[93]

But, however hard Catholic nonconformists and their clergy were pressed by the Jacobean regime, and at various points they did not hesitate to call it a 'persecution,' they did not revert to the 'evil counsellor' critiques which some of their Protestant enemies were now beginning to use. This is not to say that they did not identify specific (usually 'puritan') conspiracies against the crown and the established Church; but they did not portray them as in some sense having a lethal and corrupting control over the establishment. In that the

Elizabethan Catholic 'evil counsel' tracts demonstrate the Queen's Catholic subjects continuously repositioning themselves to take advantage of the Stuart succession when it finally came, the Catholics' abandonment of that style of political critique suggests that, albeit in a somewhat limited and contingent way, they had actually won. Some of the anti-popery discourses of the early Stuart period hint that some Protestants seemed to know it.

V

Our review of how Catholics positioned themselves towards Elizabeth has, I would argue, helped to recontextualise and reinterpret the 'myths' about her and them which we reviewed earlier. We have seen that contemporary stories and rumours about whether Catholics were loyal or disloyal, and whether they hated the Queen or not, were to a degree 'mythic' in the sense that they were not, generally, mere statements of fact. But equally we should not dispense with those stories. For we cannot say that the dis/loyalty issue had nothing to do with most early modern English Catholics as if they were people who for the most part only wanted to be left to pray in peace. For if we identify Catholicism and its discontents exclusively or even mainly with a parochial trauma caused by the disappearance of the 'old' religion under the hammer of royal injunctions and episcopal visitations, then we shall miss a good deal of the political force and essence of Elizabethan Catholicism. To be sure, as Eamon Duffy and others have shown, we can be sure that the extirpation of the old rites was frequently pretty unpopular. The *Treatise of Treasons* itself denounced the burning of 'all the Relics, Images, and holy ornaments of Christ and his Saints'.[94] But that in itself cannot explain how contemporaries identified Catholicism as a powerful and often dangerous force within the Elizabethan settlement and polity. This may seem to run completely counter to the sense of much recent historiography of post-Reformation Catholicism which tends to regard the 'old religion' as primarily a 'popular' phenomenon, a gut plebeian instinct which reacted badly to the elitist premises and nanny-statishness of the official Protestant Reformation. Insofar as this sort of religiosity was contiguous with 'Catholicism', it made sense to equate the decay of that kind of popular culture with a decline of English Catholicism *tout court*. But a rereading of some of the leading Catholic polemical texts of the period, notably of the 'evil counsellor' variety, permits us to reintegrate the principal lines of political thought and modes of agitation which contemporaries most readily referred to as 'Catholic' into the extant master narratives of the period from which those lines and agitators have often been excluded.

Seen in this light, the oppositionalism and irritability of English Catholics towards the Queen look a good deal more serious and significant than many historians allow. For even as Catholics protested a kind of loyalty towards the person of the monarch, they both articulated a series of limitations on her authority and described how they ought to be reintegrated into the commonwealth from which they were in many senses excluded. Now, the stories about the Queen and her 'evil counsellors' were themselves in some ways 'mythical' or at least they contributed to the various historiographical 'myths' about Catholic loyalism which we have rehearsed above. But their essential accuracy in communicating to contemporaries the realities of the political relationship between Elizabeth and her Catholic subjects was such that it frequently sent many of those contemporaries into paroxysms of fear and fury. We may conclude that myths had and, for historians of the period, still have their uses.

NOTES

I am particularly grateful to Dr Simon Adams, Professor John Bossy, Professor Pauline Croft, and Professor Peter Lake for their assistance in the writing of this chapter.

1 S. Doran and T. Freeman (eds), *The Myth of Elizabeth* (London, 2002).

2 See, e.g., J. E. Paul, 'The Hampshire Recusants in the Reign of Elizabeth I with Some Reference to the Problem of Church Papists', PhD dissertation, University of Southampton, 1958, pp. 109–10.

3 Richard Challoner, *Memoirs of Missionary Priests*, ed. J. H. Pollen (London, 1924), p. 176.

4 William Allen, *An Admonition to the Nobility and People of England* ([Antwerp ?], 1588, RSTC 368), sigs. A6r, D3v. For a broadside version summarising Allen's text, printed in order to be distributed by the Spanish troops after landing in England, see William Allen, *A Declaration of the Sentence and Deposition of Elizabeth* ([Antwerp ?], 1588, RSTC 22590).

5 See, e.g., T. F. Knox (ed.), *The Letters and Memorials of William Cardinal Allen* (London, 1882), pp. xxix–xxx.

6 For this reading of anti-popery, see, e.g., C. Z. Wiener, 'The Beleaguered Isle. A Study of Elizabethan and Early Jacobean Anti-Catholicism', *PP*, 51 (1971), 27–62.

7 C. Read, *Mr Secretary Walsingham*, 3 vols (London, 1925), 3: 278–9.

8 M. L. Carrafiello, 'English Catholicism and the Jesuit Mission of 1580–1581', *HJ*, 37 (1994), 761–74.

9 William Cecil, *The Execution of Justice in England*, printed in *Harleian Miscellany*, 10 vols (London, 1808–13), 2: 137–8.

10 See, e.g., William Allen, *A True, Sincere, and Modest Defence* (Rouen, 1584, RSTC 4902), replying to Burghley's *Execution of Justice*.

11 See, e.g., P. Hughes, *The Reformation in England*, 3 vols (London, 1954), 3: 342.

12 H. Trevor-Roper, *Historical Essays* (London, 1957), pp. 113–18.

13 Christopher Haigh, 'The Continuity of Catholicism in the English Reformation', *PP*, 93 (1981), 37–69, at pp. 55–7.

14 E. Carlson, review of Thomas M. McCoog, S.J., *The Society of Jesus in Ireland, Scotland, and England 1541–1588: 'Our Way of Proceeding?'* (Leiden, 1996) in *EHR*, 113 (1998, 1301–3).

15 See, e.g., Peter Lake, 'Religious identities in Shakespeare's England', in D. Kastan (ed.), *A Companion to Shakespeare* (Oxford, 1999), pp. 57–84; Alexandra Walsham, *Church Papists: Catholicism, Conformity, and Confessional Polemic in Early Modern England* (Woodbridge, 1993); Frances Dolan, *Whores of Babylon: Catholicism, Gender, and Seventeenth-Century Print Culture* (Ithaca, 1999).

16 J. Neale, *Elizabeth I and her Parliaments*, 2 vols (London, 1953), 1: 225–34.

17 Peter Lake and Michael Questier, 'Agency, Appropriation and Rhetoric under the Gallows', *PP*, 153 (1996), 64–107, at p. 71.

18 G. B. Harrison (ed.), *De Maisse* (London, 1931), pp. x, 55–8. For cases where Elizabeth appears to have extended her personal protection to convicted recusants, see Historical Manuscripts Commission (HMC), *Calendar of the Manuscripts of the Most Honourable the Marquess of Salisbury (Salisbury)*, ed. M.S. Giuseppi et al. (London, 1888–1976), 8: 541; 16: 288; 24: 30.

19 P. Caraman, *William Weston* (London, 1955), p. 33, cited in John Bossy, *The English Catholic Community, 1570-1850* (London, 1975), p. 154.

20 Challoner, *Memoirs*, p. 211.

21 K. Longley, *Saint Margaret Clitherow* (Wheathampstead, 1986), p. 168.

22 Ziliah Dovey, *An Elizabethan Progress: The Queen's Journey into East Anglia, 1578* (Stroud, 1996), p. 54. Dovey points out that the only detailed account of the events at Euston comes from Richard Topcliffe, and may not be entirely reliable. Simon Adams has suggested to me that such performances on the 1578 progress were a coded message to the duke of Anjou that the regime would not change its official line on religion and conformity for his benefit.

23 R. Simpson, *Edmund Campion* (London, 1996), p. 449.

24 H. Foley, *Records of the English Province of the Society of Jesus*, 7 vols in 8 (London, 1875–83), 3: 37–8.

25 D. Lunn, *The Catholic Elizabethans* (Bath, 1998), p. 156.

26 A. Marotti, 'Manuscript Transmission and the Catholic Martyrdom Account in Early Modern England', in A. Marotti and M. Bristol (eds), *Manuscript, Print and Performance* (Ohio, 2000), p. 180.

27 J. H. Pollen, *Acts of English Martyrs* (London, 1891), p. 108.

28 Ibid., pp. 214–16, 220.

29 Hatfield House, Cecil MS 70, fol. 9r–v.

30 HMC, *Salisbury MSS*, 15: 41.

31 S. Kaushik, 'Resistance, Loyalty and Recusant Politics: Sir Thomas Tresham and the Elizabethan State', *Midland History*, 21 (1996), 37–72, at p. 62.

32 C. C. Breight, 'Caressing the Great: Viscount Montague's Entertainment of Elizabeth at Cowdray, 1591', *Sussex Archaeological Collections*, 127 (1989), 147–66, at p. 160.

33 Archives of the Archdiocese of Westminster, Series A, VII, no. 54. For a major new thesis on the identity of 'Rivers' and the mechanics of late Elizabethan and early Jacobean Catholic newsletter networks, see the forthcoming research of Patrick Martin and John Finnis.

34 Read, *Mr Secretary Walsingham*, 1: 30–1.

35 Patrick Collinson, 'Windows in a Woman's Soul: Questions about the Religion of Queen Elizabeth I', in his *Elizabethan Essays* (London, 1994), pp. 87–118.

36 Christopher Haigh, *Elizabeth I* (London, 1988), pp. 30–3.

37 Ibid., pp. 36–7. Adams has commented on this well-known episode of the Anjou Match that the evidence for it is pretty slim and the whole thing may have been mere wishful thinking on the part of Mary Stuart and the nuncio in Paris.

38 Ibid., p. 38.

39 Ibid., pp. 38–9.

40 Ibid., p. 170.

41 For an overview of the 'evil counsellor' polemical genre, see Simon Adams, 'Favourites and Factions at the Elizabethan Court', in R. G. Asch and A. M. Birke (eds), *Princes, Patronage and the Nobility: The Court at the Beginning of the Modern Age, c. 1450–1650* (Oxford, 1991), pp. 265–87, reprinted in Simon Adams, *Leicester and the Court* (Manchester, 2002).

42 Adams, 'Favourites,' p. 268.

43 For the quasi-'republican' historical and literary forms which these authors exploited, see the chapter by Peter Lake in this volume, as well as Peter Lake, 'The Counterfactuals of Failure: Dynastic Politics, Catholic "Loyalism" and Conspiracy Theory under Elizabeth I' (forthcoming).

44 [John Leslie,] *A Treatise of Treasons against Q. Elizabeth, and the Croune of England* (Louvain, 1572, RSTC 7601), sig. a7r and *passim*.

45 Thomas Norton, *To the Quenes Maiesties Poore Deceived Subiectes of the North Countrey* (London, 1569, RSTC 18680).

46 *Treatise of Treasons*, sig. a1v.

47 Ibid., sig. a3r–v, fols. 106v, 108r, 109r, 110r, 110v. For the Greys (Suffolk), see fols. 126r–7r, 127v–8v; Adams, 'Favourites', p. 269. For the Cecils' kinship link with the Greys, see M. Levine, *The Early Elizabethan Succession Question 1558–1568* (Stanford, 1966), pp. 80–1.

48 *Treatise of Treasons*, fol. 14r.

49 Ibid., fols. 17r–18v.

50 S. Alford, *The Early Elizabethan Polity* (Cambridge, 1998), chs. 7–8. See also J. E. A. Dawson, 'William Cecil and the British Dimension of Early Elizabethan Foreign Policy', *History* 74 (1989), 196–216.

51 A marginal note on fol. 11v says 'all the privy council allowed the intent, the Lord Keeper [Bacon] except [i.e. excepted],' thus stating baldly that even Cecil was in the know.

52 *Treatise of Treasons*, fols. 11v–12r; Adams, 'Favourites', p. 270.

53 *Treatise of Treasons*, sigs. e3v–6r.

54 Ibid., sig. a4r.

55 Adams, 'Favourites', pp. 268–9.

56 *Treatise of Treasons*, fols. 28v–9r, 31r–2v.

57 Ibid., sigs. e1v, i4r–v.

58 Ibid., fol. 94r.

59 Ibid., fol. 91v. For John Stubbs's likening, in his *A Discoverie of a Gaping Gulf*, of

Elizabeth to Eve, see I. Bell, '"Souereaigne Lord of Lordly Lady of This Land": Elizabeth, Stubbs, and the *Gaping Gvlf*', in J. M. Walker (ed.), *Dissing Elizabeth* (London, 1998), pp. 108–9.

60 Adams, 'Favourites', p. 271.

61 For the debate about the authorship of the book, see *Leicester's Commonwealth*, ed, D. C. Peck (Athens, Ohio, 1985), introduction; Peter Holmes, *Resistance and Compromise: The Political Thought of the Elizabethan Catholics* (Cambridge, 1982), pp. 129–34; Peter Holmes, 'The Political Thought of the Elizabethan Catholics', PhD dissertation, University of Cambridge, 1975, pp. 149–53.

62 I am very grateful for Dr Adams's and Professor Bossy's advice on this point. Adams's forthcoming biography of Leicester will deal with these authorship issues in detail. See also Peter Holmes, 'The Authorship of "Leicester's Commonwealth"', *JEH*, 33 (1982), 424–30.

63 See John Bossy, 'The Heart of Robert Persons', in Thomas M. McCoog, S.J. (ed.), *The Reckoned Expense* (Woodbridge, 1996). I am very grateful to Professor Bossy for discussing the tract with me.

64 I am grateful to Professor Peter Lake for this point.

65 Adams, 'Favourites', pp. 276–8.

66 Peck, *Leicester's Commonwealth*, p. 74.

67 Ibid., pp. 76–7, 78–9.

68 Ibid., pp. 124, 130–1.

69 Ibid., pp. 94, 104, 127.

70 Ibid., p. 37.

71 Lake, 'The Counterfactuals of Failure', citing Peck, *Leicester's Commonwealth*, p. 169.

72 Peck, *Leicester's Commonwealth*, pp. 103–4.

73 Ibid., p. 120. Adams suggests that Catholic usage of the word 'puritans' in this context is a shorthand term for Mary's enemies rather than an informed comment on contemporary ecclesiastical divisions among English Protestants.

74 For a review of this literature, see V. Houliston, 'The Lord Treasurer and the Jesuit: Robert Persons' Satirical *Responsio* to the 1591 Proclamation', *Sixteenth Century Journal*, 32 (2001), 383–401.

75 Ibid., pp. 385–6, 393–4; Robert Parsons, *Elizabethae Angliae reginae haeresim Calvinianam propugnantis* (Antwerp, 1592).

76 Houliston, 'The Lord Treasurer', p. 387.

77 Richard Verstegan, *A Declaration of the True Causes of the Great Troubles, Presupposed to Be Intended against the Realm of England* (Antwerp, 1592, RSTC 10005), sig. A2r, pp. 7–8, 52–3; Adams, 'Favourites', pp. 267–8, 272; Holmes, *Resistance*, pp. 138, 141.

78 For the mid-Elizabethan Catholic court faction, see John Bossy, 'English Catholics and the French Marriage, 1577–81', *Recusant History*, 5 (1959–60): 2–16.

79 Verstegan, *Declaration of the True Causes*, pp. 9, 17–18.

80 *Treatise of Treasons*, sig. a8r.

81 Adams, 'Favourites', p. 272.

82 Holmes, *Resistance*, p. 134.

83 Verstegan, *Declaration of the True Causes*, sigs. A7v–8r, B1–v.

84 Patrick Collinson, 'The Elizabethan Exclusion Crisis and the Elizabethan Polity', *Proceedings of the British Academy*, 84 (1994), 51–92. The problem for Mary's enemies was that her claim was so strong. After the death of Catherine Grey in 1568, she was really the only candidate; her right had statutory authority, and her marriage to Darnley had merged her claim and that of the Lennoxes. For discussion of her claim, see Levine, *The Early Elizabethan Succession Question*. (I am grateful to Pauline Croft for discussions of this point.)

85 J. Watkins, '"Out of her Ashes May a Second Phoenix Rise": James I and the Legacy of Elizabethan Anti-Catholicism', in A. Marotti (ed.), *Catholicism and Anti-Catholicism in Early Modern English Texts* (London, 1999), pp. 116–36.

86 John Bossy, 'English Catholicism: The Link with France', PhD dissertation, University of Cambridge, 1961, p. 156.

87 Lake, 'Leicester his Commonwealth'.

88 D. R. Woolf, 'Two Elizabeths? James I and the late Queen's Famous Memory', *Canadian Journal of History*, 20 (1985), 167–91, at pp. 176–9.

89 M. A. Tierney, *Dodd's Church History of England*, 5 vols (London, 1839–43), 4: ciii.

90 ARSI, Rom. Anglia 37, fol. 308r.

91 I am grateful to Professor Lake for this point. For an account of how 'commonwealth' polemic in 'evil counsellor' mode was generated in the early 1620s by Thomas Scott, see Peter Lake, 'Constitutional Consensus and Puritan Opposition in the 1620s: Thomas Scott and the Spanish Match', *HJ*, 25 (1982), 805–25, at p. 818. See also, Alastair Bellany, *The Politics of Court Scandal in Early Modern England: News Culture and the Overbury Affair, 1603–1660* (Cambridge, 2002), pp. 208, 210.

92 R.C. Johnson, M. F. Keeler, M. Jannson Cole, and W. B. Bidwell (eds), *Commons Debates 1628*, 6 vols (New Haven, 1977–83), 4: 172. For Buckingham and concepts of evil counsel, see Thomas Cogswell, 'The People's Love: The Duke of Buckingham and Popularity', and R. Cust, 'Charles I and Popularity', both in Thomas Cogswell, Richard Cust and Peter Lake (eds), *Politics, Religion and Popularity: Early Stuart Essays in Honour of Conrad Russell* (Cambridge, 2002).

93 C. Hibbard, *Charles I and the Popish Plot* (Chapel Hill, 1983), pp. 232–3, and *passim*.

94 *Treatise of Treasons*, fol. 28r.

Chapter 5

Construing martyrdom in the English Catholic community, 1582–1602

Thomas M. McCoog, S.J.

INTRODUCTION

O ver the past decade scholars have successfully liberated martyrs and martyrologies from a confessional bias that had permeated the field. The papers collected in the Society of Ecclesiastical History's *Martyrs and Martyrologies* examined various cultural, sociological, and theological aspects of the phenomenon within the Christian tradition.[1] Well aware of the confessional studies that had dominated the field, Brad Gregory's rightly acclaimed *Salvation at Stake* argued that the 'corrective to traditional confessional history is not atheistic history of religion, which substitutes one bias for another ... [but] ... an approach that does justice to any and all evidence ... without distorting the convictions of any of its protagonists'.[2] Such cross-confessional studies have opened new vistas for future research. The British Academy established its John Foxe Project to produce a new, critical edition of the most famous and influential martyrologist. In the process, members of the Project, especially David Loades and Thomas Freeman, are producing articles and monographs with significance beyond Foxe. Yet studies of English Catholic martyrs have, as Anne Dillon has noted, 'attracted less attention from the academy.'[3] This lack of interest, however, cannot be explained simply because Catholics were the 'losers' but because their confessional, hagiographical bias proved to be stronger. As John Foxe became an international business, recusant martyrologies remained a self-satisfied cottage industry. Anne Dillon's recent *The Construction of Martyrdom in the English Catholic Community, 1535–1603* has done much to correct this omission. But, like all good books, it leaves the reader with more questions than answers.

Forty years ago, Thomas H. Clancy, S.J., observed that 'from 1582 to the end of Elizabeth's reign the martyr books formed one of the most important classes of Recusant writings, second in volume to the books of piety and devotion. Indeed, for a time the martyrologies almost outnumbered the martyrs.'[4] No one can deny the significance of martyr books. But how many were there? Fortunately, because of the essential guide to recusant writings compiled by A. F. Allison and D. M. Rogers, we can now be more precise.[5] Working with these volumes, Brad Gregory calculated 163 editions in Latin, French, Spanish, Italian, German, and Dutch on the persecution of English Catholics between 1580 and 1619. But, he added, there were 'at least *twenty* different works in *English* on the same subjects ... between *1564 and 1630*' (emphasis mine).[6] These figures raise some questions. Why were there eight times as many non-English editions within a period of thirty-nine years as there were English volumes within sixty-six years? Where were the books published? In England? On the continent? Who were the targeted audiences? Was the interest in martyrs and martyrologies constant between 1558 and 1640, or were there specific periods of excitement that generated more publications? Because, as Brad Gregory reminded us, martyrs are never disembodied: 'Contextual understanding compels us to relate religion to other aspects of life – social, political, economic, cultural – while resisting absorption by any of them.'[7] The same is true of martyrologies. A fuller appreciation requires a greater understanding of their context.

Interestingly, there is little evidence that English Catholics were eager to construct an Elizabethan martyrological tradition on Henrician foundations. Perhaps they were still hopeful of an eventual settlement in their favour and thus did not wish to antagonise Elizabeth or her ministers. Eleven priests and laymen were executed between 1570 and 1580, but no published account proclaimed their status as martyrs with the exception of Nicholas Sander's *De Visibili Monarchia Ecclesiae*.[8] Sander described both John Story and John Felton as martyrs for the 'primacy of the Roman Pontiff in England' ('*pro pontificis Romani primatu in Anglia*' [Felton] and '*pro ecclesiae Romanae primatu*' [Story]). In the same chapter, Sander named nobles and gentlemen currently in exile for taking up arms against Elizabeth because of 'the Catholic faith and the primacy of the Roman Church' ('*ob fidem catholicam & Romanae ecclesiae primatum arma ceperunt*').[9] Other Catholic writers, not as forward as Sander, may have preferred to ignore the martyrological credentials of candidates so involved in political and potentially treasonous activities. Of the eleven possible martyrs, four had dubious associations: John Felton had publicised *Regnans in Excelsis*, Pope Pius V's excommunication of Elizabeth in 1570; John Story had been active in the prosecution of heretics during the reign of Mary Tudor; Thomas Percy, Earl of Northumberland, and Thomas Plumtree had been involved in the Northern Rebellion of 1569. But why no account of Cuthbert Mayne, the proto-martyr of the English College in Douai, condemned for bringing a papal bull into the country, or of Thomas Woodhouse, who refused to acknowledge the Queen's spiritual supremacy? Perhaps more surprising was the general failure (or refusal) of early Elizabethan Catholics to associate their sufferings with those endured by Sir Thomas More, John, Cardinal Fisher, and the London Carthusians, whose martyrdoms had been narrated in Maurice Chauncy's *Historia Aliquot Nostri Saeculi Martryum* (1550) for a continental audience during the reign of King Edward VI. In 1573, a 'V. a Dulken' joined Chauncy's *Historia* with an earlier anonymous defence of Mary, Queen of Scots, *Proditionis ab Aliquot Scotiae Perduellibus ... Narratio* to produce *Illustria Ecclesiae Catholicae, ex Recentibus Anglicorum Martyrum, Scotiae Proditionis, Gallicorumq.*[10] But neither a biography nor a hagiography nor a martyrology was printed in English.

Once the passion ignited by the death of Edmund Campion had passed,[11] there was a similar silence. Accounts of different trials and executions did, in fact, exist. For example, Henry Garnet forwarded to Father General Claudio Acquaviva reports on Robert Southwell's and Henry Walpole's ordeals in Latin and in Italian. English versions may have circulated in manuscript within the Catholic community, but none has been identified. More important, neither martyr was extolled in print in English. Joseph Creswell published an account of Walpole in Spanish,[12] which was translated into French the following year.[13] An English translation never appeared. Between 1580 and 1600, only three English martyrologies were published, all in 1582: Robert Parsons's *An Epistle of Persecution*,[14] William Allen's *A Briefe Historie of the Glorious Martyrdom*,[15] and Thomas Alfield's *A True Reporte of the Death & Martyrdome of M. Campion Iesuite.*[16] The next martyrology in English was Thomas Worthington's 1601 *A Relation of Sixteen Martyrs: Glorified in England in Twelve Monethes. With a Declaration. That English Catholiques Suffer for the Cathlique Religion. And that the Seminarie Priests Agree with the Iesuites.*[17] Why was there nothing for an English audience for twenty years?

In his investigation of recusant lists of martyrs, John Hungerford Pollen, S.J., was perplexed by vacillation between periods of intense activity and almost utter silence. 'I am not able to say with any certainty', Pollen observed regarding renewed interest in 1608,

> what the reason of this was; perhaps it was due to the publication, by the Fathers of the Society of Jesus, of the lists of their first century of Martyrs, which took place in that year. Perhaps it was suggested by the first publication of the Roman Martyrology in English.[18]

Perhaps. But it is more likely that both publishing events relate to struggles within the Catholic community over its identity and direction as is suggested by the subtitle of Worthington's treatise: *With a Declaration. That English Catholiques Suffer for the Cathlique Religion. And that the Seminarie Priests agree with the Iesuites.* But before investigating the late Elizabethan revival of interest in Catholic martyrologies, can we offer any explanation for the earlier waning?

Thomas M. McCoog

THE CAMPION AFFAIR: CONFESSOR OR CONSPIRATOR?

Edmund Campion's arrest in July and eventual execution on 1 December 1581 fuelled and redirected a 'public'[19] confrontation which extinguished the dying embers of a proposed match between Queen Elizabeth and François, Duke of Anjou; introduced more severe legislation against recusancy; and popularised an identification of Catholicism with treason.[20] As Protestant preachers denounced the proposed match, Elizabeth considered stacking her Privy Council with Catholics in order to advance the marriage. Campion's and Parsons's missionary antics, however, confirmed Protestant apprehensions that a revived Catholicism intended the destruction of the Established Church. Parsons claimed that he knew nothing about the Hispano-papal invasion of Ireland until the arrival of the missionary band in the Low Countries. Historians, relying more on Parsons's popular Machiavellian image than on concrete data, question his sincerity. But, even assuming the veracity of his claim, there was no need for his prior knowledge. The mission of Campion and Parsons depended not on Spanish military force or an Irish insurrection, but on a favourably disposed faction at court with extravagant expectations that a marriage treaty would decriminalise Catholicism within certain restrictions. With this relative freedom, Catholic priests could further the marginalisation of advanced Protestantism by exposing its theological errors and historical inaccuracies. One common theological error concerned attendance at Protestant services. The government demanded attendance as a demonstration of political allegiance. Parsons, on the other hand, argued that attendance at church had nothing to do with political loyalty but demonstrated religious profession. Catholics, despite their fidelity to the monarch, could not obey her command to attend services because such behaviour testified to their acceptance of the Protestant creed. Study of recent history, as Parsons and other Catholic writers reiterated, revealed a Protestant predilection for rebellion and a Catholic allegiance to authority.

Despite Parsons's disclaimer, the conflict in Ireland, illustrating as it did another aspect of revived Catholicism, cast a dark shadow over the mission. The collapse of the coalition favouring the marriage (skilfully engineered by Robert Dudley, Earl of Leicester, in mid-winter 1580–81) and Leicester's subsequent discovery of irrefutable evidence that Catholics not only exploited the negotiations to advance their cause but would resort to other tactics later if necessary, raised a general alarm to the real threat posed by Catholics. The proclamation 'Ordering Return of Seminarians, Arrest of Jesuits' of 10 January 1581 declared that Jesuits 'lately repaired into this realm by special direction from the pope and his delegates, with intent not only to corrupt and pervert her good and loving subjects in matter of conscience and religion, but also to draw them from the loyalty and duty of obedience and to provoke them, so much as shall lie in them, to attempt somewhat to the disturbance of the present quiet that through the goodness of Almighty God and her majesty's provident government this realm hath these many years enjoyed'.[21] On 25 January, Sir Walter Mildmay explicitly linked the arrival of the Jesuits with papal support for the northern rebellion in 1569 and for the current troubles in Ireland. With the clandestine presence of Jesuits in England, Pope Gregory XIII had opened another front in his campaign:

> you see how the Pope hath and doth comfort their [Catholics'] hollow hearts with absoluc[i]ons, dispensations, reconciliations, and such other thinges of Rome, you see how lately he hath sent hither a sort of hipocrites naming themselves Jesuites, a rable of vagrant fryers newly sprung upp and comyng throught the world to trowble the Church of God, whose principall errand is, by creeping into the howses and familiarityes of men of behaviour and reputacion, not only to corrupt the realme with false doctrine, but also under that pretence to stirr sedition to the perill of her Majestie and her good subiectes.[22]

The subsequent 'Act to Retain the Queen's Majesty's Subjects in Their Due Obedience' (23 Eliz. I, c. 1) increased fines for Catholic recusants and threatened with high treason anyone reconciled to the Church of Rome and anyone responsible for said reconciliation. The new law completed what Father General Everard Mercurian had long feared in his opposition to a Jesuit mission to England: the identification of Jesuit apostolic activity with treason.

The capture of the Jesuit with the highest profile and the greatest notoriety provided the government with an ideal platform to demonstrate the treason inherent in Catholicism. According to Robert Parsons, of the various priests paraded to the Tower of London as a public spectacle, only Campion wore a hat with an attached sign describing him as 'Edmund Campion Jesuit Traitor'.[23] The anonymous authors of *An Advertisement and Defence of Trueth Against Her Backbiters* (1581) and *A Triumph for True Subjects and a Terror unto all Traitors* (1581) disseminated the official line to a wider public: priests were executed for treason and not for religious dissent. Anthony Munday, ex-Catholic informer and future playwright, and George Elliot, Campion's betrayer, specifically addressed the case of Campion. Both sought to destroy his reputation. For Munday, Campion was a braggart, a dissembler, a hypocrite eager to issue challenges but fearful of appearing on the field of battle. Munday denigrated Campion's alleged learning and claimed that the truly learned actually detested him but tolerated him because of Christian kindness.[24]

Parsons's *De Persecutione Anglicana*,[25] an English translation of which appeared the following year as *An Epistle of the Persecution of Catholickes in Englande*,[26] dismissed the official pronouncement that Catholics suffered for treason and not for religion. The translator's introduction extolled the loyalty of Catholic subjects 'most readie both withe lyfe & goods to serve their

Princesse, and your honours [the Privy Councillors], with all dewtifall and faithful goodwill'.[27] Moreover Campion, a 'great lerned clerk, a harmelesse and verie Innocent man', was subjected to base treatment and torture on the rack. With mildness, modesty, and a cheerful, Christ-like countenance, Campion endured all and emerged a martyr for his faith.[28] Alfield's *A True Reporte* described Campion as 'the flower of Oxford', 'an honor to our country, a glasse and mirror, a light and lanterne, a paterne and example to youth, to age, to lerned, to unlerned, to religious, and to the laytie of al sort, state & condition, of modestie, gravitie, eloquence, knowledge, vertue, and pietie'.[29]

Other priests were executed in May of 1582. William Allen combined accounts of their martyrdom with Alfield's earlier report in *A Briefe Historie of the Glorious Martyrdom*. For all, treason was simply a pretence to hide the true religious motives for the executions. As continental presses produced Latin and vernacular accounts of the suffering endured by English Catholics, the Elizabethan government sought to control the damage of such widespread negative publicity with official *apologiae*. *A Declaration of the Favourable Dealing of Her Maiesties Commissioners* (1583), with a Latin translation the following year, explained the crown's case. *The Execution of Iustice in England* (1583), with translations into French, Italian, Latin, and Dutch, substantially developed the argument. William Cecil, Lord Burghley, was the author of both. Despite the lenient treatment allotted to priests arrested, many Catholics 'do falsely allege that a number of persons, whom they term as martyrs, have died for the defense of the Catholic religion, the same in very truth may manifestly appear to have died (if they will have it) as martyrs for the Pope but yet as traitors against their sovereign and queen in adhering to him, being the notable and only openly hostile enemy in all actions of war against Her Majesty'.[30] Allen's *A True, Sincere and Modest Defence, of English Catholiques*[31] refuted Cecil's argument, exonerated the reputations of the executed priests, and established their credentials as true martyrs. New editions and translations continued to argue the Catholic interpretation to their co-religionists on the continent. More Catholics were executed or died in prison. But neither new English martyrologies nor reprints of older English ones appeared.

JASPER HEYWOOD AND JESUIT POLICY

During the late Elizabethan, intra-Catholic 'Appellant Controversy', John Mush castigated the style and demeanour of the English Jesuit Jasper Heywood. In 1601, he reprimanded the Jesuit for claiming the authority of a papal legate, summoning provincial synods, abrogating traditional fasts, and forbidding publication of a martyrology approved by William Allen.[32] Parsons immediately dismissed the complaints as 'partly plaine calumniations, and partly odious and malitious wrestings of his doings'.[33] The following year, 1602,

Parsons asked for proof that Heywood had prohibited reading lives of martyrs and forbidden their promulgation.[34] No one provided the evidence requested, but William Clarke repeated the accusation in 1603.[35]

One could easily, and justifiably, consider Mush's, Clarke's, and Humphrey Ely's claims as unfounded allegations generated by the heat of the conflict, or as intentional misconstructions of Heywood's perhaps relatively minor indiscretions, or as official propaganda disseminated by the government's collaborators. One can conclude that the Appellants did not provide the requested evidence because it simply did not exist, especially since no such evidence has come to light subsequently. But circumstantial evidence makes the allegations more credible.

In 1580, Pope Gregory XIII granted permission to Campion and Parsons to publish Catholic books without the names of the author, place, and publisher.[36] Perhaps, as a result, Parsons worked closely with Stephen Brinkley whose press at Greenstreet House, East Ham, had already published Thomas Hide's *A Consolatorie Epistle to the Afflicted Catholikes*[37] under the author's name but with a false imprint (Louvain).[38] From different locations, Parsons and Brinkley published approximately six works before the former's escape to France and the latter's capture in the summer of 1581.[39]

Another Catholic press under the direction of Richard Rowlands (alias Verstegan) published Alfield's *A True Reporte* at the end of February of 1582. In the consequent government crack-down, Alfield and the volume's distributors, Edward Cooke, William Dean, and Edward Osborne, were arrested. Rowlands, warned of his imminent arrest, escaped to the continent and continued his work for the Catholic cause as Richard Verstegan.[40]

Printing and distributing Catholic literature in general became even more dangerous as the government sought to silence these voices of opposition, but controversial and martyrological literature intensified the problem. Somewhere in the heart of London lay a potent weapon that challenged official propaganda on such highly contested subjects as church attendance and public executions. After Rowlands's flight, Catholic presses in England remained silent until the arrival of the Jesuits Henry Garnet and Robert Southwell in July 1586. After their arrival, volumes once again flowed from secret presses, but they avoided controversial areas. The new press at Arundel House in the Strand published H. B.'s *A Consolatory Letter to All the Afflicted Catholikes in England*[41] and Southwell's *An Epistle of Comfort.*[42]

A strange silence had descended upon the clandestine Catholic presses in England during Heywood's tenure as superior of the Jesuit mission, a silence that cannot be attributed solely to government vigilance. In 1590, Heywood submitted to Father General Acquaviva a critical evaluation of Parsons's influence on the English mission. Heywood and Parsons had consistently disagreed on almost every aspect of the mission, an apparent consequence of which was Heywood's removal from England. In his memorial, Heywood argued that Parsons's publications had offended many, insulting, as they did, the Queen and her councillors. These books, written presumably for the benefit of English Catholics, Heywood argued, only made life more difficult for them. Good men, such as the Jesuit brother Ralph Emerson, suffered imprisonment for smuggling Catholic works into the kingdom. As long as Catholics produced volumes that ridiculed specific nobles, challenged the established religious order, or depicted the Elizabethan government as blood-thirsty persecutors, Heywood – and he claimed that the Spanish ambassador Bernardino de Mendoza supported him on this – doubted any improvement in the general lot of Catholics.[43]

Heywood opposed inflammatory Catholic publications as counter-pro-ductive. As he subsequently explained to Acquaviva, Catholics could not expect any relief as long as their writers antagonised the government and the nobility. Had he therefore refused to establish a another secret press in England after Rowlands's had been destroyed by the government? Had he, as the Appellants asserted, refused to authorise the anonymous publication of Allen's *A Brief Historie of the Glorious Martyrdom*?

Father General Claudio Acquaviva's personal hesitations about martyro-logical literature may have been another factor in the abrupt cessation of such treatises for the English market. Admittedly the evidence for this is, at best, ambivalent. In his first letter to Parsons after learning of Campion's capture, Acquaviva exhorted Parsons to be prudent and careful as he exercised his priestly ministry in England. Although Jesuits should always be ready to suffer, 'intemperate trust' was foolish and displeased God.[44] Later, as Parsons was writing a life of Campion, Acquaviva advised him to include not only details of Campion's imprisonment and execution, both readily available in the published accounts of his martyrdom, 'but also what he was able to accomplish before his imprisonment, which I hear was considerable and tremendously edifying'. Acquaviva wanted Parsons to collect information about Campion's earlier life 'so that something complete and entire may be published for the comfort of Jesuits and, especially, for the glory of God'.[45] A month later, despite his awareness of the good that the martyrs would do for the English cause because 'encouragement by deeds is far weightier and more effective than encouragement by words', Acquaviva repeated his wish that Parsons produce an account of what Campion 'had achieved not only at his death but also while in prison, before his imprisonment, and in his earlier life as well'.[46]

Parsons never completed his life of Campion, perhaps, as John Bossy has suggested, because of his inability to understand precisely what Acquaviva wanted.[47] What he wanted, apparently, was a mission focused on ministering to Catholics and not on dying on scaffolds. He wanted Parsons to record not just the edifying death of Campion but the edifying ministry that had preceded it. In July 1584, Acquaviva asked for specific information regarding living conditions of Jesuits in England, 'the probability of results and of not being discovered'. If the Jesuit's motive was 'to suffer and to edify others by this', his presence could prove harmful to many and increase persecution for Catholics 'without any gain'.[48] Acquaviva's concern about living conditions, the possibility of effective ministry, and the potential consequences for other Catholics steered Parsons away from a preoccupation with martyrs and martyrologies. Instead of a life of Campion, Parsons completed *The First Booke of the Christian Exercise*, better known as *The Book of Resolution* or *The Christian Directory*, in which martyrdom is not exalted as a goal but as a possible consequence of resolution.[49]

To return to the original allegation: John Mush et al. contended that Jasper Heywood forbade publication and distribution of Allen's martyrology. Parsons's demand for evidence went unanswered. Nonetheless, Heywood's clear opposition to such treatises as counter-productive makes their complaint plausible. Moreover, Acquaviva did not wish to encourage a perspective, a spirituality, that considered England a killing field instead of an apostolic vineyard. For a domestic audience at least, the Society of Jesus was not interested in producing martyrologies. Others, of course, could have been printed without the assistance and resources of the Society of Jesus, but, on the evidence of Allison and Rogers's index, they were not.

CONTINENTAL INTEREST IN THE ENGLISH MARTYRS

Anne Dillon has noted the absence of an Elizabethan Catholic equivalent of John Foxe's *Acts and Monuments*. 'The nearest contemporary Catholic equivalent, the *Concertatio*', Dr Dillon suggested, 'aspired to this but it remained in Latin without illustration, remote and inaccessible, as did much of the printed martyr material produced by Catholics'.[50] After 1582, Catholic martyrological literature did remain 'remote and inaccessible', generally without 'illustration'. But was this an unfortunate accident as Dillon insinuates or was the literature simply not intended for the English market? With the number of clergy educated in Flanders, Rome, and later Spain, the English mission did not lack potential translators for Spanish, Italian, French, and Latin martyrological tracts. If the *Concertatio* and other volumes 'remained in Latin', we cannot attribute this to an absence of translators.

Throughout the 1580s, Catholic presses on the Continent, many associated with Jesuit colleges or located in cities where Jesuit influence was strong, consistently produced horrifying accounts of the sufferings endured by English Catholics for a non-English market. Parsons's *De Persecutione Anglicana* had five Latin editions, three French, one or two Italian, and one German.[51]

Allen's *A Briefe Historie of the Glorious Martyrdom* went through four Italian editions.[52] Alfield's *A True Reporte of the Death & Martyrdome of M. Campion Iesuite* was not reprinted as such but the anonymous *L'Histoire de la Mort que le R.P. Edmond Campion* was thrice published in French, twice in Latin, four times in Italian, and once in German.[53] Thomas Bourchier's *Historia Ecclesiastica de Martyrio* had three Latin editions and two German abridgements.[54] Richard Verstegan's *Descriptiones Quaedam Illius Humanae et Multiplicis Persecutionis* appeared twice in Latin and once in French.[55] The Jesuit John Gibbons's *Concertatio Ecclesiae Catholicae in Anglia*, the volume suggested by Dillon as a Catholic equivalent for Foxe, had three Latin editions;[56] Maurice Chauncy's *Historia Aliquot Nostri Saeculi Martyrum*, two Latin editions;[57] and *Ecclesiae Anglicanae Trophaea*, two Latin editions.[58] Nicholas Sander's *De Origine ac Progressu Schismatis Anglicani* appeared five times in Latin and thrice in French.[59] The Jesuit Pedro de Ribadeneira's adaptation of *De Origine*, the *Historia Ecclesiastica del Scisma del Reyno de Inglaterra*, appeared ten times within two years.[60] Adam Blackwood's proclamation of the martyrdom of Mary, Queen of Scots, *Martyre de la Royne d'Escosse,* was published five times in French.[61] Thomas Stapleton's *Tres Thomae*, one of whom was Sir Thomas More, appeared once in Latin.[62] *Relatione del Presente Stato d'Inghilterra* published documents regarding the persecution from the English College then in Rheims, including Richard Barret's list of 91 martyrs executed between 1577 and 1590.[63] Parsons's *Relacion de Algunos Martyrios* had one Spanish, two French, and two Italian editions.[64]

Sander's *De Origine ac Progressu* remained the dominant account in the 1590s. G. Pollini based his *Historia Ecclesiastica della Rivoluzione d'Inghilterra* on Sander and dedicated it to William Allen. There were three editions.[65] A. da Sciacca used the same source for his *Relazione dello Scisma Anglicano*.[66] Ribadeneira extended Sander's *De Origine* to cover the years 1587 to 1593 in *Segunda Parte de la Historia del Scisma de Inglaterra*. Over the next two years this volume went through five more editions. A German translation, *Warhaffte Engellaendische Histori*, appeared in 1594.[67] J. Mayr derived his *Kurtzerbericht aller gedenckwuerdigen Sachen ... in Engelland* from Sander among others.[68] Gibbons's *Concertatio Ecclesiae Catholicae in Anglia* was republished only once in the 1590s.[69] Joseph Creswell, S.J., published a Spanish account of the martyrdom of Henry Walpole, the first martyr from one of the English seminaries in Spain, *Historia de la Vida y Martyrio que Padecio en Inglaterra* (1596). It had a second Spanish edition and, surprisingly, a French translation.[70]

The last martyrologies or accounts of persecution of the sixteenth century were Diego de Yepes's *Historia Particular de la Persecucion de Inglaterra* and *Relacion del Martirio de los Dos Sacerdotes*.[71] Richard Verstegan returned to the genre with *Brief et Veritable Discours, de la Mort d'Aucuns Vaillants et Glorieux*

Martyrs, translated into Flemish as *Cort Ende Waerachtich Verhael van Het Lijden van Sommighe Vrome Ende Glorieuse Martelaers*.[72]

Some important observations can be made after this survey. Bourchier's *Historia Ecclesiastica* was translated into German but not into English; Sander's *De Origine ac Progressu* had translations, or derivative accounts, in French, Spanish, German, and Italian, but nothing in English. Parsons's *Relacion de Algunos Martyrios* appeared in Spanish, French, and Italian, but not in English. Creswell's *Historia de la Vida y Martyrio que Padecio en Inglaterra* had a French edition but not an English one. Only the *Relacion del Martirio de los Dos Sacerdotes* was translated into English as part of Worthington's *A Relation of Sixteen Martyrs*. Continental presses produced their martyrologies in Latin, Italian, French, Spanish, and German for a Continental audience. The treatises not only informed Continental Catholics of the unjust sufferings endured by their co-religionists for their faith alone, but were de facto propaganda intended to arouse Catholic powers to take action either by reaching into their pockets for financial assistance or by fomenting alliances for total liberation. Copies of Parsons's *De Persecutione Anglicana* were distributed to Jesuit provincials, and most likely other ecclesiastical leaders, before special collections to aid the English College, Rome, and English Catholics in general.[73] Apparently fundraising lay behind Joseph Creswell's works on the martyrs as he sought benefactors eager to endow bursaries for 'future' martyrs.[74]

Before 1588, France was the centre of the literary productions of English Catholics. Henry, Duke of Guise, as head of the Catholic League, skillfully exploited French translations of English martyrologies to warn the nation of the possible consequences of a Protestant king. As a Guise, Henry was concerned about the welfare of his kinswoman, Mary, Queen of Scots. Dissemination of such horrifying reports also justified his active role in coalitions directed against Elizabeth's government in the early 1580s. Most martyrologies published in German lands were printed in Ingolstadt and Dillingen, two cities with influential Jesuit colleges (in fact, the Society administered the university in Dillingen) within the duchy of Bavaria, whose Duke William IV, married to Renée de Guise, was another participant in coalitions against Elizabeth.[75] With the exception of the two editions of Chauncy's *Historia Aliquot Nostri Saeculi Martyrum* published in 1583, no volume concerning the English persecution was published in Spain until 1588, the year of the Armada. Henceforth Spain also became the champion of English Catholics on the literary front. France's role diminished to insignificance as the fortunes of the Catholic League collapsed and the now former Huguenot Henry IV assumed control over his kingdom.

Approximately ninety lives of martyrs, martyrologies, and accounts of the persecution of Catholics in England were published in the sixteenth century.

Only three were in English, Parsons's *An Epistle of Persecution*, Allen's *A Briefe Historie of the Glorious Martyrdom*, and Alfield's *A True Reporte of the Death & Martyrdome of M. Campion Iesuite*, all in 1582. No further work was produced for the English market until 1601. Dr Dillon observed that the martyrs 'became a powerful ideological tool with which to encourage the community to maintain its own separated existence and identify and to support its priests'. However true this observation may be at some future point in the community's history, the Catholics of Elizabethan England seem to have been intentionally deprived of that tool. The English martyrs principally served as an 'international Catholic banner ... to rally [Catholic European powers] against the threat of international Calvinism' and not as paradigms offered for emulation by religious exiles to English Catholics.[76]

'THE DESIGNED MARTYRS OF OUR COUNTREY'

Subsequent Catholic controversialists often exaggerated the halcyon days of the English mission before the death of William Allen in 1594. Under his benign governance, the lion may not have lain with the lamb but disparate elements had worked together for the good of the mission. As the universally acknowledged leader, his personal authority maintained a delicate tranquillity which collapsed shortly after his death on 16 October 1594. The search for a successor aggravated old sores as factions formed around a reluctant Robert Parsons, the elderly Thomas Stapleton, and the experienced Owen Lewis, Bishop of Cassano. In England, the 'Wisbech Stirs' between late 1594 and early 1595 purportedly provided new evidence of Jesuit ambitions to dominate the secular clergy as William Weston assumed an ambiguous position of religious authority within the community of imprisoned clerics. At the same time in Belgium, Charles Paget, Thomas Morgan, and other lay exiles, many former associates and friends of individual English Jesuits, lamented Jesuit devotion to Spain, especially Spanish pretensions to the English throne, and Jesuit control over distribution of Spanish pensions. Finally, in Rome some students denounced the pro-Hispanic Jesuit administration of the English College. By 1597 the three battles had become fronts in the same war. Personal conflicts, theological disagreements, and ecclesiastical rivalries united in one general struggle encompassing all aspects of the mission. In the conflict between Jesuits and Appellants, no weapon was too dirty. Each side sought to discredit its opponents with allegations of lewd behaviour, violations of religious poverty, and conduct unbecoming clergy.[77]

William Wiseman, a prominent recusant layman, friend of the Jesuit John Gerard, and patron of the Society of Jesus, wrote 'A Triple Farewell to the World or Three Deaths in Different States of Soul' while he was in prison in the mid-1590s.[78] Writing for his wife and family, Wiseman explained the pivotal role of a spiritual director in the life of a serious Christian through three parables: the first, the story of a good, virtuous man, who sought to live as a Christian without any director; the second concerned a good, devout woman who had assumed her own spiritual direction after she had been deceived by the Devil into abandoning her priest; and the third told of the holy death of a good man who accepted the direction of his spiritual father. Wiseman's spiritual guide received a wider circulation than he had intended. Some readers interpreted his description of the ideal spiritual director as a barely disguised endorsement of Jesuits. Such readers interpreted Wiseman as suggesting that the laity should turn to the secular clergy for counsel only if Jesuits were not available. Even then, the godly should select a secular priest friendly with Jesuits and, presumably, approved by them.

The secular priest John Mush, formerly a candidate for the Society of Jesus and generally considered friendly towards it, complained to Wiseman about this apparent partiality. Not wishing to denigrate the Jesuits, Mush exhorted Wiseman to esteem secular clergy as highly as he did the Society of Jesus. Neither had a monopoly on virtue:

> Comparisons of good men are ever odious & disgustfull to vertuous eares: And this extraordinary magnifyinge, extollinge, & preferringe of Jesuits above priests, or this man above that man, specially when they be all good men argueth no litle vanitie, indiscretion, & fonde affection. Jesuits be good religious men, & ye better, ye meaner conceipt they carry of themselfes in respect of others as well religious as secular priests. They labour well, they be fitt spiritual guides. the secular preists, also be all vertuous men (except myself) they laboure well; they be sufficient spirituall guides, as appeareth by the effects of their travailes in every corner of the realm. Both sorts spend their lives, & yeeld their blood with equall courage & constancy for one & ye same cause. Let not then theire children contend emulously for ye preferringe or more credit of either, but reverence love, and honor all ... Of all sorts some are better and more perfect then others, but yet all profitable, & worthy of more love comfort, estimacion, & honor then is given them. Of all sorts there wilbe som badde. Apostata Jesuits, Apostata secular priests: ut omnes timeant dominium: nec se quisque commendet, sed in domino glorietur.[79]

Wiseman either showed Mush's letter to Henry Garnet, Jesuit superior in England, or repeated the secular priest's comment about apostate Jesuits. Garnet demanded specific names. Mush replied: Thomas Langdale, Christopher Perkins, and Thomas [*vere* George] Durie.[80] The first two were English; the third, a Scot. Garnet countered that all three had apostatised after their dismissal from the Society and, thus, could not be labelled apostate Jesuits. Either provide names of persons who had apostatised as Jesuits, or rescind the charge, Garnet argued. In January of 1598, Garnet asked Robert Parsons to confirm his assertion that all three had abandoned their faith after their departure from the Society.[81]

Eager to preserve the reputation of the Society of Jesus, Garnet refuted the very suggestion that a Jesuit was ever less than faithful, orthodox, and honourable. Comparisons of good men may have been odious to the ears of the virtuous but in the subsequent controversy between English Jesuits and secular clergy, accusations of apostasy took second place to accusations about vice and quality of life. Each side positioned themselves on the moral high ground and accused their opponents of moral turpitude, treason, or collusion. So vitriolic did the conflict become that not even the martyrs were safe.

William Gifford, the English Dean of Lille, apparently first introduced the question of martyrs into the conflict in the summer of 1597. In a letter to Robert Markland at the English College, Rome, Gifford asserted that Jesuit attempts to dominate all aspects of the English mission resulted in a persecution of Catholics more grievous than any campaign conducted by the government. Moreover, Gifford continued, those who suffered at the hands of the Jesuits were punished 'on account of their virtue'.[82] Markland reformulated this charge in a petition to Pope Clement VIII with a significant addition 'Jesuits persecuted some priests, now martyrs, in such a way that their death has been attributed partly to the heretics and partly to the fathers'.[83] Unfortunately he did not specify the martyrs for whose deaths he held Jesuits partially responsible. Robert Fisher dropped the accusation from his more (in)famous memorial submitted to Pope Clement VIII via the apostolic nuncio in Brussels, Ottavio Mirto Frangipani, in September 1597. Nonetheless, it was not forgotten: Christopher Bagshaw repeated it in 1601.[84] Fisher's only comment about martyrs in the memorial was almost an aside in his denunciation of Jesuit political involvement. Because of such activity, the heretics understood 'our martyrs' as traitors to their fatherland, culpable of *lèse-majesté* even though they suffered for their faith.[85]

On 2 April 1597, Easter Saturday, Robert Parsons addressed the scholars at the English College. Summoned from Spain to assume the rectorship in the hope that he could resolve the problems then plaguing the college, Parsons recommended that all meditate on certain scriptural passages with marked resemblance to the current state of the college: Israel wandering in the desert, Israel exiled in Babylon, and the early church in Corinth. There were difficulties; there was resentment; there were factions. Cardinal Allen 'who was in deede our Moyses, our Esdras, our Nehemias, and as I may saye in a certayne sort our first and cheefe Apostle in thys affayre',[86] had competently coordinated activities performed by 'two hands'. From the start there was tension between nationalities, between social classes, etc. But the situation had deteriorated. Parsons avoided specific names but he informed his audience 'that these twoo handes are now manifestlye knowen to the world'. Their differences were apparent:

for first yt ys evident that there was before thother which ys the difference noted before by our Saviour in the Gospell betweene the twoo seedes, good and badde: and betweene the twoo sowers hym self and hys enimye; to wytte that th'one sowed first and th'other came after and oversprinkled the same.

The good hand has worked for the benefit of England from the start. It included:

our late good Cardinal Doctor Sanders, Sir franncys Inglefield and the rest of that ranke now deade, and there frindes and comparteners yet alive of the learnedest and gravest of our nacion: And with them have jeoned ever all the fathers of the Societye, all the Seiminaryes, all the priests within and withowt Ingland. All the Catholikes in prison and other abrode withowt exception.

By their fruits, the members of the right hand were known: the martyrs, the confessors, the benefactors and founders of seminaries, colleges and residences. And the left hand? What have they done? Among their accomplishments were:

the overthrow of the poore quene of Scots, that otherwyse myght yett have lyved manye a fayre yeare, with the ruyne of those fourteene Inglische Gentilmen that dyed with hyr and for hyr, in trapped by the rashe and undiscrete treatie of Ballarde, wherin I can assure yow, the right hand had nether part nor knowledge. The fall in lyke maner of Gylbert Gifford and hys treatye with the enime were by thys hand; as also the twoo bookes wytten by hym and hys compagnion, The one againste our Cardinals epistle for the deliverye of Deventrye,[87] and the other against the ffathers of the Societye, which were so fondlye and malitiously written as Walsingham hym self was assahaymed to lett them be printed.

Like his companion Edmund Campion,[88] Parsons claimed the martyrs for his side. United with the Jesuits around the Standard of Christ, were the founders of the colleges, all Catholics in prison, confessors and 'above a hundred martyrs: twyse or thryse as manye Confessors'. Their opponents included double-dealers, plotters and traitors to the Catholic cause. Their rash acts resulted in the death of fourteen English gentlemen. Markland blamed the Jesuits for the deaths of some martyrs; Fisher accused the Society of devaluing the religious witness of martyrs because of Jesuit political involvement. Parsons held the unnamed 'second hand' responsible for fourteen deaths. The Appellants portrayed Jesuits as overweening political Machiavellians whose involvement in state matters prolonged the persecution of Catholics. Jesuits, on the other hand, depicted their opponents as schismatic trimmers so eager to conclude an agreement with the English government that they were disloyal to Rome. Seculars accused Jesuits of debasing martyrs through their political machinations; Jesuits lamented that seculars betrayed the martyrs through their willingness to negotiate with the government. Parsons claimed the martyrs as supporters of the Jesuit position and alleged that the intrigues of 'the second hand' caused the deaths of many loyal Catholics. Opponents of the Jesuits countered that some martyrs had suffered almost as much at the hands of the Jesuits as they had at the hands of the government.

In 1599, Parsons repeated many of the comments made in his speech in an anonymous defence of the Society of Jesus against Sir Francis Hastings's *A Watch-Word to all Religious, and True Hearted English-Men* (1598). The majority of Catholics, Parsons explained, loved and esteemed Jesuits. Only heretics, infidels, atheists, and a few Catholics – and then for reasons of cowardice and lack of zeal – opposed the Society. The willingness of so many Jesuits to suffer torture and martyrdom in the Indies, Ethiopia, Japan, England, and France testified to their quality and validated their position in the hearts of true Catholics.[89] True Catholics, among whom he numbered the martyrs, supported the Society of Jesus; by implication, he undermined the religious integrity of Jesuit opponents. Parsons's *A Temperate Ward-Word to the Turbulent and Seditious Wach-Word of Sir Francis Hastings* proclaimed in the public sphere what had originally been restricted to lectures and letters. In early 1599, the Jesuit Thomas Lister provided the final straw when he infamously labelled secular clergy who had questioned the establishment of a novel ecclesiastical structure, the archpresbyterate, 'schismatics'.

Secular clergy considered Wiseman's treatise, Parsons's adaptation of the Ignatian two standards, and Lister's denunciation as examples of the same arrogance. Perhaps because Wiseman's treatise circulated more widely, Appellant writers cited it more frequently. John Mush, Christopher Bagshaw, William Watson, William Clarke, and an anonymous editor[90] refer to the treatise. Jesuits, they reminded their readers, never denied Wiseman's suggestion nor attempted to moderate his zeal. Despite the protests of secular clergy, Henry Garnet did nothing. Perhaps, as the editor of *Copies of Certaine Discourses* suggested, Jesuits allowed such exaltation of their spiritual prowess in order to dislodge mere secular clergy from comfortable residences and their replacement with Jesuits and their associates.

To defend their impugned reputation, secular clergy took the initiative. In 1601, Anthony Copley, a lay Catholic cousin of the executed Jesuit Robert Southwell, pointed out that between the time of the founder of the Jesuits and this treatise, 'which is now well nigh a hundred yeeres [sic]', 'there is not so much as one Canonized Saint of the order, Confessor, or Martyr; no not their founder himselfe ...' Within England, Copley contended, for every one Jesuit martyr, there were at least twenty secular priests. Nonetheless, the Society sought to usurp all the honour.[91] Copley also calculated the number of Jesuit martyrs as two or three. Instead of martyrs willing to suffer for their faith, the Society produced priests such as Parsons, who 'ranne away most cowardlie from the like honour', and Heywood, 'who got himselfe to be banisht, giving thereby the first president (if I mistake not) to others of the like frailtie'.[92]

Thomas Bluet, another secular priest, also commented on Jesuit aversion to martyrdom. Secular priests, 'the designed Martyrs of our countrey', were more ready than Jesuits to shed their blood to prevent the loss of one soul. How, therefore, he asked the nobility to whom he addressed his opening letter, could secular clergy have offended them?[93] Jesuits, not secular clergy, were the cause of the persecution. Their intrigues and machinations, their harangues and tirades forced the government to legislate against Catholics. Anthony Copley reminded his cousin that Protestants suffered for 'their errours in Religion', during the reign of Queen Mary I. In some ways, they should be commended and imitated because of their respectful approach to the very powers that persecuted them. 'Let us withall hope', Copley continued, 'that (seeing bloud will have bloud) the Protestants hand which he are now under, will one day be satisfied for the Protestant bloud, in my opinion, too profusely shed, and other theeir vexations in the aforesaid good Queens daies, and so perhaps appeased'.[94] Copley repeated his censure of the Society for their paucity of martyrs in *Another Letter of Mr A. C. to his Dis-Iesuited Kinsman.* But, more important, in his work he questioned their claims to martyrological status: 'Why may not we aswell by the same reason calumniate even those three or 4. Martyrs (which are all that have bin of their Societie here in England) to have died rather to their shames for their seins, then to gods glorie, which (though unconfirmed as yet by myracles for Saints) God defend that absolutely we should[?]'[95]

Jesuits were not the mortified, spiritually motivated spiritual directors that they and their supporters claimed. In fact, as described by the Society's opponents, Jesuits were money-loving, ingratiating, hypocritical traitors, responsible for the persecution suffered by Catholics. Christopher Bagshaw noted:

> no Iesuit goeth but to visite any one, or travelleth from one place to another, but he is richly apparrelled, he is attended on with a great trayne of servants, as if he were a Baron, or an Earle, which is not necessary, but playnely riduculous and absurd. The secular Priests themselves do go also Gentlemen-like because of danger; but not arayed in that sumptuous manner, nor guarded with so many attendants, as the Iesuites. They wrangle, and reprove the Priests garments, and spending; whereas the expences of one Iesuite were able to mayntayne twentie Priests, plentifully, and richly.[96]

Unlike secular priests who 'dissent from the State in the profession of our Religion; yet we are her Maiesties borne subjects' and in no way conspire against her interests, their 'trayterous adversaries of the Societie, not indeede of Iesus, but of the Divell', Bagshaw said slandered her and sought her overthrow.[97] Not surprisingly many in England believed that Jesuit pride and sedition alone prevented some form of tolerance.[98] Appellant literature, seeking to redirect official wrath away from Catholics in general to Jesuits in particular, blamed the Society of Jesus for the persecution of Catholics within

England. To various degrees, the authors extolled the mercy of their sovereign and wondered rhetorically whether Elizabeth had any alternative if she wished to preserve her life and her realm. To Jesuit allegations that their enemies were always heretics, infidels, or schismatics, the Appellants countered not only that some English martyrs had opposed the Society but also that the martyrological credentials of Jesuits executed by the Elizabethan government were undermined by the traitorous activities of their colleagues.

Repeated regularly as a mantra was the accusation that Jesuits defamed and, in fact, persecuted some secular priests now venerated as martyrs. Despite Parsons's efforts to characterise the Society's opponents as wicked Protestants or lukewarm Catholics, many innocent men and martyrs opposed the Society of Jesus. John Mush remarked that secular clergy opposed to the Society were 'no lesse patient in torments and prisons, and no lesse courageous in shedding their blood for defence of Christs cause, than any of the Iesuites'. The editor of *Copies of Certaine Discourses* echoed this observation: 'some of our brethren as forward in dislike and disclaiming from such proceedings as we be (if not more forward) have ended their peregrination and troubles, with most glorious martydome, giving a greater testimony thereby of their sincere intentions in such matters as they took in hand ...'[99] John Mush was more specific: he named John Ingram, Thomas Portmort, and M. Lanton [presumably Joseph Lambton] as 'reckoned in the number of the Iesuits adversaries, yea, and not a little afflicted and disgraced by them for the same'.[100] William Clarke added Francis Jones, John Pibush, and Mark Barkworth to the list of anti-Jesuit martyrs. Jesuits, he contended, especially calumniated the Franciscan Jones (alias Buckley).[101] According to Bagshaw, Parsons repeated a story that the great Cesare, Cardinal Baronio, dismissed some English martyrs: they might brag of martyrdom but they, according to Baronio, 'had no part of Martyrs spirit, which was in humilitie and obedience' and were too 'refractory' ('*refractarii*'). Worse still, Parsons allegedly repeated how the pope and some cardinals suspected that some martyrs and confessors suffered 'not so much for vertue and love to Gods cause, as of a certaine choler and obstinate will to contradict the magistrate there'.[102]

The Appellants reinterpreted the history of the English mission to highlight the disastrous influence of the Jesuits. Before their arrival, England was a vibrant mission, staffed by secular clergy willing to die for their faith but unwilling to meddle in political matters. The publication of outrageous attacks on the government, intemperate meddling in political matters such as the succession to the crown of England, and treacherous involvement in plots and conspiracies, forced the government to crack down on Catholics. More strongly and clearly than others, William Watson affirmed 'that both her Maiesties lawes and proceedings against all sorts of catholikes, have been milde and mercifull (the opinion and iudgement of her Highnesse in religion one way, and their foresaid practices against her another way duly considered)'.[103] Given the seditious activities of the Jesuits, what else, asked Thomas Bluet, could the queen have done?[104] More extreme than other Appellants, Christopher Bagshaw summarised Jesuit activity:

> For of late yeeres many of that order take such a course, as if religion were nothing else but a meere politicall devise, conceived, framed, and upheld only by humane wisdome, and sleights of wit: and they were the men that by Machivels rules are raysed up to mayntayne it by equivocations, detractions, dissimulation, ambition, contention for superioritie, stirring up strife, setting kingdomes against kingdomes, raising rebellions, murthering of Princes, and by we know not how many stratagems of Sathan, comming out of hell, and tending to confusion ... Matters of State, titles of Princes, genealogies of Kings, rights of succession, disposing of scepters, and such affaires, are their chiefe studies. Some fear that they ate more cunning in *Aretine, Lucian,* and *Machivell,* then either in their breviaries, diurnals, or portwise: assuredly they do not behave themselves like any other religious men.[105]

Jesuit activity, in some ways, justified the government's claim that priests were executed for political and not religious reasons. They were, therefore, traitors and not martyrs. Watson lamented that so many Englishmen suspected all clergy because of Jesuits.[106] As Appellants distanced themselves from Jesuit intriguers, they slowly transferred the government's characterisation of Catholic martyrs to Jesuits alone in order to win some form of tolerance for Catholics at the expense of the Society of Jesus.

Appellants employed the memory and authority of William Allen in their campaign against the Jesuits. Allen, they claimed, feared Jesuit involvement in the English mission from the very start. He believed that their pride and ambition, as subsequently demonstrated, of course, in their governance of the English colleges and their attempt to assume superiority over secular clergy in Wisbech, would mark the downfall of the church. By implication, Jesuits should be removed from the colleges and their toadies should not be placed in authority over secular clergy. Allen anticipated trouble and was certain that Jesuits could be better employed in India than in England. Again, by implication, they should be excluded from the mission.[107]

Their continued involvement was proving disastrous. If the secular clergy had not laid down a strict policy of recusancy before the arrival of the Society, John Mush asserted, English Jesuits would have followed the example of their Scottish confrères and have tolerated Catholic attendance at Protestant services: the Jesuits 'could not without great confusion and discredit runne any other course than that wherein they saw our priests to have led them the way'. These critics portrayed Jesuits not as advocates of recusancy but as defenders of some form of occasional conformity. Nonetheless, Mush knew of a Jesuit in England who had promised a gentleman that if he became a Roman

Catholic 'hee should have licence to eat flesh in Lent, and in all fasting dayes, among Lollards and Protestants; that by so doing, hee might live without suspition of being a Catholicke, and escape daunger of the lawes'.[108]

Robert Parsons almost single-handedly defended English Jesuits against the Appellants as he reinterpreted the history of the mission. In *A Temperate Ward-Word*, Parsons expounded the deleterious consequences of Protestantism. As noted earlier, he claimed that most Catholics, especially Cardinal Allen, esteemed Jesuits; for those who opposed the Society, Parsons offered unflattering explanations for their rejection. Writing anonymously, he contended rather disingenuously that Parsons was never involved in any attempt on the Queen's life. Indeed, he downplayed Catholic political activity and stressed their fundamental loyalty to the crown. Unlike Huguenots in France, English Catholics never rebelled against their Queen nor invaded the kingdom. In fact Catholics had helped Elizabeth ascend the throne. Their refusal to attend Protestant services resulted not from any disloyalty to their sovereign but from a scrupulous religious conscience. Parsons argued:

> a mannes conscience is to be followed, though it did erre, and much more when it erreth not, and the reason for the former is, that forasmuch as our conscience is nothing but the voice and determination of our reason and iudgement, about matters to be donn or not to be donne, it followeth that we are bound to obey that direction (be it right or wrong) so long as we have no other light to guyde us.[109]

He cited the recent example of France as a model for England: peace and prosperity returned to the realm after Henry IV had returned to Rome. Elizabeth should emulate him and grant the same liberty of conscience to Catholics in her realm. Individuals of different confessions may eventually agree with each other 'or at leastwise to agree in some good temperature for this publique afaire of the common-wealth, which is impossible to do while matters of religion are pursued with such hostilitie, as for many yeares they have bin'.[110]

Robert Parsons, hiding this time behind the initials S. N., defended himself in the third person in *The Copie of a Letter Written to a Very Worshipful Catholike Gentleman in England*.[111] Arguing from various scriptural examples, he warned English Catholics of the dangers and horrors of discord and stressed how well secular clergy and Jesuits worked together. As examples he cited Allen's and Gregory Martin's letters to Campion in the 1570s. Jesuits, he explained,

> have byn the most rediest & willingest in all countreyes to help us, their houses have byn our houses, their frends our frends, their credit our credit, their word alwayes ready to comend us, their hands to help us, their labors to assist us in all kinds of busines and necessityes, that have befallen unto us, they have byn our Masters, our Doctors, our confessors, our frends, our fathers every where, they have published the worthines of our cause, recommended the persons exalted the worke, procured us patrons and benefactors where they have byn able, and more then this, they have

ioyned with us in the very action it selfe, laborred with us in England and passed torments and imprisonments with us, and shed their bloud with us.[112]

Only gross ingratitude prevented some from acknowledging this. Parsons himself performed many commendable services for the mission. On a more conciliatory note, the author minimised the difference between Jesuit and secular to stress that both ministered to Catholics and sought to strengthen their bond with the church: 'what is Iesuit, and what is priest? are not we all *Ministri eius cui credunt Catholici*: and to whose Catholike church we do our endeavour to draw all?'[113] Can one hear here a faint echo of Mush's remark to Wiseman?

In the anonymous *A Briefe Apologie, or Defence of the Catholike Ecclesiastical Hierarchie*, Parsons replied to Appellant criticism of the Society and drafted a Jesuit interpretation of the history of the mission. Their arrival in England heralded a new day: 'by whose comming matters of religion beginning to go with more fervour (for that divers other grave and ancient priests by their example, and persuasion, went with them or soone after) the counsel beganne to be more vigilant & not only to persecute them above the rest, but also to set others against them so much as they might'.[114] The intensified persecution, Parsons insinuated, resulted from the increased religious fervour and resolution that followed the arrival of the Jesuits. But more important for Parsons's immediate concerns was the opposition to the Society, forged by the government among Catholics. Parsons blamed this faction for the death of Mary, Queen of Scots, and an attack on Allen's defence of Sir William Stanley. Exploited and misled by the English government, this faction now believed that they could obtain some form of tolerance for Catholics under certain conditions, one of which was the exclusion of Jesuits from the mission.[115] Fundamentally the Society's enemies suffered from 'the disease of emulation': laity against clergy and secular priests against religious. They repeated, without producing any evidence, allegations that Cardinal Allen supported them in their opposition to the Society, whereas they, in fact, sent Prior Arnold to Spain to set up a network of agents in opposition to the network erected by Allen and the Jesuits. Within England they proposed to establish an association of secular clergy directed against the Society.[116] Parsons specifically attacked John Mush and John Colleton, and defended himself (at length and particularly against the charge that he fought with everyone!), William Holt, and Jasper Heywood against all accusations.[117] He noted how closely the Appellants worked with Richard Bancroft, Bishop of London, and how they sought to make the Jesuits scapegoats for all the ills and persecution suffered by Catholics.[118]

Not surprisingly Parsons's *A Briefe Apologie, or Defence of the Catholike Ecclesiastical Hierarchie* did not silence his critics. In *A Manifestation of the Great Folly and Bad Spirit of Certayne in England Calling Themselves Secular*

Priestes, Parsons, again anonymously, reiterated his fundamental contention that the Appellants hated Jesuits for their virtue. This envy, 'fostered by ambition, anger, revenge, and other such Assistants', fuelled their attacks. Even if their claim were true that the Society wanted to exercise jurisdiction over the secular priests in Wisbech – a claim Parsons zealously refuted – did the Appellants truly believe that the Society would have expanded this governance to include all secular clergy within England?[119] Although the government pursued Jesuits more vigorously than others, Parsons denied that they were responsible for the persecution. If, he asked, the Appellants wanted to blame the Society for the persecutions and martyrdoms, how did they account for the persecution during the twenty years between the accession of Elizabeth and the arrival of the Jesuits?[120] More important, Parsons detected an appropriation of the official governmental position on the execution of priests. He accused Appellants of defending heretics and persecutors, and accusing persecuted Catholics of imaginary crimes.[121] Protesting that they were the 'designed martyrs' and 'worthy confessors', the Appellant controversialists, according to Parsons, impugned the kingdom's true martyrs. Because they flatter the government so much, there was little danger that these writers would be asked to risk their lives. If the Appellants implemented what they wrote, they would denounce to the authorities true martyrs, recognised and venerated as such by Catholics:

> And yf these blessed men whome we hold for true martyrs already were alive againe, and their opinions and cogitations knowne to these men, they were obliged according to their protestations made in this book [*Important Considerations*] to reveale them to the persecutors & then thinke you what goodly designed martyrs and worthie confessors these men are, that doe willingly put themselves in this obligation?[122]

This was the context for the appearance of the first English martyrology since 1582. The author, Thomas Worthington, succeeded Richard Barret as president of the English College, Douai, on 28 June 1599. Many colleagues in Douai, in the words of Godfrey Anstruther, 'considered him too much under the thumb' of Parsons. After a turbulent administration, he resigned in 1613, three years after the death of Parsons.[123] Worthington may not have been 'under the thumb' of Parsons but his martyrology was clearly intended to substantiate Parsons's interpretation of post-Reformation English Catholic history, his defence of the Society of Jesus, and his assault on his opponents. Worthington seized upon John Rigby, executed in Southwark on 21 June 1600, and other recent victims to sabotage Appellant arguments that 'both her Maiesties lawes and proceedings against all sorts of catholikes, have been milde and merci-full'.[124] During his interrogation, Rigby even admitted, in reply to the 'Bloody Questions',[125] that he would take up arms to defend Elizabeth against a papally sponsored invasion. He remained silent, however, when asked on which side he would serve if the invading armies 'should come to settle the Catholique Religion'.[126] Rigby, Worthington summarised, 'acknowledged and yelded al temporal powre, and authoritie to the Quene, stil professing and behaving him selfe as a faithful and loyal subiect, serving her, and praying for her, and even to death denying and detesting al treasons and traytors'.[127] All Catholics, 'but also most Protestants, and in maner al Puritanes', acknowledged that he and others were executed for matters of religion and not, as the government 'with a few more that folow the sway of authoritie' claimed, for treason.[128] No kingdom but England executed believers who frequented Catholic services. No kingdom but England punished anyone 'for refusing to sweare, that they think in their conscience that the King, Quene, or Prince, is and ought to be supreme head, or supreme governour of the Church, immediately under Christ, in al causes as wel spiritual as temporal'.[129]

Worthington also reported how, before his execution in York on 28 March 1600, Christopher Wharton was asked about current discord among English Catholics. Although there may be disagreements among Catholics, 'either Priests or others,' he replied, 'those differences are not in Articles of their faith; but in other matters, of some particular Iurisdiction, right or title, spiritual or temporal, and the like'. For his part, he had not been involved in any disputes nor had he a 'breach of charitie' with any living person.[130] Wharton thus dismissed disagreements over titles and jurisdiction, e.g. the controversy over the Archpriest, as relatively unimportant.

Worthington digressed from a report on Wharton to an exposition of 'the state of Catholiques, before this controversie begane'.[131] During his historical presentation, the running titles are 'That the Seminarie Priests Agree with the Iesuits'. The Society of Jesus became involved in the English mission at the insistence of William Allen. Jesuits, seminary priests, and old Marian clergy worked so well together that Catholicism increased 'in number, and in corage, and more [Catholics] were willing to suffer and to die for their faith' as the government sought to stiffle this increase with new proclamations, more strict legislation, and more intense persecution.[132] But, alas, Satan, fearing that godly religion would prosper in England, aroused envy in the hearts of some Catholics. Worthington asked them:

> But I pray you (deare brethren and freinds) that would be more esteemed than you are, tel me what fault is in the fathers, or in other men for this? Is not honour and estimation the reward of vertue? especially amongst good men: such as you can not deny these Catholiques to be, who ordinarily prefer Iesuits before you? will you blame them for being more vertuous, and for deserving better than you? for if they did not deserve better, so manie good men would not more esteem them. Or els wil you blame the whole Catholique world and al other countries, that beginne, or returne to be Catholiques, for embracing the Iesuits labours more then yours? Wil

you barre mens iudgments in making their owne choice, by what spiritual men they wil be chiefly directed? Or wil you abridge their liberties, and force them to leave the Fathers, whose conversation, and discretion they like better then yours; and to be directed by you, of whom they have not so great an opinion? Is this the libertie you talke of, and which your promise, if you may have your wills, that ghostly children shal first forsake their ghostly fathers whom they most desire, and then be bond to those which you like best? ... Perhaps you would have them, whet they are willed to do such good offices, to refuse to do them, and to send them to you; as though al such affayres depended upon your wills, who should manage them.[33]

Worthington had no doubts about who was responsible for the dissension. Instead of ranting and raving about Jesuits, Worthington advised the Appellants to emulate them. Faithfully following Parsons's interpretation of the origins of the discord, Worthington blamed everything on Thomas Morgan, Charles Paget, and a few others. They opposed Parsons, Sir Francis Englefield, 'and al others, that agreed with D. Allen, because they would not leave him, and the whole nation, and hang upon them'.[34] Now they refused to accept George Blackwell as Archpriest because he worked so well with Parsons. Instead they demanded the expulsion of Jesuits from English mission and their dismissal from the administration of the colleges. But this faction remained a minority. The overwhelming majority of seminary priests and Catholics were well aware of the good work done for the English mission by the Society of Jesus in general and by Parsons in particular.

After this historical digression, Worthington returned to Wharton. This 'ancient ... grave ... and ... learned' graduate of the University of Oxford acknowledged Blackwell as archpriest and 'most sincerely alwayes agreed with the reverend fathers of the Societie of Iesus'.[35] Worthington related the stories of the other Catholics executed in 1600 and the first months of 1601 to demonstrate that they 'suffered meerly for Religion.'[36]

A MARTYR FOR WHOM?

Unlike contemporary historians who investigate martyrs phenomenologically across confessional lines, early modern Christians denied the status of martyr to members of opposing ecclesial communities. Martyrologies did not simply establish the credentials of individual martyrs, but dismissed the pretensions of executed members of other Churches. Each agreed, in the words of St. Augustine, '*Martyres veros non facit poena sed causa*' ('It is not the punishment but the cause that makes true martyrs'). Each confession advanced theological reasons underlining the authenticity of their martyrs and exposing the heresies of their foes. Heretics, by definition, could not be martyrs. Few would even express as much sympathy for their plight as Anthony Copley. No one would go further: to concede martyrdom to an opponent recognised implicitly some value in the confession (*causa*) for which he died. Conflicting martyrologies and debates about martyrs and pseudo-martyrs played an important role in late sixteenth-century theological controversy. Rarely, however, was there a 'pseudo-martyr' debate within the same Church. In fact the debate within English Catholicism may be unique.

In late sixteenth-century England, two factions sought to establish themselves as the authentic heirs and interpreters of English Catholicism. Each group appealed to Cardinal Allen for legitimation. Each group espoused a quasi-official interpretation of post-Reformation English Catholic history. Each group blamed the other for the intensive persecution, accused the other of specific vices and moral turpitude, and labelled the other as colluders or traitors. One group hoped to win some form of toleration through the expulsion of the other. In the controversy, the Appellants adopted some of the government's traditional arguments regarding executed Catholics. Some Jesuit 'martyrs' had been so tainted by intrigue and political involvement that their execution was not, in fact, for religious reasons. Against these complaints, Jesuits and their supporters such as Worthington repeated many arguments earlier made against official and semi-official government *apologiae*. The Appellants, defining more precisely the *causa* required for martyrdom along specific ecclesiological and ideological lines, excluded unnamed Jesuits from their list of martyrs. Jesuits retaliated with moral innuendo against suspected opponents and accusations of complicity in official action against the martyrs.

Anne Dillon observed that, at the end of Elizabeth's reign, the 'symbol of the Catholic martyr, seen until now as a unifying symbol of Catholic persecution by Protestants, was used as a stick with which the clergy, both Jesuits and the Appellants, beat each other'.[137] But the Jesuits and the Appellants did more than exploit a symbol. Their conflict played a formative role in the creation of the symbol. Even after the Appellants had successfully excluded Jesuits from any role in the governance of the Archpriest, the struggle continued over a new issue: the possibility of Catholic bishops in England. Henceforth each side sifted through the literary and mortal remains of each martyr as they searched for allies in their battle over the past, present, and future of English Catholicism. Jesuits circulated rumours that Robert Drury, a known Appellant, had been received into the Society of Jesus a few days before his execution. The Jesuit Robert Jones testified that the martyr Roger Cadwallader, another known opponent of the Society, had bequeathed his personal library to the Jesuits because one had ministered to him in prison. In 1612 secular clergy spread the account that the heart of the martyred John Almond had leapt from the fire then consuming his entrails. A year later, they disparaged the same account because some one had added an undesired conclusion: Almond's heart had leapt into the hands of a Jesuit! 'Garnet's

Straw,' a miniature representation of the Jesuit's face on a piece of straw made by a drop of his blood, demonstrated the righteousness of his cause. Opponents of the Jesuits dismissed it sarcastically. Agents of the secular clergy recounted how martyrs included endorsements for bishops in England in their dying speeches.[38] Both groups had their own criteria as they compiled lists of authentic martyrs.[39]

The construction of martyrdom as 'a powerful ideological tool with which to encourage the community to maintain its own separated existence and identity and to support its priests'[40] did not proceed smoothly and effortlessly in some quasi-Whiggish manner. Elizabethan Catholics originally manifested little interest in their Henrician predecessors. With the exception of three books in 1582, they produced no martyrologies in their vernacular. English martyrologies only became important twenty years later during the Appellant Controversy, as each side validated its claims by invoking martyrs as witnesses. Henceforth Elizabethan and Jacobean interest in English martyrs was ideologically driven. Catholicism and execution did not bring automatic inclusion in rolls of martyrs. Ideological and ecclesial correctness dictated membership as secular clergy and Jesuits exploited persecution and martyrdoms to establish their pedigree and to advance their understanding of, and plans for, the English mission.

NOTES

1 Diana Wood (ed.), *Martyrs and Martyrologies*, Studies in Church History 30 (Oxford, 1993).

2 Brad Gregory, *Salvation at Stake: Christian Martyrdom in Early Modern Europe* (Cambridge, Mass., 1999), p. 11.

3 Anne Dillon, *The Construction of Martyrdom in the English Catholic Community, 1535–1603* (Aldershot, 2002), p. 7.

4 Thomas H. Clancy, *Papist Pamphleteers: The Allen-Persons Party and the Political Thought of the Counter-Reformation in England, 1572–1615* (Chicago, 1964), p. 126.

5 I shall follow the convention of giving citations in *ARCR* by volume and entry number.

6 Gregory, *Salvation at Stake*, p. 4.

7 Gregory, *Salvation at Stake*, p. 13.

8 Nicholas Sander, *De Visibili Monarchia Ecclesiae* (Louvain, 1571), with later editions at Antwerp in 1578 and 1580, *ARCR*, I, 1013–15.

9 Ibid., pp. 734, 736, 730.

10 Vitus à Dulken, *Illustria Ecclesiae Catholicae, ex Recentibus Anglicorum Martyrum, Scotiae Proditionis, Gallicorumq* (Munich, 1573), *ARCR*, I, 1455.

11 See Thomas M. McCoog, S.J., '"The Flower of Oxford": The Role of Edmund Campion in Early Recusant Polemics', *Sixteenth Century Journal*, 24 (1993), 899–913.

12 Joseph Creswell, *Historia de la Vida y Martyrio que Padecio en Inglaterra* (Madrid, 1596), *ARCR*, I, 276.

13 *Histoire de la Vie et Ferme Constance du Pere Henry Valpole Anglois Prestre, de la Compagnie de Iesus* (Arras, 1597), *ARCR*, I, 278.

14 Robert Parsons, *An Epistle of Persecution* (Douai, n.d. [1582]), *ARCR*, II, 627.

15 William Allen, *A Briefe Historie of the Glorious Martyrdom* (n.p. [Rheims], 1582), *ARCR*, II, 7.

16 Thomas Alfield, *A True Reporte of the Death & Martyrdome of M. Campion Iesuite* (n.p.d. [London, 1582]), *ARCR*, II, 4.

17 Thomas Worthington, *A Relation of Sixteen Martyrs: Glorified in England in Twelve Monethes. With a Declaration. That English Catholiques Suffer for the Cathlique Religion. And that the Seminarie Priests Agree with the Iesuites* (Douai, 1601), *ARCR*, II, 847.

18 J. H. Pollen (ed.), *Unpublished Documents Relating to the English Martyrs*, CRS 5 (London, 1908), p. 3.

19 In the sense defined by Peter Lake and Michael Questier, 'Puritans, Papists, and the "Public Sphere" in Early Modern England: The Edmund Campion Affair in Context', *Journal of Modern History*, 72 (2000), 587–627, at p. 590.

20 For a more detailed exposition see Thomas M. McCoog, S.J., 'The English Jesuit Mission and the French Match, 1579–1581', *Catholic Historical Review*, 87 (2001), 185–213.

21 P. L. Hughes and J. F. Larkin (eds), *Tudor Royal Proclamations*, 3 vols (New Haven, 1964–69), 2: 483.

22 Printed in T. E. Hartley (ed.), *Proceedings in the Parliaments of Elizabeth I*, 3 vols (Leicester, 1981–95), 1: 504.

23 ARSI, Fondo Gesuitico 651/640, published in Thomas M. McCoog, S.J., 'Robert Parsons and Claudio Acquaviva: Correspondence', *Archivum Historicum Societatis Iesu*, 68 (1999), 93–7.

24 *A Breefe Discourse of the Taking of Edmund Campion* (London: 1581), sigs. A3r, A4r–v; Anthony Munday, *A Discoverie of Edmund Campion* (London, 1582), sigs. B1v, B7v, C2r, C5r, C7v, D3r, D7r, G1r–2r.

25 Robert Parsons, *De Persecutione Anglicana* (Bologna [vere Rouen], 1581), *ARCR*, I, 874.

26 Robert Parsons, *An Epistle of the Persecution of Catholickes in Englande* (Douai, n.d. [1582]), *ARCR*, II, 627.

27 Parsons, *An Epistle of the Persecution*, p. 8.

28 Ibid.

29 Alfield, *A True Reporte*, sigs. B3v–B4r.

30 I have cited the modern edition, *The Execution of Justice in England by William Cecil and A True, Sincere, and Modest Defense of English Catholics by William Allen*, ed. Robert M. Kingdon (Ithaca, 1965) p. 15.

31 William Allen, *A True, Sincere and Modest Defence, of English Catholiques* (n.p.d. [Rheims, 1584]), *ARCR*, II, 14.

32 'Quinetiam & actuum Martyrum nostrotum duodecim, ab ipso *Alano* approbatorum & eiusdem iussu editorum promulgationem eidem placuit prohibere': [John Mush],

Declaratio Motuum ac Turbulationum (Rouen [vere London], 1601) *ARCR*, I, 838.1, pp. 8–9.

33 Robert Parsons, *A Briefe Apologie, or Defence of the Catholike Ecclesiastical Hierarchie* (n.p.d. [Antwerp, 1601]), *ARCR*, II, 610, fo. 164v.

34 Robert Parsons, *A Manifestation of the Great Folly and Bad Spirit of Certayne in England Calling Themselves Secular Priestes* ([Antwerp], 1602), *ARCR*, II, 631, fos. 38r–v.

35 William Clarke, *A Replie unto a Certaine Libell, Latelie Set Foorth by Fa. Parsons* ([London], 1603), *ARCR*, II, 139, f. 58r. Humphrey Ely claimed that the prohibition was enacted by Heywood at his 'provincial synod': Humphrey Ely, *Certaine Briefe Notes upon a Briefe Apologie Set Out under the Name of the Priests United to the Archpriest* [Paris, (1602)], *ARCR*, II, 187, p. 31.

36 PRO SP 12/137/46, printed in A. O. Meyer, *England and the Catholic Church under Queen Elizabeth* (London, 1916), pp. 486–8.

37 Thomas Hide, *A Consolatorie Epistle to the Afflicted Catholikes* (Louvain [vere London], 1579) two editions, *ARCR*, II, 430–1.

38 On the importance of the printed word for the Jesuit mission, see Nancy Pollard Brown, 'Robert Southwell: The Mission of the Written Word', in *The Reckoned Expense: Edmund Campion and the Early English Jesuits*, ed. Thomas M. McCoog, S.J., (Woodbridge, 1996), pp. 193–6.

39 For the books published by this secret press, see *ARCR*, II, 225. Is the disappearance of the author's name from the title page a consequence of the papal instructions?

40 See Anthony Petti, 'Stephen Vallenger (1541–1591)', *RH*, 6 (1962), at 251.

41 H. B., *A Consolatory Letter to All the Afflicted Catholikes in England* (Rouen [vere London], n.d. [1587–88]), *ARCR*, II, 33.

42 Robert Southwell, *An Epistle of Comfort* (Paris [vere London], n.d. [1587–88]), *ARCR*, II, 714.

43 See Thomas M. McCoog, S.J., *The Society of Jesus in Ireland, Scotland, and England 1541–1588: 'Our Way of Proceeding?'* (Leiden, 1996), p. 217.

44 'Ut enim, cum res postulat, nobis ipsi parcere non debemus, et libenter depositum reddere, quod accepimus, ita intempestiva fiducia stulta est, et illi ipsi pro cuius honore suscipitur ingrata', ARSI, Franc. 1/I, fo. 109r (published in McCoog, 'Parsons and Acquaviva', 97).

45 'Sed etiam quae gessit antequam comprehenderetur; quae audio multa esse et magnae aedificationis ... et praeterea, si quid sit illustre in eius vita anteacta, ut aliquid plenum ac perfectum ad nostram consolationem, et in primis ad Summi Dei gloriam prodeat', ARSI, Franc. 1/I, fo. 122r (published in McCoog, 'Parsons and Acquaviva', 113).

46 'Cum gravior et longe efficacior sit exhortatio factorum quam verborum ... non modo quid P. Edmundus in morte gessisset, sed etiam quid in carcere, quid ante carcerem, atque adeo etiam de superiore eius vita aliquid scribi cupiebamus', ARSI, Franc. 1/I, fo. 130v (published in McCoog, 'Parsons and Acquaviva', 114).

47 John Bossy, 'The Heart of Robert Persons', in McCoog, *The Reckoned Expense*, ed. McCoog, pp. 146–7. Brad Gregory contests some of Bossy's data (Gregory, *Salvation at Stake*, p. 486n). I have amended the hypothesis in light of Gregory's criticism.

48 'Bene havei desiderato intendere in particolare, qual modo s' ha da tenere nel mandarli et nel loro stare in Inghilterra; che probabilità di frutto et di non essere scoperti; però che

se solo si mandano per patire, et per edificare gli altri per tormenti; ancora la loro andata potrebbe esser dannosa a molti et moltiplicare danni et tormenti a Catholici senza altro frutto', ARSI, Franc. I/I, fo. 198r (published in McCoog, 'Parsons and Acquaviva', 138).

49 Robert Parsons, *The First Booke of the Christian Exercise, Appertayning to Resolution* (n.p. [Rouen], 1582), *ARCR*, II, 616.

50 Dillon, *Construction of Martyrdom*, p. 7.

51 Robert Parsons, *De Persecutione Anglicana* (Bologna [*vere* Rouen], 1581), (Paris, 1582), (Rome, 1582), (Rome, 1582), (Ingolstadt, [1582]), *ARCR*, I, 874–8; (Paris, 1582), (Paris, 1583), (Paris, 1586), *ARCR*, I, 879–81; (Bologna, 1582), *ARCR*, I, 883. Another possible edition is *Raccolta d'Alcuni Avvisi della Dura Persecutione d'Inghilterra contra Catholici* (Brescia, 1582), *ARCR*, I, 884; (Ingolstadt, 1582), *ARCR*, I, 882.

52 Allen, *A Briefe Historie of the Glorious Martyrdom* (Macerata, 1583), (Milan, 1584), (Naples, 1584), (Macerata, 1585), *ARCR*, I, 8–11.

53 *L'Histoire de la Mort que le R.P. Edmond Campion* (Lyons, [1582]), (Paris, 1582), (Paris, [1582]), *ARCR*, I, 196–8; (Louvain, 1582), (Paris, 1585), *ARCR*, I, 203–4; (Turin, 1582), (Milan, 1582), (Bologna, 1581 [1582]), (Venice, 1582), *ARCR*, I, 199–202; (Dillingen, 1588), *ARCR*, I, 204.

54 Thomas Bourchier, *Historia Ecclesiastica de Martyrio Fratrum Ordinis Divi Francisci ... qui Partim in Anglia sub Henrico Octavo Rege* (Paris, 1582), (Ingolstadt, 1583), (Paris, 1586), *ARCR*, I, 106–8; (Ingolstadt, 1584), (Ingolstadt, 1585), *ARCR*, I, 109–10.

55 Richard Verstegan, *Descriptiones Quaedam Illius Humanae et Multiplicis Persecutionis quam in Anglia Propter Fidem Sustinent Catholice Christiani* (n.p.d. [Paris, 1583–84]), (Rome, 1584), (n.p.d. [Paris, 1583–84]), *ARCR*, I, 1283–5.

56 John Gibbons, *Concertatio Ecclesiae Catholicae in Anglia* (Trier, 1583), (Augsburg, 1588), (Augsburg, 1589), *ARCR*, I, 524–6.

57 Maurice Chauncy, *Historia Aliquot Nostri Saeculi Martyrum* (Burgos, 1583), (Burgos, 1583), *ARCR*, I, 235–6.

58 *Ecclesiae Anglicanae Trophaea* (Rome, [1584]), (Rome, [1585–90]), *ARCR*, I, 944–5.

59 Nicholas Sander, *De Origine ac Progressu Schismatis Anglicani* (Cologne [*vere* Rheims], 1585), (Rome, 1586), (Ingolstadt, 1586), (Ingolstadt, 1587), (Ingolstadt, 1588), (n.p. [Pont-à-Mousson?], 1587), (Augsburg [false imprint], 1587), (n.p., 1587), *ARCR*, I, 972–6, 980–1, 983.

60 Pedro de Ribadeneira, *Historia Ecclesiastica del Scisma del Reyno de Inglaterra* (Madrid, 1588), (Madrid, 1588), (Lisbon, 1588), (Lisbon, 1588), (Barcelona, 1588), (Zaragoza, 1588), (Valencia, 1588), (Antwerp, 1588), (Madrid, 1589), ([Lisbon], 1589), *ARCR*, I, 993–1002.

61 Adam Blackwood, *Martyre de la Royne d'Escosse, Douariere de France* (Edinburgh [*vere* Paris], 1587), (Edinburgh [*vere* Paris], 1588), (Antwerp, 1588), (Edinburgh [*vere* Paris], 1589), (Paris, 1589), *ARCR*, I, 98.1–100.

62 Thomas Stapleton, *Tres Thomae* (Douai, 1588), *ARCR*, I, 1159.

63 *Relatione del Presente Stato d'Inghilterra* (Rome, 1590), *ARCR*, I, 312.

64 Robert Parsons, *Relacion de Algunos Martyrios, que e Nuevo Han Hecho los Hereges en Inglaterra* (Madrid, 1590), (Paris, 1590), (Lyons, 1590), (Rome, 1590), (Brescia, 1590), *ARCR*, I, 894–8.

65   G. Pollini, *Historia Ecclesiastica della Rivoluzione d'Inghilterra* (Florence, 1591), (Bologna, 1591[?1592]), (Rome, 1594), *ARCR*, I, 990–2.

66   A. da Sciacca, *Relazione dello Scisma Anglicano* (Palermo, 1597), *ARCR*, I, 1011.

67   Pedro de Ribadeneira, *Segunda Parte de la Historia del Scisma de Inglaterra* (Alcalá, 1593), (Madrid, 1594), (Lisbon, 1594), (Lisbon, 1594), (Antwerp, 1594), (Madrid, 1595), *ARCR*, I, 1004–9; (Salzburg, 1594), *ARCR*, I, 984.

68   J. Mayr, *Kurtzerbericht aller gedenckwuerdigen Sachen, so sich in Engelland in den nechsten hundert Jaren verlauffen* (Munich, 1600), *ARCR*, I, 989.

69   Gibbons, *Concertatio* (Augsburg, 1594), *ARCR*, I, 527.

70   Creswell, *Historia de la Vida y Martyrio* (Madrid, 1596), (Zaragoza, 1596), (Arras, 1597), *ARCR*, I, 276–8.

71   Diego de Yepes, *Historia Particular de la Persecucion de Inglaterra* (Madrid, 1599), *ARCR*, I, 284; Diego de Yepes, *Relacion del Martirio de los Dos Sacerdotes* (Seville, 1600), *ARCR*, I, 91.

72   Richard Verstegan, *Brief et Veritable Discours, de la Mort d'Aucuns Vaillants et Glorieux Martyrs* (Antwerp, 1601), (Antwerp, 1601), *ARCR*, I, 1280–1.

73   See Thomas M. McCoog, S.J., '"The Slightest Suspicion of Avarice": The Finances of the English Jesuit Mission', *RH*, 19 (1988), 103–23, at 104–5.

74   See Martin Murphy, *St Gregory's College, Seville, 1592–1767*, CRS 73 (London, 1992), p. 22.

75   See McCoog, '"The Flower of Oxford"', 908–10; McCoog, *Society of Jesus*, pp. 178–99.

76   Dillon, *Construction of Martyrdom*, p. 370.

77   See Peter Lake with Michael Questier, *The Antichrist's Lewd Hat: Protestants, Papists & Players in Post-Reformation England* (New Haven, 2002), pp. 281–314.

78   This manuscript is no longer extant. Almost all our knowledge of it comes from the memoirs of John Gerard. See Philip Caraman (ed.), *John Gerard: The Autobiography of an Elizabethan* (London, 1951), pp. 87–9.

79   Inner Temple, Petyt MS 38, fos. 331r–332v, printed in Thomas Graves Law (ed.), *The Archpriest Controversy*, 2 vols (London, 1896–98), 1: 60–1.

80   On Langdale and Perkins, see Thomas M. McCoog, S.J., *English and Welsh Jesuits 1555–1650*, 2 vols (London, 1994–95), 2: 228, 265. On Durie, see Thomas M. McCoog, S.J., '"Pray to the Lord of the Harvest": Jesuit Missions to Scotland in the Sixteenth Century', *Innes Review*, 53 (2002), 127–88, at 167.

81   Archivum Britannicum Societatis Iesu [ABSI], Anglia II, 33, printed in Henry Foley (ed.), *Records of the English Province of the Society of Jesus* (Roehampton/London, 7 vols in 8, 1855–84), 4: 50.

82   His and others' comments were collected into the 'Abstract of the Memorial and of sundry Letters against the Jesuits. Sept.–Dec., 1597', in Law (ed.), *Archpriest Controversy*, 1: 9.

83   Law (ed.), *Archpriest Controversy*, 2: 9.

84   'The Iesuites have so persecuted some Priests that are now Martyrs, as that their death hath bin imputed partly to the hereticks, and partly to the Iesuites': Christopher Bagshaw, *A True Relation of the Faction Begun at Wisbitch* (London,1601), *ARCR*, II, 39, p. 78.

85 'Brevis declaratio miserrimi status Catholicorum in Anglia iam degentium' [Fisher's Memorial], Archives of Archdiocese of Westminster, VI, 57.

86 The full English text may be found in ABSI, Coll. N II 125–59. The relevant section is pp. 151–3.

87 This is William Allen's *The Copie of a Letter Written by M. Doctor Allen* (Antwerp, 1587), *ARCR*, II, 8. Robert Southwell also commented about a rejoinder to Allen's defence. To my knowledge no one has identified the treatise. See McCoog, *Society of Jesus*, pp. 230–3, especially n. 36.

88 In the tenth reason, Campion listed individual martyrs as witnesses for the authenticity of the Catholic Church: Edmund Campion, *Rationes decem* (n.p.d. [Stonor Park, 1581]), *ARCR*, I, 135.1, fos. 30r–38r.

89 Robert Parsons, *A Temperate Ward-Word to the Turbulent and Seditious Wach-Word of Sir Francis Hastings* ([Antwerp], 1599) *ARCR*, II, 637, pp. 57–64.

90 *The Copies of Certaine Discourses* (Rouen [*vere* London], 1601), *ARCR*, II, 913, [sig. *ijr].

91 Anthony Copley, *An Answere to a Letter of a Iesuited Gentleman* ([London], 1601), *ARCR*, II, 115, pp. 15, 18.

92 Copley, *An Answere to a Letter of a Iesuited Gentleman*, p. 107.

93 Thomas Bluet, *Important Considerations, Which Ought to move All True and Sound Catholikes* ([London], 1601), *ARCR*, II, 62, sig. **2v.

94 Anthony Copley, *Another Letter of Mr A. C. to His Dis-Iesuited Kinsman* ([London], 1602), *ARCR*, II, 156, p. 19.

95 Ibid., p. 26.

96 Bagshaw, *A True Relation of the Faction Begun at Wisbitch*, p. 70. According to Anthony Copley, a Jesuit was a fisherman not of souls but of money (Copley, *An Answere to a Letter of a Iesuited Gentleman*, pp. 82, 84), and similar claims were commonplace.

97 Bagshaw, *A True Relation of the Faction Begun at Wisbitch*, p. 67. Anthony Copley recounted the insults levelled at the Appellants by 'these Fathers, these Courtiers, these souldiers; unworthie of the name of Apostles, of Religious, or Iesus' (*An Answere to a Letter of a Iesuited Gentleman*, p. 95). Thomas Bluet asserted that Jesuits were dangerous to their sovereign and to all English subjects, including Catholics (Bluet, *Important Considerations*, sig. *2v). William Watson urged Catholics to imitate saints who died as martyrs for the conversion of their country and to have nothing to do with Jesuit sedition (William Watson, *A Decacordon of Ten Quodlibeticall Questions* ([London], 1602), p. 232).

98 Bagshaw, *A True Relation of the Faction Begun at Wisbitch*, p. 73. Copley and others believed that Elizabeth would follow the example of King Henry IV of France if she could be assured of Catholic loyalty (Copley, *An Answere to a Letter of a Iesuited Gentleman*, pp. 66–7, 71).

99 *Copies of Certaine Discourses*, p. 2. Watson claimed that more than thirty secular clergy 'most iniuriously defamed, slaundered, and detracted, by the Iesuiticall faction, ... are now glorious martyrs in heaven' (Watson, *A Decacordon*, p. 352).

100 Mush, *A Dialogue Betwixt a Secular Priest*, pp. 77–8.

101 Clarke, *A Replie unto a Certaine Libell*, fos. 17r, 58r.

102 Christopher Bagshaw, *A Sparing Discoverie of Our English Iesuits* ([London], 1601), pp. 67–8.

103 Watson, *A Decacordon*, pp. 267–8.

104 Bluet, *Important Considerations*, pp. 36–7.

105 Bagshaw, *A Sparing Discoverie*, pp. 6–7.

106 Watson, *A Decacordon*, p. 352.

107 Bagshaw, *A True Relation of the Faction Begun at Wisbitch*, p. 6; Bagshaw, *A Sparing Discoverie*, p. 18; Mush, *A Dialogue Betwixt a Secular Priest*, pp. 26–7, 77–80; Copley, *An Answere to a Letter of a Iesuited Gentleman*, p. 38.

108 Mush, *A Dialogue Betwixt a Secular Priest*, p. 99.

109 Parsons, *A Temperate Ward-Word*, p. 75. On Jesuits and recusancy see Alexandra Walsham, *Church Papists: Catholicism, Conformity, and Confessional Polemic in Early Modern England* (Woodbridge, 1993); McCoog, *Society of Jesus*, pp. 144–5; Hubert Chadwick, 'Crypto-Catholicism, English and Scottish', *The Month*, 178 (1942), 388–401.

110 Parsons, *A Temperate Ward-Word*, pp. 125–6. See also pp. 16, 57, 62–4, 71, 120–4.

111 S. N., *The Copie of a Letter Written to a Very Worshipful Catholike Gentleman in England* ([Antwerp], 1601), *ARCR*, II, 565.5. Peter Holmes argues for Parsons's authorship in 'An Epistle of Pious Grief: An Anti-Appellant Tract by Robert Persons', *RH*, 15 (1981), 328–35.

112 S. N., *The Copie of a Letter*, fo. 13r–v.

113 Ibid., fo. 23v.

114 Parsons, *A Briefe Apologie*, intro. fo. 4r.

115 Ibid., fo. 6r-v.

116 Ibid., fos. 5r–v, 7r, 29r–32r.

117 Ibid., fos. 5v, 88r, 89v, 164v, 193v–190 [*vere* 198]r.

118 Ibid., fos. 209v, 209 [*vere* 211]r.

119 Robert Parsons, *A Manifestation of the Great Folly*, fos. *2r–v, 2v.

120 Ibid., fos. 9r, 17r–v.

121 Ibid., fo. 13v.

122 Ibid., fo. 37r.

123 Godfrey Anstruther, *The Seminary Priests*, 4 vols (Ware/Durham, n.d. [1968]), 1: 388.

124 Watson, *A Decacordon*, pp. 267–8.

125 On them see Patrick McGrath, 'The Bloody Questions Reconsidered', *RH*, 20 (1991), 305–19.

126 Worthington, *A Relation of Sixteen Martyrs*, p. 11.

127 Ibid., p. 36.

128 Ibid., p. 34.

129 Ibid., p. 35.

130 Ibid., p. 48.

131 Ibid., p. 49.

132 Ibid., p. 54.

133 Ibid., pp. 61–2.

134 Ibid., p. 51 [*sic* for p. 67].

135 Ibid., pp. 80–1.

136 Ibid., p. 97. The page of the opening 'Advertisement' is given as p. 97 but it is, in fact, p. 1.

137 Dillon, *Construction of Martyrdom*, p. 326.

138 See Lake with Questier, *The Antichrist's Lewd Hat*, pp. 299–307, and *Newsletters from the Archpresbyterate of George Birkhead*, Camden Society 5th ser., vol. 12, ed. Michael Questier (Cambridge, 1998), pp. 30–4 for more illustrations.

139 Michael Questier is currently working on another volume of newsletters in which he investigates efforts by Richard Smith, Bishop of Chalcedon, to compile lists of martyrs.

140 Dillon, *Construction of Martyrdom*, p. 370.

Chapter 6

From *Leicester his Commonwealth* to *Sejanus his Fall:* Ben Jonson and the politics of Roman (Catholic) virtue

Peter Lake

O f late a variety of historians have been giving greater emphasis to the prevalence within the political culture of Elizabethan England of certain strands of civic or classical republicanism. The influence of such 'neo-Roman' strains of thought and feeling has been pictured as pervasive throughout what Patrick Collinson has termed the 'monarchical republic of Elizabeth I', suffusing not only hitherto little known tracts about town government in Tewkesbury or the governance of Ireland but also the thought and practice of men as central to the regime as William Cecil.[1] The notions of counsel, good government, and political virtue held by these men, together with their vision of England as a mixed, if not polity, then certainly monarchy, are taken to represent not only the abiding effects of a humanist education but telltale signs of a vibrant classical or civic republican tradition. Commenting on the implications both of his own research and of recent scholarship on Elizabeth's reign, Steven Alford has concluded, 'It is increasingly clear that England did experience republicanism in the middle of the sixteenth century – a republicanism on a classical model, in which Cicero and Quintillian's *vir civilis* could not only lead a *vita activa* by offering counsel and submitting advice but also involve himself in the legislative functions of parliament.' Alford goes on to endorse Markku Peltonen's claim that this form of republicanism was not a 'constitutional goal', but 'a theory of citizenship, public virtue and true nobility based essentially on the classical humanist and republican traditions'.[2] Patrick Collinson sums up current scholarly orthodoxy when he remarks that

> a suppressed, critical, neo-stoicist republicanism was the product of the late Eliza-
> bethan years, an ideology nurtured in the rather different political climate which, in
> wartime and old age, had succeeded the politics of the Exclusion Crisis, a climate
> less consensual, more dirigiste, even, in Fulke Greville's words, 'metamorphosing'
> 'into a precipitate absoluteness', the climate of the *regnum Cecilianum* (contested by
> the Earl of Essex) which was the 1590s.[3]

The result, as Smuts, Worden and others have argued, was a series of searing 'republican', Tacitean, in Skinner's terms neo-Roman, critiques of the corruptions to be found at the core of the late Elizabethan and early Stuart regimes.[4] We have then two republican modes or moments; the first the legitimating ideology of the Protestant and politique clique at the head of the Elizabethan regime and its intermittently desperate efforts to perpetuate itself in the event of the queen's sudden death (without a settled heir, other than Mary Stuart); and the second a moment of oppositional critique, directed, by a ragbag collection of outs and malcontents, at what was seen to be, at least from the outside looking in, an increasingly narrow and corrupt court.

I

It is in that second moment or context that Ben Jonson's play *Sejanus* has traditionally (and quite rightly) been placed. Performed at the very start of James' reign in 1603 and printed in 1605, Jonson's play dramatises certain events from the reign of Tiberius centred on the rise to power and subsequent precipitate fall of the Emperor's favourite, Sejanus. Both the main body and margins of the printed text of the play aggressively display Jonson's classical and historical knowledge. His sources – most importantly Tacitus but also a range of other Roman authors – are rendered explicit in ways surely designed to affirm both the author's learning and the play's historical accuracy.[5] Indeed, on this basis, some critics have even been led to read the play as simply an exercise in and display of classical scholarship. But, in fact, as a number of other scholars (Matthew Wikander and Richard Dutton and, more recently, Blair Worden and Glenn Burgess) have argued, the play is, in fact, riven with echoes of and references to far more recent happenings.[6] On this view, the stories he took with such elaborate pedantry from the pages of Tacitus and Dio provided Jonson not only with the means to comment on contemporary events but also with plausible deniability, the means to turn aside accusations of slander or sedition with the claim that his was just a history play about events from the distant past scrupulously reconstructed from the very best editions of the relevant classical sources. As Jonson himself explained, the elaborate pedantry displayed in his footnotes was designed to 'show my integrity in the story, and save myself in those common torturers that bring all wit to the rack'.[7]

Indeed with wonderful (and typically Jonsonian) irony something like these very arguments are actually rehearsed during the action of the play as the historian Cordus is, at Sejanus' and Tiberius' behest, tried before the Senate as 'a man factious and dangerous, / A sower of sedition in the state / A turbulent and discontented spirit' (III, 380–2). Cordus' offense has been to write a history of the late civil wars – times now, as Natta, one of Sejanus' creatures, observes, 'somewhat queasy to be touched' (I, 82). Cordus defends himself by claiming only to have told the truth about the past and praised ancient virtue. His eloquence saves his life but his book is ordered burnt and he borne off to prison, leaving Arruntius to decry

> the Senate's brainless diligence,
> Who think they can, with present power, extinguish
> The memory of all succeeding times!
> ... Nor do they aught, that use this cruelty
> Of interdiction, and this rage of burning,
> But purchase to themselves rebuke and shame,
> And to the writers an eternal name.

The drawing of the final moral is left to Lepidus:

> it is an argument the times are sore,
> When virtue cannot be advanced,
> Nor vice reproved. (III, 471–83)

In these exchanges Jonson has not only managed to include, in the very action of the play, his own defence against charges of sedition and libel yet to be made, he has, in the process, also placed any potential accuser in the unenviable moral position of one who would prevent the praise of virtue and the reproof of vice, a position occupied in the play by the tyrant Tiberius, his favourite Sejanus, and their creatures and parasites in court and Senate. He has also set up one of the many references to or echoes of recent history that suffuse his text. The fate of Cordus recalls the Privy Council's recent ban on unofficial vernacular history books and the bishops' ban on satirical writing, official actions in which, because of his own recent imprisonment for his part with Nashe in writing the *Isle of Dogs*, Jonson had a close personal interest. More sensationally still, the fate of Cordus could not but remind the audience of the fate of Dr John Hayward who had been threatened with a treason trial and left to rot in gaol for his history of Henry IV, dedicated in 1599, with execrable timing, to the Earl of Essex.[8]

It was precisely through multiple, multivocal parallels and resonances of this sort that I want to argue (here following a fine article by Matthew Wikander) that *Sejanus* attached itself to contemporary or near contemporary events; not by establishing anything like simple one-to-one correspondences between Jonson's in large part scrupulously Tacitean narrative and particular political actors or events but by allowing, indeed by encouraging and eliciting from the reader/audience, a set of associations or parallels between what was happening on stage or on the printed page and recent events. Let us take the following descriptions of the character and fate of Germanicus, the Emperor's virtuous and much loved heir. According to Arruntius 'if there were seeds of the old virtue left, / They lived in him' (I, 119–20) – a judgement confirmed by

Sabinus who in his turn describes Germanicus as a compound of 'Pompey's dignity, / The innocence of Cato, Caesar's spirit, / Wise Brutus' temperance, and every true virtue' (I, 150–2). 'He was', concurs Silius, ' a man most like to virtue' (I, 124). But therein lay the rub: Germanicus' virtue, combined with his high birth, won him applause and, Sabinus explains, that, in turn, won him Tiberius' enmity.

> ... When men grow fast
> Honoured, and loved, there is a trick of state
> (Which jealous princes never fail to use)
> How to decline that growth, with fair pretext,
> And honourable colours of employment,
> Either by embassy, the war, or such,
> To shift them forth into another air,
> Where they may purge, and lessen; so was he:
> And had his seconds there, sent by Tiberius,
> And his more subtle dam, to discontent him;
> To breed and cherish mutinies; detract
> His greatest actions; give audacious check
> To his commands; and work to put him out
> In open act of treason. All which snares
> When his wise cares prevented, a fine poison
> Was thought on, to mature their practises. (I, 159–74)

All of which might well remind certain observers of an Essexian account of the fate of Essex at the hands of his enemies at the Elizabethan court. But if in some ways and on some readings both the antique martial hero and servant of the state, Germanicus, is described in ways designed to evoke memories of Essex, so too is the arch villain Sejanus.

Sejanus is presented as a favourite elevated to power by the prince, until his overweening ambition utterly to dominate the favour, patronage, and business of the Crown makes him a threat to the very monarch who has raised him to such eminence in the first place. Using his position at the centre of power and daily access to the prince to play on the envy, anxiety, and insecurity of an ageing monarch, Sejanus sets out sedulously to undermine all the other claimants to the imperial crown. But Sejanus' manipulations of the Emperor do not end with exploiting his fears of his relatives and potential heirs. By playing on Tiberius' love of sexual pleasure and sensual indulgence, he plans to lure the Emperor into rural retirement on Capri, far from the centre of events in Rome. Having, in the Emperor's absence, used his virtual monopoly over the distribution of patronage and place to build himself a faction in the state, Sejanus intends finally to displace an isolated Tiberius, now deeply loathed for the very cruelties and extremities into which he has been encouraged by Sejanus himself.

By this means, Sejanus rapidly achieves a dominance of the state so great that even after Tiberius has realised the extent of his favourite's treasonous ambitions – to which he has been alerted by Sejanus' maladroit attempt to marry his way into the heart of the imperial family – the Emperor does not feel able directly to confront his erstwhile protégé. Proceeding rather by stealth, Tiberius raises another favourite – the equally vile and self-serving Macro – through whom he plans to undermine and ultimately to destroy the initial object of his favour, Sejanus. And so it proves, in a palace coup orchestrated from Capri by Tiberius and carried out in Rome by Macro who, while appearing to confer yet further honours – the tribunical power – on Sejanus, seizes military control of the city and calls an emergency meeting of the Senate. There he delivers a long and ostensibly equivocal letter from Tiberius in the course of which the Emperor betrays his full knowledge of Sejanus' plotting. Expressing himself unwilling to prejudge the case or to force the Senate's hand, Tiberius asks only for judgement and justice, at which sign of the loss of royal favour the Senate immediately switches its allegiance with servile rapidity from the old 'court-God' Sejanus to the new, Macro. Sejanus is dragged off to summary execution and then, in an orgy of popular violence, the ever-fickle people fall upon first the body and then the innocent wife and children of Sejanus.

There are obvious general parallels between the action of the play and the late Elizabethan political scene, when an increasingly polarised and desperate faction politics swirled around an ageing and remote queen, and all the major players positioned themselves for the transition to a new regime which everyone knew was coming but the queen herself refused to acknowledge. The story of a courtier attempting to monopolise the favour of the monarch, busily arrogating power over the court, patronage, and the military and using the position of dominance thus achieved to fix the succession in his own interests had clear resonances and parallels with recent Elizabethan history. The favourite's sudden unlooked-for fall from the height of royal favour to death at the hands of the executioner, having been manœuvred into increasingly erratic behaviour by the machinations of the prince and of another, emergent favourite has, of course, more than a passing resemblance to certain readings of the career and fate of Essex. The pattern of such resonances, such potential or actual moments of recognition, was far from stable or consistent. Thus, we might conceive of Germanicus (or even of Silius) as Essex, as his former friends and admirers saw him, a personification of the admirable, virtuous, and soldierly Essex, the loyal servant of the Queen and commonwealth. Sejanus, on the other hand, might be Essex the courtier and favourite as his enemies portrayed him, a personification of that decline into overweening ambition and increasingly factious, allegedly irreligious, and even atheistical irrationality that precipitated the earl's fall. In short, there are elements in the play that appear designed, at different points in the action, to recall for differently minded contemporaries different versions of certain central figures and events in recent political history.

On this view, therefore, the play does not operate as a roman à clef. It is not, to use De Luna's resonant phrase[9] coined about Jonson's *Catiline*, a simple parallelograph set up against contemporary events, requiring us to identify, in any simple or straightforward sense, either Germanicus or Sejanus with Essex. The references to and echoes of contemporary events contained within Jonson's relentlessly Roman story are brief, evanescent, indeed at times mutually contradictory. They serve not to render the play an account of recent events with a stable factionalised or personalised meaning or agenda, but rather as means to establish flashes of recognition or correspondence whereby the audience or reader is led to connect the action of Jonson's play with their own experience or memory of recent political history and to use the former to think and moralise about the latter and, of course, vice versa. The most that can be said is that the play opens up or makes available a number of (often mutually contradictory) readings of recent history and then leaves the reader/spectator to choose among them, drawing as he or she does so the appropriate moral and political lessons.

These choices, these applications of text to context and context to text, are left open-ended. The resulting processes of application or interpretation, precisely because they take place entirely between the ears of the reader/spectator, cannot be the author's responsibility and yet they are not without an attendant frisson of risk or danger; for whichever of the multifarious identifications or parallels suggested above struck a chord, they all led rather quickly to uncomfortable, even seditious, consequences or conclusions. Even a brief toying with the Essex/Germanicus parallel brought with it the identification of Essex/Germanicus' arch-enemy, political successor and the architect of the next regime with none other than the evil Sejanus himself. If, on the other hand, the seemingly safer Sejanus/Essex correspondence was preferred, the role of his/their nemesis (for whom the most obvious contemporary parallel was also Sir Robert Cecil) was now being played by the equally corrupt and appalling Macro. Moreover, whichever of the available readings or systems of reference one preferred, there was no doubt that these events were presided over by the tyrant Tiberius, and there was only one candidate for the role of ageing and increasingly both remote and suspicious monarch in late Elizabethan England.

For the reign of Tiberius is presented throughout as a tyranny pure and simple. Corruption, it seems, has spread from the top down, enveloping the court and thence the polity. The result is a politics of servile ambition and fear that, through hope of reward and fear of ruin, has infected not merely the court but the state and senate as well. All office and favour are now concentrated in the hands of the Emperor and his favourite. Sejanus. With their role in the state reduced, at best, to that of 'good-dull-noble lookers on' 'only called to keep the marble warm' (III, 16–17) – the majority of the ruling elite have become alternately terrified and servile suitors for imperial favour.

For besides the carrot of reward the regime wields the threat of summary ruin, as an army of informers and lick-spittles stand ready to denounce any sign not only of opposition but even of moral independence in terms likely to lead to ruin, expropriation, and death. 'Every minist'ring spy / That will accuse and swear is Lord of you / Of me, of all, our fortunes, and our lives', Silius tells Sabinus. 'Our looks are called into question, and our words, / How innocent soever, are made crimes: / We shall not shortly dare to tell our dreams, / Or think, but twill be treason' (I, 64–9).

The subsequent action of the play works as a practical illustration of this analysis of the moral and political corruption afflicting the Roman state. Through a number of exchanges between the likes of Sejanus, Macro, and Tiberius himself, as well as through the commenting chorus-like passages and soliloquies of the Germanicans, the play provides the spectator/reader with a veritable compendium of entirely corrupt and corrupting court maxims and apothegms; here is what passes for received political and moral wisdom at the court of absolute tyrants like Tiberius. It is as though the play were operating at once as both a moral critique of, and a practical guide for, aspiring tyrants and court politicians.

The play's lessons in amoral statecraft and self-preservation have clearly been learnt by a wide range of Romans. As Opsius observes, as he prepares (at the bidding of Tiberius and Sejanus) to lure the virtuous Sabinus into treasonous words, 'to do an office / So grateful to the state, I know no man / But would strain nearer bands than kindred' (IV, 111–13). The ambiguity in Opsius' use of the term 'state' speaks volumes here. On the one hand, it gestures at a conventional nexus of meanings surrounding the 'state' viewed as the commonwealth, the public interest, the *res publica*. It is precisely that same nexus of value that Varro attempts to mobilise against Silius when he denounces him as 'an enemy of the state' (III, 234). As we shall see below, this is a usage to which Tiberius himself regularly pays lip service. 'For the public', he proclaims at one point, 'I may be drawn to show I can neglect / All private gains' (III, 136–7). But, of course, the state to which Sabinus' downfall will be 'grateful' is not the public interest or the commonwealth but the private interest and will of Sejanus and, behind him, of Tiberius. It is in that sense that Arruntius uses the term when he claims to Lepidus that 'I'd sooner trust Greek Sinon than a man / Our state employs' (IV, 360–1). This paradox is picked up by a parallel distinction made by Silius during his trial in the Senate. When told by Afer his accuser that 'he shall have justice', Silius replies, 'nay, I shall have law' only to elicit the tellingly obtuse reply, from the *lawyer* Afer, 'would you have more?' (III, 221–2) In Tiberian Rome, will has displaced law, the private interest of the ruler has usurped the public interest of the state, and the formalities of the law have taken the place of justice. As Silius observes at one point, since the decline of the republic, 'we since became the slaves to one man's lusts / And now to many' (I, 63–4). The result is moral anarchy, a situation in which words mean their opposite and the equivalences and complementarities between moral and political virtue, between 'virtue' and *virtù*, between 'virtue' and 'honour', have completely broken down in the face of Tiberius's exercise of tyrannical power and the desperate court manœuvre for advantage and survival that his regime has engendered.

Throughout the play, it is Sejanus and latterly Macro who produce the most strident and striking statements of Machiavellian realpolitik, but the real past master of intrigue turns out to be not the upwardly mobile evil counsellor but the prince. Thus not the least of the play's ironies is that Tiberius adopts precisely the 'softly softly' approach to the destruction of Sejanus that Sejanus himself has recommended to Tiberius as the best means to bring down the Germanicans. But by this point Sejanus is so high on his own political skills, so convinced of his own invincible greatness, that he remains entirely blind to what his erstwhile master is doing to him, until it is far too late.

Again, while Sejanus both indulges and congratulates himself over his mastery of the dark arts of Machiavellian manœuvre,[10] raging at what he now takes to be the puny powers of providence and the gods, the real master of those arts, Tiberius, sedulously observes the outward forms of piety and personal and political virtue. Having set up a system of almost complete corruption, servility, and flattery, and while basking in the results, Tiberius insists on deprecating the efforts of some of his subjects to treat him as a god. Elsewhere he describes himself as but 'the creature' or 'the servant of the Senate, and are proud / T'enjoy them our good, just, and favouring lords' (I, 393–4, 439). Indeed, at one point he even affects a desire to resign his powers as Emperor, only agreeing to continue in office 'for the public', 'if the Senate still command me serve' (III, 113–17, 137–40). This performance immediately precedes the entirely rigged trial of Silius, in the course of which Tiberius again displays his punctilious observance of legal form and constitutionalist platitude.

Tiberius' powers of dissimulation are presented as a product or expression of his superior political skill – what Lepidus calls 'Tiberius' art' (IV, 453) – of his capacity, unlike the god- and/or providence-challenging upstart Sejanus, to know the limits of human political action. For Tiberius acknowledges the necessity, even for the greatest prince or most corrupt tyrant, sedulously to observe, even as he utterly ignores and subverts, the appropriate (religious, legal, and moral) norms and outward forms. It is as though Sejanus represents a form of Machivellianism gone wrong, as, intoxicated with his own powers of statecraft and policy, he conceives of himself as a Fortuna-dominating superman. In his own eyes, at least, he is a man of such prowess as to be able simply to impose his will on events. Thus he enters Act V exulting in his powers and the incipient triumph they have won him. 'Great, and high, / The world knows only two, that's Rome, and I. / My roof receives me not; 'tis air I tread – / And, at each step, I feel my advanced head/ Knock out a star in heav'n!' (V, 5–9) Tiberius, on the other hand, emerges as someone who never forgets the rules of statecraft by which he has risen and by which, if he wishes to survive, he must continue to regulate his conduct.

Sejanus' fall comes hard on the heals of a number of blasphemous refusals to heed, as omens of impending doom, a series of prodigies performed first at or by his own statue at the theatre of Pompey and then at or by the statue of his tutelary deity, Fortuna. Alarmed by these signs of the gods' displeasure, Sejanus' followers beg him 'to attempt the gods once more with sacrifice'. Sejanus views such advice with contempt; 'what excellent fools / Religion makes of men!' (V, 69–70). He does, however, concede that, alone of 'the throng that fill th'Olympian hall' – deities whose power, Sejanus claims, is 'as cheap as I esteem it small' (V, 77–8) – he has retained a soft spot for Fortuna. He therefore concedes that to satisfy the 'scrupulous fant'sies' of his clients, he will 'go offer' to her statue (V, 84–9). But this gesture goes disastrously wrong, with the goddess' statue, in the midst of the sacrifice, miraculously averting its face from the suppliant Sejanus. At this Sejanus sweeps the altar clear of offerings, proclaiming as he does so that he is the goddess' superior and master. 'Nay hold thy look / Averted, till I woo thee turn again', he tells the now contorted statute. 'And thou shalt stand to all posterity / Th'eternal game and laughter, with thy neck / Writhed to thy tail, like a ridiculous cat. / Avoid these fumes, these superstitious lights, / And all these coz'ning ceremonies' (V, 194–200). He despises, he tells the fleeing priest, 'thy blind mistress, or / Thy juggling mystery, religion' (V, 192–3). As one 'that have been titled and adored a god, / Ye, sacrificed unto, myself, in Rome', Sejanus scorns 'to do a peevish giglot rites'. 'Perhaps the thought / And shame of that made Fortune turn her face, / Knowing herself the lesser deity, / And but my servant. Bashful queen, if so, / Sejanus thanks thy modesty' (V, 203–10).

What we have here is a series of problematising gestures towards what are overtly Machiavellian themes; the opposition of the *virtù* and policy of the statesman over and against the powers of Fortuna; the atheistical contempt for religion as a form of 'superstition', a series of empty outward forms, faith in which makes 'fools' of the ordinary run of men, from the constraints of which the likes of Sejanus are free and about which they are openly contemptuous. The seemingly miraculous nature of the prodigies or providential signs and warnings, vouchsafed by 'the gods' to Sejanus – the fire belching from his own statue, the giant serpent found within it, the averting of the image of Fortuna's face from Sejanus in the very act of propitiatory sacrifice – together with the immediacy and completeness of his subsequent fall, might all be taken to imply that what is happening here is a genuinely providential punishment of the atheistic Sejanus. On the other hand, the moral impact of this 'providential judgement' visited upon the evil Sejanus might be taken to be almost completely undercut by the outcome to which it leads – that is, the triumph of the equally evil Tiberius and his new creature Macro. All of which might lead us to conclude that Sejanus is being 'punished' not for his moral faults or even his blasphemy towards the gods and providence, but for his disastrously incomplete and self-deluding understanding of Machiavellian statecraft and his scandalously public disrespect for the outward forms of both constitutional and religious piety. Having gestured in both directions, the play, typically, leaves it up to the reader/spectator to decide the issue, ensuring, as ever, that whatever subversive hermeneutic moves the play may elicit take place not on the stage or the printed page but between the ears of the consumer of the performance or text.

II

On this view, Tiberian Rome was a covert tyranny; a regime riven with faction, deadly court-based rivalries and oppressions of the rights of the subject, presided and fought over by a rout of functional atheists and Machiavels and yet dressed up in the formal pieties of true religion and the language of the law and commonwealth. If this was, in some sense, a portrait or version of the Elizabethan regime, it was an extraordinarily dark and intemperate one.

No wonder, then, that when the play appeared in print in 1605 it did so smothered in references to Tacitus and other classical authorities. As a mass of modern scholarship (magisterially summed up in Philip Ayres' Revels edition of the text) has shown, the classical texts and authorities cited by Jonson were indeed his sources; his play followed very closely the lineaments of the story told by Tacitus and Dio. But I want to argue in the rest of this paper that, just because Jonson recommends them so forcibly to us, indeed precisely because he recommends them so forcibly to us, these are not the only texts against which we should read the play. I want now to advert to a fact which has not figured so prominently in recent criticism on the play as it might have done: that when Jonson wrote Sejanus he was a recently converted Catholic. In 1598 Jonson had found himself in gaol accused of murder – he had killed another actor, one Gabriel Spencer, in a 'duel'. In the end, by pleading benefit of clergy, he got off with a brand on the hand, but in the anxiety-filled interim, lying in gaol, confronting the prospect of death on the gallows, he had been converted to Catholicism.[11] What, then, if we approach *Sejanus* as, in some sense, a Catholic play?

As more than one commentator has observed (albeit usually more or less in passing), if we do so view it, a number of discrete aspects of the plot fall into place. For instance, the emphasis on informers preying on the wealthy, and on entrapment and conviction through words rather than deeds, all strike a chord when viewed from an Elizabethan Catholic perspective.[12] After all, we have here a regime hiding its illegal, persecutory assault on the lives, property, and legal rights of its subjects behind a punctilious observance of legal forms and an insistent claim that, all evidence to the contrary notwithstanding, its victims were 'traitors' and 'enemies of the state'. Thus, whatever personal or particularising references and associations may or may not have been contained in the play, the general vision conjured there of a tyrannical and persecutory state is highly reminiscent of long-standing Catholic claims about the treatment meted out by the Elizabethan state to its Catholic subjects. For if one group had been tempted by the characterisation of the Elizabethan regime as some sort of tyranny it had been the Catholics (or at least elements among them). Since at least the early 1570s there had been a steady stream of works by Catholic authors that provided detailed readings of the political character-istics and failings of the Elizabethan regime. That series might be said to have started with *A Treatise of Treasons*, and continued with *Leicester's Commonwealth* and that clutch of pamphlets known colloquially as *Cecil's Commonwealth*.[13] Here was a mode of analysis and polemic produced by what one might term the experience of political defeat as various Catholic groups and individuals emerged, defeated and frustrated, from a variety of failed dynastic and factional court manœuvres; manœuvres designed to reverse the forward march of Protestantism through the Elizabethan state and to disrupt the current distribution of political rewards and influence at the centre of the regime. Thus, the *Treatise of Treasons* was a product of the fallout from the projected match between Mary Stuart and the Duke of Norfolk, while *Leicester's Commonwealth* was a product of the similar collapse of the match between Elizabeth and Anjou. These texts were part of the reaction of Catholic insiders to turning points that not only failed to turn but ended with the main Catholic protagonists in a far worse position than they had been in the first place; discourted, disgraced, in exile or even (like Norfolk) dead. Reacting in bitterness against these reverses, the survivors struggled to produce accounts of how and why and to whom precisely they had lost.

Viewing 'the monarchical republic of Elizabeth I' from the outside, these men saw not a group of virtuous servants of the commonweal, united in the selfless defence of the monarch, the state, and true religion. On the contrary, they saw an utterly corrupt conspiracy of low-born evil counsellors and Machiavels. The men at the head of the regime were mere politiques, to all intents and purposes atheists who merely used arguments about religion and the national interest for their own sinister ends. Cecil and Bacon had, accord-ing to the *Treatise*, conformed to whatever religion the state had required of them. They had embraced the cause of religious change in 1559 only because it presented them with an ideal opportunity to create a kind of political instability through which they could seize power and thereafter play on the natural susceptibilities and insecurities of a young queen.[14] They had then destabilised Scotland, the Low Countries, and France, disrupting the old pattern of alliances that had attached England to the Hapsburgs. They had done so quite deliberately to perpetuate a pervading sense of crisis and insta- bility, a state of anxiety through which they could solidify their hold on power by presenting themselves and their policies as the only means to keep the queen and realm safe.[15] Invoking the demands of national security against a largely illusory, indeed invented, popish threat, they had managed to exclude those natural bulwarks and counsellors of the Crown, the ancient (and largely Catholic) aristocracy, from royal favour. In so doing they had also established for themselves a virtual monopoly over the favour and patronage of the Crown.[16] In the same spirit they had also sought to detach the Queen from her Catholic subjects, pushing her into more and more openly persecutory and tyrannical policies towards them. In this way they had been able both to pervert the law against their enemies and to isolate and frighten the Queen. If any complained or dared to tell the monarch the truth about their machina- tions they were denounced as traitors and either ruined or killed.[17] Again playing the Catholic card, they dissuaded the Queen from marriage and alienated her affections from her legitimate Catholic heir Mary Stuart. They did so as part of a plot to divert the succession, with the ultimate intention of seizing supreme power for themselves.[18] Throughout, therefore, they had put their own private ambitions and will to power before the public interests of Crown and commonwealth.

The identity of these evil Machiavels shifted through the period. In the *Treatise* it was those 'two Catilines', Cecil and Bacon; in *Leicester's Common- wealth* it was Leicester (Burghley and Sussex were now depicted as being on the side of the angels); but in *Cecil's Commonwealth* we are back to Burghley. What all these accounts had in common, of course, was the claim that the Queen herself was the chief victim of these conspiracies; sequestered and misled, her trust and powers were being systematically abused and her person put in great danger by a conspiracy of self-serving evil counsellors.

This vision of the monarchical republic as a conspiracy was a simple inversion of the regime's picture of itself. It mobilised against the Elizabethan Protestant establishment precisely the same moral values, historical templates, and classical or classicising sources that the ruling clique and its clients were using to constitute themselves as virtuous and public-spirited. It is perhaps worth noting here that the figure of Catiline, deployed with such gusto in the *Treatise of Treasons* against Cecil and Bacon, was in fact taken over from Thomas Norton's tracts against the northern earls, where it was deployed with equal enthusiasm against the likes of Westmorland and Northumberland.[19] The moral polarities and dichotomies at the centre of 'republican' discourse were simply being turned inside out. Now good became evil counsel; defence of the public became pursuit of private interest, and claims to virtue, loyalty, and the defence of true religion precisely the sort of obfuscation that one would expect from the standard evil counsellor and atheistical Machiavel. In the face of this sort of stand-off, the crucial question became who was the evil and who the good counsellor, who the conspirator and who the saviour of the state; just who, in the current circumstances, was Catiline and who was Cicero? The result, just as in the showdown between Catiline and Cicero as Cicero and Sallust retold it, was as much a rhetorical as a political struggle, with each side desperately making its case to be the party of truth and virtue through the spoken or, in this case, the printed word.

I want to suggest that Jonson's play can profitably be read against this mode of Catholic political analysis, which, particularly in *Leicester's Commonwealth*, gives a detailed account of just how the Elizabethan conspiracy of evil counsel worked. Just like Cecil and Bacon before him, Leicester, it was claimed, had started with the court where he now had 'so absolute authority and commandry ... as to place about the prince's person (the head, the heart, the life of the land) whatsoever people liketh him best ... By their means casting indeed but nets and chains and invisible bands about that person whom he most pretendeth to serve, he shutteth up his prince in a prison most sure, though sweet and senseless.'[20] By these means he was able completely to control access to the Queen. So great was his monopoly there that no one at the court had dared to tell the Queen of Leicester's marriage to the Countess of Essex; a task that fell in the end to a foreigner, Anjou's agent Simier. The *Treatise*, of course, had made precisely the same point about the extent of the Queen's sequestration under the rule of Cecil and Bacon, when no one had dared tell her the truth about their machinations against Norfolk and Mary, against the King of Spain and the English Catholics.[21]

Just like Bacon and Cecil, Leicester used this situation to effect a monopoly on royal favour, telling suitors that the Queen was extremely parsimonious and that, therefore, they needed his help and intercession to get their suits granted. In this way, both he and they had managed to attach the loyalty and gratitude of satisfied petitioners to his own rather than to the Queen's person. But such transactions did not merely lead to the evil counsellor figure getting as rich as Croesus. It also enabled him 'to advance his party and to fortify his faction, which faction if by these means it be great (as indeed it is) you may not marvel, seeing the riches and wealth of so worthy a commonweal do serve him but for a price to buy the same'.[22]

Not that Leicester's (or Cecil and Bacon's) power was limited to the court; he/they had come to dominate the Council as well. 'For the most part of the

Council present, they are known to be so affected in particular, the one for that he is to him a brother, the other a father, the other a kinsman, the other an ally, the other a fast obliged friend, the other a fellow or follower in faction, as none will stand in the breach against him.'[23] This fear-factor applied even to Councillors outside, indeed opposed to, his circle, as both Sussex and Burghley were now presented as being. This situation was no accident; rather it was the product of a long-standing series of intrigues against the natural counsellors of the crown – the ancient nobility. Here, following on again from the line adopted in the *Treatise of Treasons*, the author's star exhibit was Leicester's involvement in the destruction of Norfolk, whom, on this account, Leicester had inveigled into an intrigue with Mary Stuart and then used it to ruin him.[24] Again, just like Cecil and Bacon in the *Treatise*, having established himself at the centre in court and in Council, the tentacles of Leicester's influence had then encircled the country, particularly the strategically important or vulnerable bits of it. Taken together, all these machinations and manœuvres had given Leicester a dangerous preponderance, indeed almost a monopoly, of power in the state.

That alone would be bad enough but Leicester wanted more than preponderant power as a favourite. To adopt the language of the soap opera into which these texts were turning the high politics of the reign, he wanted it all, and ever since his early machinations first to marry the Queen and then to prevent her marrying elsewhere, he had been manœuvring to get it. Again this account of Leicester's plotting about the succession merely repeated the earlier analysis of Bacon and Cecil's ambitions provided in the *Treatise*, where they too were presented as desperately blocking the Queen's attempts to marry, playing the anti-popish card to prevent her marrying abroad and using their dominance at home to prevent marriage there.

Just like Cecil and Bacon in the *Treatise*, the will to power, the drive to achieve supreme sovereignty, was presented as Leicester's only principle. Leicester himself had started out in alliance with Catholics. Only latterly had he been converted 'by Lord North by way of policy' to the puritan party.[25] 'Being himself of no religion', Leicester 'feedeth notwithstanding upon our differences in religion, to the fattening of himself and ruin of the realm.'[26] Rather than any religious principle, the guiding spirit of the Dudleys, *père et fils*, was 'seignor Machavel, my Lord's counselor'. The *Treatise*, of course, had made precisely the same point about those two Machiavel Catlines, Bacon and Cecil.27 'Policy' rather than 'religion' was the guiding light for all these low-born evil counsellors. Just like Bacon and Cecil in the *Treatise*, Leicester's espousal of the Protestant (in reality the puritan) cause enabled him to use the bugbear of popery as an excuse to cut out the Stuarts from any just claim to the throne 'under the vizard and pretext of her (Queen Elizabeth's) defence and safety, having sowed in every man's head so many imaginations of the dangers present both abroad and at home, from Scotland, Flanders, Spain and Ireland, so many conspiracies, so many intended murders'.[28]

Leicester's version of this plan involved the assertion of Huntingdon's claim to succeed; making 'open title and claim to the crown with plots, packs and preparations to most manifest usurpation, against all order, all law and all rightful succession'.[29] Just as the *Treatise* had done, so *Leicester's Commonwealth* argued that the real obstacle to the consummation of such schemes was not so much Mary Stuart as Elizabeth Tudor. Moreover, given Leicester's dominance of the court and council, it 'cannot be denied but that her majesty's life lieth much at their discretion, to take it or use it to their best commodity ... Marry, one thing standeth not in their powers so absolutely, and that is to prolong her majesty's days or favour towards themselves at their pleasures, whereof it is not unlike but they will have due consideration, lest perhaps upon any sudden accident they might be found unready.'[30]

As both the *Treatise* and *Leicester's Commonwealth* pointed out, such unforeseen circumstances had been all that had prevented Leicester's father's attempt to divert the Tudor succession to his own advantage. How likely was it that the son – 'so born, so bred up, so nuzzled in treason from his infancy' – would repeat the same mistake as the father? 'When they shall see only her Majesty's life and person to stand betwixt them and their fiery desires ... no doubt but it will be to them a great prick and spur to dispatch her majesty also.'[31] On this view the Stuart claim, far from representing a threat to Elizabeth and the continuity and stability of the English monarchical state, represented a last bulwark against the plotting of Leicester and his allies; a bulwark preserved, with great wisdom and foresight, *Leicester's Commonwealth* claimed, by the Queen herself.

Here, then, is a vision of the Elizabethan regime and court remarkably similar to that adumbrated in Jonson's *Sejanus*. Leicester's (and Cecil and Bacon's) rise to power, its modes and methods, establishing a monopoly over royal favour, control over the court and access to the monarch, building up a patronage base in court, Council, and army, while systematically depleting the power and influence of the old aristocracy and setting the members of the royal house against one another, playing up the monarch's fears of a reversionary interest while aiming to divert the succession to their own advantage, are all reminiscent of the career of Sejanus as Jonson portrayed it. The tyrannical policies towards the Catholics into which Cecil and Bacon are depicted persuading the Queen parallel perfectly the tyrannical impulses which Sejanus encourages in Tiberius. In both cases the aim is the same; so to alienate the affections of the subject from the monarch that, when the final blow is struck, no hand will be lifted to defend a now isolated, loathed and despised ruler.

Probably because of the contrast between the prim regularity of the domestic lives of Cecil and Bacon and the rather more raffish course of Leicester's love life, *Leicester's Commonwealth* gives a far more immediate and racy account of the interiority of tyranny. Like Tiberius, Leicester's tyranny is founded on and figured by his personal and sexual depravity. Leicester is presented throughout as some sort of sex monster or addict. A man who keeps a jar of erection-enhancing white ointment next to his bed, Leicester simply cannot control his lusts. 'No man's wife can be free from him, whom his fiery lust liketh to abuse nor their husbands able to resist nor save from his violence if they show dislike or will not yield consent to his doings.'[32] While he had left the details of his first wife's murder to others, he himself had played a more central role in poisoning his second wife's husband, the Earl of Essex, but not before at his behest she had aborted a bastard child conceived with Leicester for fear that Essex might find them out. These and his other unsuccessful attempts to poison Anjou's agent Simier and the Earl of Sussex were all undertaken with the help of a kitchen cabinet made up of two foreign minions, 'Julio the Italian and Lopez the Jew', whom he maintained for the express purpose of 'poisoning and destroying children in women's bellies', and two Englishmen, 'Dee and Allen (two atheists)', whom he maintained 'for figuring and conjuring'.[33] Poison and a providence-defying obsession with augory, fortune-telling, and magic were, of course, attributes of Tiberius and indeed of many another tyrant figure. Like Tiberius a classic tyrant, Leicester's personal depravity expressed itself in a restless lust not merely after sexual conquest and pleasure but also after power, and throughout *Leicester's Commonwealth* he was consistently referred to as a 'tyrant', a man bent on arrogating and monopolizing power to and for himself.

It forms no part of the argument being advanced here to claim that *Leicester's Commonwealth* or the *Treatise of Treasons* should be seen as a 'source' for *Sejanus* in the same sense as, say, Tacitus or Dio clearly were sources. There is, however, good reason to assume that *Leicester's Commonwealth*, in particular, was readily available and avidly read in the circles in which Jonson habitually moved. We know, for instance, that (as Simon Adams has shown) his schoolmaster at Westminster School and very close friend, William Camden, drew heavily on stories from *Leicester's Commonwealth* when he came to compose the portrait of the earl contained in his *Annals*.[34] So Jonson could easily have read the book. He certainly told Drummond at least one scurrilous story about Leicester being poisoned by accident by a draught he had intended for his wife, so he was clearly not uninterested in, uniformed about, or above retelling stories culled from such dubious, low, and seditious sources.[35]

But it is not necessary for the purposes of this paper to argue that Jonson had ever read the the *Treatise*, or *Leicester's* or *Cecil's Commonwealth*. It is enough to be able plausibly to claim that both he and some of his audience – in particular, the informed part about which he cared most – were familiar both with the penumbra of libellous and lascivious stories surrounding the doings of the great and the good, and with the strand of Catholic thinking which deployed such libellous materials to describe and denounce the Elizabethan regime as effectively a tyranny. For it is on the basis of that assumption that we can see both sets of texts as a legitimate context within which to read Jonson's play. At the most general level, the mass of libels circulating in the period, each of them offering to tear the veil away from the great events of the day, to reveal what was really happening, just as Tacitus was deemed to do for the politics of the imperial court, provide a context which would, independent of anything said or done on stage, have invited Jonson's audience to apply his classical story to current affairs. More particularly, for at least some contemporaries, the mode of Catholic analysis and argument outlined above would have set Jonson's Roman materials into an altogether more precise and politically pointed polemical context. In both cases, Jonson's parade of his intense engagement with his classical sources allowed him to tap into and play off such disreputable, low, 'popular', and, indeed, seditious or even treasonable genres and modes of argument, while appearing only to be telling a story about the classical past, according to the highest standards of scholarly accuracy.

III

But if we start to read the play in an explicitly 'Catholic' context, what sort of 'Catholic' text does the play become? Jonson gives his audience some very obvious clues with which to answer that question, for some of the major issues of political casuistry confronting Elizabethan Catholics receive direct discussion and pretty explicit resolution in the play. Of these the central question involves the right legitimately to resist monarchical power, an issue which confronts the Germanicans in the play with quite as much force and urgency as it did Elizabethan Catholics. For the Germanicans find themselves confronted with a raging tyrant who, convinced of their ill will, is bent throughout on their destruction. They do so moreover in a polity that a mere seventy years previously had been a republic, only recently reduced to an absolute hereditary monarchy; that monarchy is now run by a tyrant and his evil counsellor and favourite, a favourite who, as at least some of the more perspicacious among them realise, is aiming to usurp the throne for himself. From the outset they betray themselves as well aware of all these political and constitutional realities and by the end have come to a bitter appreciation of the extremity of their own danger.

But if the Germanicans' situation and, indeed, that of Rome itself is as clear as day, what to do about that situation is most definitely not. At certain points the Germanicans toy with the idea of resistance, but it is always rejected. Significantly, by far the most strident and explicit statement of the need for violent action against imperial tyranny, couched in the uncompromising language of lost republican liberty and virtue, is put by Jonson into the mouth of Latiaris, a government spy and agent provocateur trying to tempt Sabinus into treasonous words. Having lured Sabinus into the usual moaning session about the moral and political condition of the times, Latiaris makes his pitch.

> Methinks the genius of the Roman race
> Should not be so extinct, but that bright flame
> Of liberty might be revived again,
> Which no good man but with his life should loose....
> The cause is public, and the honour, name,
> The immortality of every soul
> That is not a bastard or a slave in Rome,
> Therein concerned. Whereto, if men would change
> The wearied arm, and for the weighty shield
> So long sustained, employ the ready sword,
> We might have some assurance of our vows.
> This ass's fortitude doth tire us all.
> It must be active valour must redeem
> Our loss, or none.

In the face of this call to arms Sabinus recoils in horror.

> Twere better stay
> In lasting darkness, and despair of day.
> No ill should force the subject undertake
> Against the sovereign, more than hell should make
> The gods do wrong. A good man should and must
> Sit rather down with loss, than rise unjust –
> Though, when the Romans first did yield themselves
> To one man's power, they did not mean their lives,
> Their fortunes, and their liberties should be
> His absolute spoil, as purchased by the sword. (IV, 142–70)

The same conclusion is reached by Agrippina who, desperately advising her faction and family to disperse in the face of Tiberius' terror campaign against them, starts to toy with the idea of meeting force with force, only immediately to reject it. She ends by telling her sons to 'stand upright; / And though you do not act, yet suffer nobly. / Be worthy of my womb, and take strong cheer. / What we do know will come, we should not fear' (IV, 73–6).

Nor are either Agrippina or Sabinus merely practising a prudent dissimulation here. Agrippina is musing to herself in private and, later in the same conversation with Latiaris in which he has so roundly rejected the notion of violent resistance, Sabinus lets slip the pious wish that Tiberius 'bogged in his filthy lusts' 'might ever sleep'. As he well knows, that sentiment alone is quite enough to provoke against him the charge of 'treason to Caesar' (IV, 216–8). Having loyally renounced action, Sabinus is condemned for mere words.

These passages are surely designed to show with crystal clarity how precisely the Germanicans observe the line between active and passive resistance, maintaining their political and moral independence – an attenuated version of both political and personal virtue, which is all their circumstances allow them – while avoiding the merest hint of real treason. However clear their appreciation of Tiberius' tyranny and Sejanus' treason becomes, they sedulously leave the punishment of the prince and his chosen creatures to heaven. As they come to know and at least half acknowledge, and as Sabinus' arrest for treason certainly demonstrates, such a sophisticated and subtle performance of passive resistance, such a carefully modulated combination of moral independence with political loyalty, is not going to save their skins, since it is based on a series of distinctions which the regime tyrannously refuses to recognise. The Germanicans' behaviour will, however, preserve their honour, demonstrating their impeccable moral and political virtue and correctitude, as virtue and correctitude were defined by, among others, James VI and I.

In the face of tyranny the only legitimate oppositional act is talk. Ideally one should talk to the prince, telling him the truth and thus dispelling the clouds of evil counsel, disinformation, and flattery that surround all monarchs and especially tyrants. Since it was in the intimate exchanges of mutual admiration and advantage between flatterers, would-be favourites, and princes that the origins of tyranny lay, telling truth to princes was the highest form of service to the commonwealth, the greatest exercise of political virtue. But for such a truth-telling strategy to work, indeed for it to be anything other than a pointless and suicidal display of private virtue, one needed, if not a virtuous prince, then at least a prince with enough vestiges of virtue to offer the rational hope that he might be able to recognise and act on good counsel when he heard it. And this, the play makes clear, Tiberius was not. Thus, having just realised the extent of Sejanus's designs on supreme power, the intemperate and politically clueless Arruntius cries, 'He (Tiberius) should be told this ... He shall be told it' and makes to rush off to confront the emperor with the moral enormities of his rule and the machinations of his favourite. It is Sabinus himself who restrains him. 'Stay, Arruntius, / We must abide our opportunity, / And practise what is fit, as what is needful. / It is not safe t'enforce a sovereign's ear: / Princes hear well, if they at all will hear' (I, 425–34).

Tiberius, of course, has no wish to hear anything that the likes of Sabinus, Silius, and Arruntius might have to say; the court is dominated by Sejanus and his faction and the Senate has been completely corrupted and cowed (just as many Catholics claimed the Parliament and court had been under Elizabeth). This left the Germanicans with no arena or stage from which they could safely or effectively address either prince or people. What, then, were they to do? Jonson sketches a range of responses. If they cannot talk to the prince, they can at least talk to themselves and one another, and throughout the play they do indeed do a good deal of talking; standing, as they think, aloof from events, they provide an ironic and horrified moral commentary on the corruption of both 'men' and 'the times'. They do so, huddled together around Agrippina's dinner table, in full knowledge that they are being watched. Under the circumstances their conduct represents a form of protracted suicide, both political and actual, as the regime picks them off one by one through a series of trumped-up charges and rigged trials.

We have here a view of politics in which the enabling condition for the exercise of an active political virtue on the part of the subject and in particular on the part of the would-be courtier or counsellor was a virtuous prince. Indeed, in the first half of the speech quoted above Silius goes out of his way to praise the rule of such a prince as the best possible polity. To Tiberius' claim (cited above) to be but 'the servant of the senate', Silius replies,

> If this man
> Had but a mind allied to his words,
> How blest a fate were it to us, and Rome!
> We could not think that state for which to change,
> Although the aim were our old liberty:
> The ghosts of those that fell for that would grieve
> Their bodies lived not now, again to serve.
> Men are deceived who think there can be thrall
> Beneath a virtuous prince. Wished liberty
> Ne'er lovelier looks than under such a crown. (I, 393–409)

Thus not only does the play present the rule of a virtuous prince as the best of all possible worlds, it also emphasises that on the level of political practice in Tiberian Rome (and surely in Elizabethan England too) the sort of political and personal virtue that alone might make a republic viable is almost entirely lacking. In his account of the final fall of Sejanus, Jonson goes out of his way to emphasise the servile corruption of the senate and the fickle and irrational violence of the mob. In neither senate nor people, therefore, is there any alternative source of virtue upon which to refound a viable popular state or republic. On Jonson's account, only the Germanicans possess anything like virtue and it is, of course, that very fact that has contributed to their status as a persecuted, marginalised, and politically impotent minority.

As a number of critics have pointed out, Jonson does not represent the Germanicans responding in the same way to their common predicament. What the Germanicans do have in common, and what I think we can say that the play does more or less enthusiastically endorse, is a shared assent to some of the central orthodoxies of what we might term an emergent Jacobean (absolutist) political style.

Despite the recent republican history of the Roman state, they accept without question the legitimacy of Tiberius' claim to be Emperor and of the absolute powers and prerogatives which that title confers upon him. Clearly, once transferred from the subject or in this case the Roman people and Senate, 'absolute and dilate' royal power can never be taken back again. Even in the face of a clearly republican political past and an utterly tyrannical political present, presided over by a prince who did indeed act as though his subjects' 'lives, fortunes and liberties' were his 'absolute spoil', there could be no legitimate recourse to resistance or force. Thus the Germanicans refuse utterly to contemplate any form of overt resistance and they display to the end a dedication (albeit an increasingly grudging one) to the person of the Emperor and the claims of his legitimate heirs. They do all this, moreover, in the face of their own clear knowledge of the personal depravity and evil of Tiberius himself, of the nature and seemingly inevitable course of what one might term his serial tyranny, and the depredations of his equally evil and vicious creatures and agents, Sejanus and Macro. They also manage to combine this commitment to political loyalty and obedience with a refusal to become complicit with the regime's utterly illegal and immoral purposes or ends. Most of them end up paying the price of maintaining these contradictory commitments with their lives.

Thus Professor Burgess is no more than half right when he argues that in *Sejanus* Jonson is relatively unconcerned with the formal structures of state power and government, his attention firmly focused instead on questions of morality, of personal and political vice and virtue, on the moral roots of both corruption and good government.[36] For Jonson certainly is concerned with such moral issues but he is also eager to locate his discussion of these questions inside a really rather precise ideological, legal, and constitutional framework; a framework to which the differences between absolute and limited monarchy, between monarchy and republicanism, between a vision of political authority that allowed a residual right to resist and one which did not were all central. The ideal state posited by Jonson's text, the legitimate alter ego to Tiberius' entirely illegitimate tyranny, is not a republic nor even a formally limited or mixed monarchy, but rather the rule of a virtuous prince within the essentially imperial absolutist structures of Tiberian Rome. Only in that context can good counsel triumph over bad, as truth-telling men of virtue and honour like the Germanicans move from the periphery back to the centre, returning to royal favour at court where, in alliance with the prince's best instincts, they might hope to control the natural tendencies toward corruption and tyranny inherent in all (monarchical) states. Now the prince can start to receive good as well as evil counsel, virtue can led to action, and action in the service of the state and prince can lead to honour and reward. The tide of corruption that has beset both 'men' and 'the times' can start being rolled back by virtuous men and, as the examples of Sosia and Agrippina make clear, women, active in the service of the commonwealth. But without such a princely lead from the top, there can be no way out of the cycle of corruption and cruelty, servility and suspicion that has enveloped the Roman state. And that is the situation that confronts and defeats the Germanicans.

Moreover, in the play we have a group of old aristocrats, grouped around a central female figure, forming there what turns into a much loathed and feared reversionary interest. As such, they attract the hostile attention of an increasingly paranoid and tyrannical regime, presided over by an ageing and corrupt monarch and his low-born favourite. In Act IV Agrippina laments her fate, left slowly twisting in the wind of Tiberius's unappeasable suspicion and Sejanus's implacable enmity, in terms strongly reminiscent of the slow Passion of Mary Stuart. 'Is this the happiness of being born great? / Still to be aimed at? Still to be suspected? / To live the subject of all jealousies? / At least the colour made, if not the ground / To ever painted danger? Who would not / Choose once to fall, than thus to hang forever?' (IV, 9–14) Constantly spied on, provoked beyond endurance into treasonable words, slowly but surely nearly all Agrippina's relatives and intimates are denounced and either destroyed or driven into exile as traitors and enemies of the state, and all this despite their innocence of any active plotting against the regime. Even as they confront the virtual certainty of their own destruction at the hands of Tiberius' tyranny, Agrippina's party refuse to consider active resistance. Taking their punishment like the patriots they are, they wait patiently for Heaven to revenge them by punishing the sins of their enemies and oppressors.

Viewed from the perspective of previous Catholic writing on the Elizabethan political scene, it is not hard to discern here a portrait of Mary Stuart and her partisans and supporters suffering under the hostile attentions of Elizabeth and her low-born 'Catilines', Cecil, Bacon, and latterly Leicester. Viewed from this perspective, then, the play becomes an attempt both to rehabilitate Mary and her party from Elizabethan accusations of treason and to indict the Elizabethan regime as even more seriously tyrannical than previous Catholic accounts had made out. For, with their insistence on the role of evil counsellors such as Cecil or Leicester, those earlier Catholic analyses of Elizabethan corruption had left the person of the Queen relatively untouched. Her favour might be the enabling condition for the predominance of whoever the Catiline of the moment might be, but the assumption, perhaps the legal fiction, underpinning these accounts was that Elizabeth herself was an innocent dupe of an otherwise entirely malign conspiracy of politique evil counsellors. Unlike his predecessors, Jonson was writing after the death of the Queen and at the moment when Mary Stuart's son was about to mount the English throne. And so, through his wonderfully astute and sinister account of the relationship, the politico-moral co-dependence, that bound Tiberius to both Sejanus and Macro, he was able to reach the parts of the Elizabethan regime that previous Catholic writing had been unable to reach, fingering

Elizabeth herself (or at least the Emperor-function who stood in for Elizabeth in Jonson's description of Tiberian Rome) as a tyrant indeed. On this view, the evil-counsellor analyses propagated by previous Catholic observers had been a function or reflection of the political arts of Elizabeth, who, just like Tiberius, had been careful in public scrupulously to observe the formal niceties of morality, piety, and legality and thus had been able to deflect the blame for her enormities onto her creatures and favourites.

Now the old Queen was dead and the truth could be told. But in writing his play, Jonson was surely looking as much forward as back. For not only did Jonson's exercise in Roman history allow him to tear the veil of evil counsellor rhetoric from previous Catholic loyalist analyses of Elizabethan tyranny, it also enabled him to make a pitch for patronage and support from the incoming monarch who, when all was said and done, was Mary Stuart's son. Out from under Elizabeth, with no real patrons to speak of, we might see *Sejanus* as Jonson's (typically intemperate and high-risk) pitch for support from the new regime. Corroboration for such a view comes from other parts of Jonson's output, written at precisely the same time to celebrate the accession of the new monarch. Here two texts are central: Jonson's 'Part of King James His Royal and Magnificent Entertainment' and 'A Brief Panegyre of His Majesty's First … Entrance to His High Court of Parliament'. Together with an 'Entertainment of the Queen and Prince' at Althorp, these were printed in 1604, and were hence available to contemporaries (and, if *Sejanus* was performed at court, available also to James himself, if he was paying attention) as a gloss on Jonson's recently performed play.[37] As both Robert Evans and Blair Worden have argued, these texts echo and pick up central themes and images from *Sejanus*, providing, as it were, a vision of the Jacobean 'after', to be juxtaposed against the tyrannical Tiberian (or, indeed, Elizabethan) 'before' outlined in *Sejanus*. Here, in these panegyric texts, is the counterpoint, the mirroring positive image of good kingship, to the vision of tyranny depicted in the play.[38] Thus in 'An Entertainment' the figure of the Thames welcomes 'greatest James', 'no less great than good', to his new capital. 'I tender thee the heartiest welcome, yet / That ever king had to his empire's seat. / Never came man, more long'd for, more desir'd: / And being come, more reverenc'd, lov'd, admir'd.' James is hailed as bringing in a new golden age of peace, plenty and liberty. His reign has brought

> sweet peace to sit in that bright state she ought,
> Unbloody, or untroubled; hath forc'd hence
> All tumults, fears, and other dark portents
> That might invade weak minds; hath made men see
> Once more the face of welcome liberty.
> And doth (in all his present acts) restore
> That first pure world, made of the better ore.

Now innocence shall cease to be the spoil
Of ravenous greatness, or to steep the soil
Of raised peasantry with tears, and blood;
No more shall rich men (for their little good)
Suspect to be made guilty; or vile spies
Enjoy the lust of their so murdering eyes:
Men shall put off their iron minds, and hearts;
The time forget his old malicious arts
With this new minute; and no print remain
Of what was thought the former ages stain.[39]

The dam of other evils,
Shall here lock down her jaws, and that rude vice
Of ignorant, and pitied greatness, pride,
Decline with shame; ambition now shall hide
Her face in dust, as dedicate to sleep,
That in great portals wont her watch to keep.
All ills shall fly the light; thy court be free
No less from envy, than from flattery;
All tumult, faction and harsh discord cease
That might perturb the music of thy peace:
The querulous nature shall no longer find
Room for his thoughts: one pure consent of mind
shall flow in every breast, and not the air,
Sun, moon or stars shine more serenely fair.[40]

Here, then, we have a view of a golden age of good government juxtaposed against a vision of tyranny, associated with the recent past, a vision which is very reminiscent of the state of affairs depicted in *Sejanus*. In both texts we are presented with a regime riven with faction and fear, with spies and informers let loose to terrify honest men and to place the rich at the mercy of either their enemies or the ruler and his creatures. In 'A Panegyre' Jonson returned obsessively to the sort of tyrannical rule to which James represented the polar opposite, conjuring images redolent of the persecution undergone by English Catholics and of the sorts of misgovernment about which a variety of Catholic tracts had complained so bitterly during the 1590s. Jonson pictured the eyes of the new monarch sending out

a thousand radiant lights, that stream
To every nook and angle of his realm ... to pry
Into those dark, and deep concealed vaults,
Where men commit black incest with their faults;
And snore supinely in the stall of sin:
Where murder, rapine, lust do sit within
Carousing human blood in iron bowels,
And making their den the slaughter house of souls:

> From whose foul reeking caverns first arise
> Those damps, that so offend all good men's eyes;
> And would (if not dispersed) infect the crown,
> And in their vapour her bright metal drown.[41]

Turning from this image of a royal gaze penetrating into the most secret dungeons, where sin, cruelty, and soul murder lurk – images that might be taken to conjure the sites and methods whereby English Catholics had been incarcerated and tormented under the previous regime – Jonson then pictures the King, as he processes to parliament, being introduced by Themis to the tyrannical excesses and legal abuses of his predecessors.

> The men she did report:
> And all so justly, as his ear was joy'd
> To hear the truth, from spite, or flattery void.
> She showed him, who made wise, who honest acts;
> Who both, who neither: all the cunning tracts,
> And thriving statutes she could promptly note;
> The bloody, base and barbarous she did quote;
> Where laws were made to serve the tyrant' will.
> Where sleeping they could save and waking kill;
> Where acts gave license to impetuous lust
> To bury churches, in forgotten dust,
> And with their ruins raise the pander's bowers:
> When, public justice borrowed all her powers
> From private chambers; that could then create
> Laws, judges, confessors, yea, prince and state.[42]

Again, then, we have a pointed version of a tyranny located in the English past, eerily reminiscent both of Jonson's own picture of Tiberian Rome and of Catholic critiques of Elizabeth's reign – with the law used to 'bury churches' and convert the ruins to corruptly secular ends or to divert the succession and thus to threaten the very 'prince and state' themselves.

James, however, is pictured as a ruler of an altogether different stripe. As he delights to hear the enormities of his predecessors described and excoriated, as part of an object lesson in how not to do it, he shows that while 'he owned their crowns, he would not so their crimes. / He knew that princes, who sold their fame / To their voluptuous lusts, had lost their name; / And that no wretch was more unblest than he, / Whose necessary good 'twas now to be / An evil king.' But James also knew that

> those who would, with love, command,
> Must with a tender (yet a steadfast) hand
> Sustain the reynes, and in the check forebear
> To offer cause of injury, or fear.
> That kings, by their example, more do sway

Than by their power; and men do more obey/
When they are lead, then when they are compell'd.[43]

Given that James was a prince who knew all this, Jonson felt able to proclaim

what a fate
Was gently fallen from heaven upon this state;
How dear a father they did now enjoy
That came to save, what discord would destroy:
And entering with the power of a king,
The temp'rance of a private man did bring,
That won affections, ere his steps won ground;
And was not hot, or covetous to be crown'd
Before men's hearts had crown'd him.[44]

On this account, then, James is the very anti-type of Tiberian (or, for that matter, Elizabethan) tyranny. Under his rule, England will experience the best of all possible regimes, the rule of a virtuous prince. Accordingly, Jonson felt able to tell James that, because of his outstanding virtue, 'blind fortune' would 'be thy slave / And may her store / (The less thou seek'st it) follow thee the more'.[45] Here, in marked contrast to the unmarried and barren Elizabeth, Jonson pictures the house of Stuart as 'a broad spreading tree, / Under whose shade, may Britain ever be. / And from this branch, may thousand branches more / Shoot o're the main, and knit with every shore / In bonds of marriage, kindred and increase; / And style this land the navel of their peace.'[46] Significantly, 'An Entertainment' echoes almost to the word the sentiments of Silius cited above from *Sejanus*. There he had lauded the rule of a virtuous prince as the best of all possible regimes: 'cherished liberty ne'er lovelier looks then under such a crown'. In 'An Entertainment', as we have seen, James is hailed as having 'made men see / Once more the face of welcome liberty'. Elsewhere Jonson uses precisely the same quotation from Claudian that in *Sejanus* he had placed in Silius' mouth, to gloss a scene featuring both 'Eleutheria or Liberty' and 'Doulosis or Servitude' to prove that under a virtuous prince there was in fact no opposition or even tension between the two: 'liberty could never appear more graceful, and lovely, then now under so good a prince'.[47]

Viewed, in this light, as the first half of a one-two punch of criticism and compliment, Jonson's play takes its place alongside a whole raft of petitions and performances whereby a range of English Catholics made a variety of different pitches to the new King for what we might term renegotiated terms and conditions of loyalty.[48] But Jonson was not making a case for some sort of generalised Catholic cause. On the contrary, the nature of his political message was really quite precise. For on the account being put forward in *Sejanus*, it was only the Germanicans, a.k.a. the Catholic loyalist, Marian aristocracy, that had preserved the cause of virtue, honour, and political legitimacy against the rout of popular and court corruption that had enveloped Protestant England and the Elizabethan regime. There was no room here for erstwhile plotters and resistance theorists, for Jesuits and Hispanophiles. We can, in fact, be quite precise about the Catholic targets of Jonson's loyalist fire, chief among which was surely the populist (quasi-'republican'?) theory of power, of elective monarchy and resistance theory, put forward by Robert Parsons in his great tract of the mid-1590s, *A Conference about the Next Succession*: a tract designed, of course, to deflate and demote Stuart claims to the English succession in the face of a host of other such claims, the most significant of which belonged to the Infanta.[49] In allying himself so explicitly with the cause of non-resistance, Jonson was in fact taking sides in a recent intra-Catholic dispute of rare intensity (the so-called Archpriest controversy) as well, of course, as agreeing volubly with the political philosophy of James VI and I, as recently set out in his *True Law of Free Monarchies* (a text which, as I hope to argue at length elsewhere, was itself written at least in part in reply to Parsons).[50]

Indeed, we can establish some tentative connections between the Catholic loyalist position, the circles around the Earl of Essex, and Jonson himself in precisely the period in which *Sejanus* was written. For a number of scholars have speculated that the instrument of Jonson's prison conversion to Catholicism was none other than Thomas Wright. Wright was a renegade Jesuit who enjoyed the patronage and protection of the Earl of Essex while he purveyed an extreme version of Catholic loyalism, designed to unite all loyal English people (both Catholic and Protestant) against the Hispanophile, papalist threat represented by the Jesuits, the Catholic League and Philip II, and their English and French supporters.[51] On Jonson's account, then, in making a pitch for royal favour under the new regime only loyalist Marians and Stuart legitimists need apply. Having stayed loyal and virtuous for so long – far more loyal and virtuous than the time-servers and politiques who under Elizabeth had sought their ruin – the descendants and/or the surviving members of this group now deserved their time in the sun as virtuous counsellors and servants of the equally virtuous prince, newly arrived from Scotland to save England from the abuses and corruptions of the previous reign.

In making such a move in and through the drama, indeed through the tragic drama, Jonson was, of course, fulfilling the age old role of the tragic poet. For as Rebecca Bushnell, among others, has reminded us, it was widely acknowledged in humanist circles that the purpose of tragedy was to present the prince with a picture of tyranny and its consequences so awful and so moving that he or she would never be tempted to become a tyrant him or herself. It was also what Richard Dutton calls an 'established neo-classical principle that tragedies must be based on true historical facts if they were to be convincing and effective'.[52] And here was Jonson, at the very beginning of a new reign, presenting the new ruler with just such a vivid, alternately disgusting and moving picture of tyranny; a picture that was historically grounded not once but twice over; obviously so, in its relation to Tiberian Rome, and, if there is anything to the argument being pursued here, implicitly so in its no less close, if rather more oblique, relationship with more recent English history. In the process, Jonson was providing James with an object lesson both in how not to do it and in what to do next; in other words, with the outlines of an immediate religio-political programme. On this view, James Stuart was the virtuous prince whose rule was about to transform the moral and political temper of the times. The expulsion of the corrupt, low-born, and self-serving clique of evil counsellors that had dominated the previous reign and their replacement by steadfastly loyal and virtuous aristocratic (and, on the current reading, often, if not always or necessarily, loyalist Catholic) Germanicans, were the means whereby that process of house cleaning could be effected.

Even given the opportunities and instabilities incident upon wholesale political change and dynastic transition, saying such things on the public stage was not without its risks, and the play accordingly did not demand to be read in this way. As both Jonson and Cordus pointed out, it was about Roman history. As an exercise in the praise of virtue and the excoriation of corruption and vice, the play was designed for the moral instruction and edification of the audience, but not for their immediate political education or agitation. It spoke to current concerns, certainly, but only in general moral, archetypal, rather than particularising or event-specific terms. And yet the play did not refuse, indeed it might even be said to have invited or elicited, such readings and applications from its audience and later its readership.

And we know that it did indeed receive at least one such reading from a very centrally placed reader. Under normal circumstances, it is virtually impossible to reconstruct how contemporaries reacted to the performance or publication of plays during this period. But in the case of *Sejanus* we know that at least one contemporary did indeed read the play in precisely the way I have suggested it could be read. Years later, Jonson told William Drummond that on the basis of *Sejanus* none other than the Earl of Northampton cited Jonson before the Privy Council for popery and treason.[53] Northampton, of course, knew whereof he spoke. In his former incarnation as Henry Howard, brother of the 'traitor' Norfolk, Catholic loyalist intimate of Mary Stuart, and ardent supporter of the Anjou match, he had been at the centre of the circles out of which *Leicester's Commonwealth* had emerged in 1584. He was also deeply learned in the politic histories of the age, in the works of Machiavelli, Guicciardini and, of course, of Seneca, Sallust, and Tacitus.[54] Northampton was, therefore, in an almost uniquely qualified position to decode or discern rather precisely both what Jonson was saying and how he was saying it.

V

In conclusion I want to make a number of connected points. I want first to argue that the preceding analysis shows the value for historians of literary or fictive sources. Properly contextualised, read with an eye to the nuances and resonances likely to have been available to a relatively aware contemporary observer or reader, such sources can greatly enhance and enlarge our sense of what was sayable and thinkable in early modern England.[55]

But what, we might ask, constitutes a legitimate, historically defensible, or meaningful context? Using Jonson's Catholicism, I have suggested that we can legitimately read *Sejanus* against a pre-existing tradition or mode of Catholic loyalist political analysis and polemic. If we do, certain echoes and resonances appear and we can reconstruct an intertextual context within which we can not only legitimately situate and read Jonson's text but within which we can plausibly posit that at least some of his contemporaries read and glossed it too.

But contexts are not only made up of texts, of traditions of thought and argument, they are also comprised of events; particular political and polemical conjunctures which can and did radically alter, if not in some ultimate sense what a given text might 'mean', then certainly how it might be read and received by contemporaries. In 1603, by painting so starkly hostile and dark a portrait of what had been, Jonson was surely trying to flatter and to shape what was to come. Certainly, if there is anything at all to the 'Catholic' analysis of what Jonson was doing in *Sejanus* conducted here, it gives us a precious glimpse not only of how the accession of James looked to certain Catholics, but also of what sorts of (lightly coded) messages and stances those same Catholics felt able, under the changed circumstances of James accession, to send to both prince and people through the very public media of the stage and cheap print. And that, in turn, has much to tell us about the hopes and fears stirred up by such public pitch-making among a range of Protestant and puritan observers, many of whom had themselves attached their own agendas for reform and hopes of preferment to the new regime. In short, we can start to recapture the alarms and excursions, the excitements and anxieties, the outbreaks of public case-making and posing, that made the accession of James I a good deal more uncertain, exhilarating, and frightening an event for contemporaries than it has tended to seem in the writings of modern historians.

Finally, I would want to argue that the preceding analysis shows the value of taking Catholicism seriously as a political, ideological, and cultural force in post-Reformation England. By reintegrating a variety of different Catholic perspectives, texts and voices into our account, the whole period can be made to look different: relatively familiar texts and events can be made to appear unfamiliar; established chronologies can be disrupted; the seemingly stable can be rendered unstable, the peripheral central and the central peripheral;

the 'conservative' 'radical' and the 'radical' 'conservative'. In particular, both the promise and threat felt by contemporaries at the prospect of turning points and transitions (like the accession of James I), the outcomes of which are only too familiar to historians, can be recaptured and placed somewhere near the centre of our accounts. To put it crudely: throughout the period after the Reformation, Catholics played the game of politics and fairly consistently lost, so viewing things from their perspective inserts an automatic and salutary counterfactual element into our analysis and provides an almost instant corrective against the sorts of teleological whiggery to which hindsight renders all historians susceptible.

Through a Catholic contextualisation of *Sejanus* we can, I think, work the 'Catholic effect' on that *mélange* of texts, attitudes and phrases that has come to be known in recent scholarship as 'republicanism'. I am not arguing that the origins of the radically disillusioned, Tacitean vision of politics to be found in *Sejanus* was somehow 'Catholic' rather than 'Protestant', 'religious' rather than 'neo-Roman' in its origins or nature. After all, many of the men at the centre of the circles which produced the Catholic texts under discussion here were – like Henry Howard – soaked in stoic, Tacitean, and Machiavellian texts and apothegms. However, the radical alienation from the workings of the regime experienced by certain Protestant (and Catholic) followers of the Earl of Essex and others during the 1590s had been experienced first by a series of Catholic would-be insiders and wannabe courtiers; men who, having been discourted by the machinations of a (as they saw it) corrupt, low-born, and self-selecting Protestant elite, produced an analysis or account of the political and moral corruption of the regime, an analysis that then became available to both Protestant and Catholic observers and victims of the Elizabethan political scene. Viewed from the inside looking out, the narrow clique of Protestants and politiques running the Elizabethan state no doubt looked and felt like a monarchical republic: a group of virtuous, learned, and godly men united in the service and defence of the commonwealth and true religion against the machinations and conspiracies of a corrupt, antichristian, popish other. Viewed from the outside looking in, however, that same republic of virtue and true religion looked rather more like a corrupt and corrupting conspiracy of self-serving and low-born evil counsellors and heretics on the make. Both sides to the resulting polemical exchanges were, of course, deploying the same classical, 'republican' materials to make their view of the situation stick.

With its entirely classical setting and pointed references to the political events and tensions of the later 1590s, Jonson's play might be taken to have provided a sort of bridge[56] across which a vision of the Elizabethan regime, previously held largely (and certainly most intensely) by Catholics, could make its way into the political mainstream. In *Sejanus* we can see those earlier (Catholic) experiences and insights coming together, in the disturbed and disturbing political and moral atmosphere of the 1590s, with other more modishly Tacitean and Stoic strands of thought and feeling,[57] to create a confessionally neutral version of what had hitherto been a recognisably 'Catholic' way of looking at and describing the Elizabethan political scene: a version or critique that now might well appeal to far wider bodies of opinion as, in fear and expectation, anxiety and hope, both Protestants and Catholics eyed the prospect of a new reign and of a new, distinctively Stuart, religio-political dispensation.

In its sources, central attitudes, and values, Jonson's text must surely qualify as solidly 'republican' as that term has come of late to be used. And yet it is perhaps worth remembering that Jonson's 'republican' critique of imperial and Elizabethan corruption and tyranny was attached to, indeed underpinned by, an entirely absolutist account of political power, its nature, origins, and exercise. Indeed, one might argue that for Jonson, here following earlier Catholic writers, the high point of Collinson's 'monarchical republicanism' had not marked an equally high point of liberty, political virtue, and good government, but rather a low point of faction and corruption, of evil counsel, tyranny, and persecution, a dark age of bad government from which (miraculously) the advent of the straightforwardly monarchical, indeed self-consciously absolutist, rule of the first Stuart was about to rescue not only England but also loyalist English Catholics. Jonson's play thus mobilises what was, in the terms set out in recent scholarship, a recognisably 'republican' mode of political and moral discourse and analysis, in order to produce a critique of an Elizabethan experiment in 'monarchical republicanism' which had produced only tyranny and persecution. It then harnesses that same 'republican' critique of Elizabethan 'republicanism' gone wrong to a quintessentially Jacobean absolutist account of monarchical rule and a Catholic loyalist pitch for royal succour and support under the rule of Mary Stuart's son. Jonson's text provides us, therefore, with a strikingly absolutist and Catholic version of the 'civic republican tradition'. It is, perhaps, a rather odd place to find some of the first stirrings of 'liberty before liberalism'.

NOTES

The first version of this paper was a lecture given in a course at Princeton on literature, politics, and religion, that I taught in collaboration with Nigel Smith. It forms part of a continuing investigation, in collaboration with Michael Questier, into Catholic modes of political analysis and critique in the period after 1560. Versions have been given to scholarly audiences in London, Chicago, Keele, and at conferences on myths of Elizabeth and the accession of James I at St Mary's College Twickenham and the University of Hull respectively. I should like to thanks the members all those audiences and in particular Julie Sanders, James Knowles, Roger Pooley, Tom McCoog, and Blair Worden for their kindness and tolerance towards a neophyte in matters Jonsonian and Catholic, not to mention some extremely useful comments, criticisms and suggestions.

1 Patrick Collinson, 'The Monarchical Republic of Queen Elizabeth I' and 'Puritans, Men of Business and Elizabethan Parliaments', both in his *Elizabethan Essays* (London, 1994); Patrick Collinson, 'The Elizabethan Exclusion Crisis and the Elizabethan Polity', *Proceedings of the British Academy*, 84 (1994); M. Peltonen, *Classical Humanism and Republicanism in English Political Thought, 1570-1640* (Cambridge, 1995); M. Peltonen, 'Citizenship and Republicanism in Elizabethan England', in M. van Gelderen and Q. Skinner (eds), *Republicanism: A Shared European Heritage* 2 vols (Cambridge, 2002), vol. 1; Stephen Alford, *The Early Elizabethan Polity: William Cecil and the British Succession Crisis, 1558–1569* (Cambridge, 1998). For a gendered reading of this nexus of themes and concerns, centred on contemporary anxieties about female rule, see A. McLaren, *Political Culture in the Reign of Elizabeth I: Queen and Commonwealth, 1558–1585* (Cambridge, 1999).

2 Alford, *Early Elizabethan polity*, p. 116.

3 Collinson, 'Elizabethan Exclusion Crisis', p. 82.

4 M. Smuts, 'Court-Centred Politics and the Uses of Roman Historians, c.1590–1630', and Blair Worden, 'Ben Jonson among the Historians', both in K. Sharpe and P. Lake (eds), *Culture and Politics in Early Stuart England* (London, 1994).

5 I use and cite the Revels edition by Philip Ayers of *Sejanus His Fall* (Manchester, 1990).

6 M. Wikander, '"Queasy to be touched": The World of Ben Jonson's *Sejanus*', *Journal of English and Germanic Philology*, 79 (1980); Richard Dutton, 'The Sources, Text and Readers of *Sejanus*: Jonson's Integrity of the Story', *Studies in Philology*, 75 (1978); Worden, 'Ben Jonson among the Historians'; Blair Worden, 'Ben Jonson and Monarchy', Glenn Burgess, 'The "Historical Turn" and the Political Culture of Early Modern England: Towards a Postmodern History?', and R. Wymer, 'Jacobean Pageant or Elizabethan Fin de Siecle? The Political Context of Early Seventeenth Century Tragedy', all in Robin Headlam Wells, Glenn Burgess, and Rowland Wymer (eds), *Neo-Historicism: Studies in Renaissance Literature, History and Politics* (Cambridge, 2000).

7 *Sejanus his Fall*, To the readers, p. 51, ll. 25–6.

8 Cyndia Clegg, *Press Censorship in Elizabethan England* (Cambridge, 1997), ch. 9.

9 B. N. De Luna, *Jonson's Romish Plot* (Oxford, 1967).

10 For the compelling argument that the mode of statecraft at stake here was genuinely Machiavellian, i.e. directly and consistently based upon the works and insights of Machiavelli, see Daniel C. Boughner, *The Devil's Disciple* (New York, 1968), esp. ch. 7.

11 D. Riggs, *Ben Jonson, a Life* (Cambridge, Mass., 1989) pp. 51–2; Ian Donaldson, *Jonson's Magic Houses: Essays in Interpretation* (Oxford, 1997), ch. 4.

12 See, for instance, the typically suggestive remarks of Blair Worden, in his 'Ben Jonson and monarchy', pp. 76, 81–3.

13 *A Treatise of Treasons* (Louvain, 1572); *Leicester's Commonwealth: The Copy of a Letter Written by a Master of Art of Cambridge (1584)*, ed. D. C. Peck (Athens, Ohio, 1985); Robert Parsons, *Elizabethae Angliae reginae haeresim Calvinianum propugnatis* (Antwerp, 1592); R. Verstegan, *A Declaration of the True Causes of the Great Troubles, Presupposed to Be Intended against the Realm of England* (Antwerp, 1592); *An Advertisement Written to M. L. Treasurer of England* (1592); also see *The Copy of a Letter Lately Written by a Spanish Gentleman* (1589) and *News from Spain and Holland* (1592). This last is a trailer for Parsons', next great tract, *A Conference about the Next Succession* of 1594/5. On this last

group of tracts see V. Houliston, 'The Lord Treasurer and the Jesuit: Robert Persons's Satirical Responsio to the 1591 Proclamation', *Sixteenth Century Journal*, 32 (2001), 383–401. For a preliminary analysis of this strand of Catholic writing see my essay '"The Monarchical Republic of Elizabeth I" Revisited (by Its Victims) as a Conspiracy', to be published in a book of essays on conspiracy and conspiracy theory in early modern Europe edited by Barry Coward and Julian Swan, forthcoming from Ashgate. I hope to deal with this tradition of thought more extensively in a monograph, provisionally entitled *Bad Queen Bess*.

14 *Treatise of Treasons*, pp. 139, 97a; Preface to the English reader, sigs. A5r–v, E6r.

15 Ibid., pp. 96, 104a, 28a–9; for more on Scotland, France and Spain see pp. 160–2.

16 Ibid., Preface to the English reader, sigs. I3v, I5r; pp. 31, 93a–4, 149a, 29a, 31, 96–7, 106.

17 Ibid., Preface to the English reader, sigs. A8r, I4r; pp. 84–5, 134.

18 Ibid., pp. 106a–109a; Preface to the English reader, sigs. I4r, A3v.

19 See, for instance, Thomas Norton, *A Warning against the Dangerous Practises of Papists*, sigs. G3r–4v, in *All Such Treatises as Have Been Lately Published by Thomas Norton* (London, 1569).

20 *Leicester's Commonwealth*, p. 93.

21 *Treatise of Treasons*, pp. 44, 52a–3, 123.

22 *Leicester's Commonwealth*, p. 96.

23 Ibid., p. 99.

24 Ibid., pp. 172–3.

25 Ibid., p. 73.

26 Ibid., p. 72.

27 Ibid., pp. 132, 193.

28 Ibid., p. 186.

29 Ibid., pp. 179, 131.

30 Ibid., p. 141.

31 Ibid., pp. 137, 73, 177.

32 Ibid., p. 88.

33 Ibid., p. 116.

34 Simon Adams, 'Favourites and Factions at the Elizabethan Court', in his *Leicester and the Court* (Manchester, 2002).

35 This one involved the death of Leicester through a dose of poison intended for his wife, see C. H. Herford and Percy Simpson (eds), *Ben Jonson*, 11 vols (Oxford, 1925–52), I: 142.

36 Burgess, 'The "Historical Turn"', pp. 38–47.

37 *B. Jonson His Part of King James His Royal and Magnificent Entertainment through His Honourable City of London* (London, 1604).

38 Robert C. Evans, 'Sejanus: Ethics and Politics in the Early Reign of James I', in J. Sanders et al. (eds), *Refashioning Ben Jonson: Gender, Politics and the Jonsonian Canon* (Basingstoke, 1998), esp. pp. 76–82; Worden, 'Ben Jonson among the Historians', esp. p. 84.

39 Herford and Simpson (eds), *Ben Jonson*, 7: 102–3.

40 Ibid., 7: 108

41 Ibid., 7: 113.

42 Ibid., 7: 115–16.

43 Ibid., 7: 116.

44 Ibid., 7: 117.

45 Ibid., 7: 104.

46 Ibid., 7: 94.

47 Ibid., 7: 98–9. On this see Evans, 'Ethics and Politics', pp. 77–8.

48 For Catholic petitions to the king at the outset of the reign see P. Milward, *Religious Controversies of the Jacobean Age* (London, 1978), pp. 72–6.

49 Robert Parsons, *A Conference about the Next Succession* (1595).

50 For other suggestions of echoes of James' works – in this instance *Basilicon Doron* – in *Sejanus* see Worden, 'Ben Jonson and Monarchy', p. 78, and Evans, 'Ethics and Politics', esp. pp. 82–5.

51 T. A. Stroud, 'Father Thomas Wright: A Test Case for Toleration', *Biographical Studies*, 1 (1951–2), and 'Ben Jonson and Father Thomas Wright', *English Literary History*, 14 (1947). Also see Donaldson, *Jonson's Magic Houses*, ch. 4. Wright's text arguing that English Catholics could legitimately come to the aid of the regime against Spanish invasion is reprinted in J. Strype, *Annals of the Reformation*, 4 vols in 7 (Oxford, 1824), 3: pt. 2, 583–97. I owe these points and references to the kindness of Thomas McCoog and James Knowles.

52 R. Bushnell, *Tragedies of Tyrants* (Ithaca, NY, 1990), p. 1; R. Dutton, *Ben Jonson* (Cambridge, 1983), p. 54.

53 Herford and Simpson (eds), *Ben Jonson*, 1: 141.

54 For Northampton's career in general see L. L. Peck, *Northampton: Patronage and Policy at the Court of James I* (London, 1982); for his intellectual interests see L. L. Peck, 'The Mentality of a Jacobean Grandee', in L. L. Peck (ed.), *The Mental World of the Jacobean Court* (Cambridge, 1991).

55 As Blair Worden has observed, 'If we want to recover the values and ideals by which, in their public lives, men of the English Renaissance lived, there is no surer or richer source than its imaginative literature': Blair Worden, 'Mingling Freely at the Mermaid', *London Review of Books*, 25, no. 21 (6 November 2003), at p. 25.

56 There were, of course, many such, not the least important of which was the circle around Essex containing loyalist Catholics, whose vision of the regime as a (Cecilian) conspiracy of evil counsel, determined to exclude Essex from royal favour, do a deal with Spain, and ditch James VI for the Infanta, the earl himself had come to share by the end of his career. See Helen Stafford, *James VI of Scotland and the Throne of England* (New York, 1940), ch. 7.

57 For an account of the parallels between the political attitudes to be found in *Sejanus* and the political thought of Lipsius, whose edition of Tacitus Jonson used when writing the play, see Evans, 'Ethics and Politics', esp. pp. 86–8. For a discussion of Jonson's debt to Lipsius's edition of Tacitus see Daniel C. Boughner, 'Jonson's Use of Lipsius in *Sejanus*', *Modern Language Notes*, 73 (1958).

Chapter 7

Papalist political thought and the controversy over the Jacobean oath of allegiance

Johann P. Sommerville

In 1918, C. H. McIlwain published an edition of the political works of James I. It was accompanied by a long introduction, in which he set the king's views in their ideological context. A great deal of what McIlwain had to say concerned the debate over the oath of allegiance, enacted in 1606. He stressed the importance of this controversy not just for understanding James, but also, and far more significantly, for British and indeed European history as a whole. 'In the history of western political thought', he declared, 'no more critical time can be found than the opening years of the seventeenth century and at no time in her whole history was England so prominent in that world of thought as in the early part of the reign of James I'. The Jacobean oath of allegiance, he proceeded, gave 'rise to a paper warfare in Europe the like of which has never been seen since and is hardly likely to be seen again'. The dispute, he asserted, 'was a carefully planned campaign for the conquest of intellectual Europe'. The main issue which divided the two sides in the contest was whether people ultimately owed allegiance to the secular governments of their countries, or, at least in some circumstances, to an international institution separate from individual states, namely the Roman Catholic Church, and its leader the pope. Manifestly, this is of the highest relevance to the problem of state formation in early modern Europe, and to the linked issue of modernisation. Arguably, it was in the course of the controversy over the Jacobean oath of allegiance that modern ideas about the relationship between the state and the individual triumphed.[1]

Though it is now over eighty years old, McIlwain's introduction remains the fullest account in print of the debate on the oath of allegiance. Some dissertations on the topic have been written, but not published.[2] Again, discussions of other subjects sometimes touch on the oath in important ways.[3] This applies to works on literature as well as history. Donna Hamilton has argued that the oath controversy is highly relevant to understanding a number of Shakespeare's later plays,[4] and writings on John Donne frequently say something about the debate – not surprisingly, since Donne himself contributed to it. Yet no systematic attempt has been made to update McIlwain's account in print. And for reasons of space, no such attempt will be made here. The goal of the present chapter is the rather more modest one of describing and analysing just one side in the dispute – the Catholic case, or rather, one particular Catholic case, for there were several Catholic approaches to the problems raised by the oath. The first section below gives a brief account of how the oath came to be formulated and enacted, and how dispute about it arose. It also draws attention to a number of diverging modern interpretations of the oath and the debate which it provoked between apologists for the Jacobean regime and their Catholic opponents. The second discusses what might be called the official Catholic line on the oath – that is to say, the line approved at the time by Catholic authorities, including the pope. The third offers some reflections on the controversy, and on modern views of it.

THE OATH AND THE CONTROVERSY

On 27 May 1606, the House of Commons passed two bills against recusants, the Lords did likewise, and the King pronounced his assent to them. Along with the rest of the laws made in this parliamentary session, the two acts appeared in print on 25 June. One of the two was an act 'for the better discovering and repressing of Popish Recusants'. It included a clause allowing a bishop, or two justices of the peace, to tender a new oath to recusants – people who refused to attend the services of the established church. The oath rejected the pope's claims to a power to depose temporal rulers from their thrones. In addition to convicted recusants, anyone who had not taken the sacrament of the Lord's Supper in the established church at least twice during the previous year, and travellers who refused to swear that they were not recusants, could also find themselves faced with the oath. Moreover, the act provided that people who went abroad to serve a foreign government would be deemed felons if they did not first take the oath. The penalty for refusing to swear was imprisonment until the next assizes or quarter sessions, when the oath would be tendered again. A second refusal resulted in the penalties of praemunire – loss of goods, and imprisonment at the king's pleasure.[5]

Roman Catholics were by far the most common kind of recusant in Jacobean England, and it was against them that the oath was directed. The main reason why parliament introduced new legislation against Catholics in 1606 was the discovery of the Gunpowder Plot in November of the previous year. A small group of Catholics had plotted to blow up parliament and to restore Catholicism by force. It turned out that Henry Garnet, the superior of the Jesuits in England, had been aware of the conspiracy, and it was widely believed that he, and perhaps other highly placed Catholics, had authorised it. The Gunpowder Plot was regarded as the latest in a series of Catholic attempts to overthrow the established government and religion, a series extending back at least to 1570. In that year, Pope Pius V issued the bull *Regnans in excelsis*, deposing Elizabeth I from the English throne. The bull licensed Catholics to remove the Queen by violent means, and a number of them made the effort, with uniformly negative results. In the eyes of many Protestants, it was divine providence which was responsible for these deliverances. But, though they trusted that God would defend them against their foes, they also believed that it made sense to take more mundane precautions against Catholics. Elizabeth's parliaments passed laws fining lay recusants, and condemning Catholic priests as traitors. Some Protestants believed that Catholicism was a totally corrupt, idolatrous, and antichristian religion, and that all Catholics ought to be extirpated. But others held that it was possible to distinguish between different varieties of Catholic, and that the harshest treatment should be reserved for those whose religion led them into disloyalty to the state. The Gunpowder Plot convinced many that still more severe legislation was needed to check Catholic plotting: hence the introduction of the oath.

In the last years of Elizabeth's reign, a major split developed among Catholic priests serving on the mission to England. Some resented the influence of the Jesuits, and appealed to the pope to establish a bishop with authority over the mission. These Appellants were opposed by the Jesuits and their supporters, who successfully advocated the establishment not of a bishop but of a less powerful archpriest. The English government attempted to capitalize on the dispute by encouraging the Appellants in their attacks on the Jesuits, and some Appellants came to hope that they might gain toleration for Catholics if they distanced themselves sufficiently from ideas of violent resistance. In January 1603 thirteen priests signed a Protestation, acknowledging that the Queen had 'as full authority, power and sovereignty over us, and over all the subjects of the realm, as any her highness's predecessors ever had'. They also condemned violent attempts to restore Catholicism, and declared that they would defend 'our prince, and country' regardless of whether the pope excommunicated the Queen or her subjects.[6] The Protestation was not an oath and, though it stressed that the pope could not justly depose Elizabeth in current circumstances, it did not altogether deny papal claims to the deposing power, which is precisely what the oath of allegiance did. Yet some contemporaries believed that the oath was based on the Protestation. The leading Jesuit Robert Parsons (or Persons) told Cardinal Bellarmine that the oath was derived from the doctrine of the Appellants, which he loathed.[7] More convincingly, the important Catholic *defender* of the oath Thomas Preston claimed that the 'Protestation of the thirteene Catholike Priests ... was the ground and foundation from whence the Parliament ... framed the forme of this new Oath of Allegiance', and cited the authority of Richard Bancroft for this assertion.[8] Bancroft, the Archbishop of Canterbury, was probably involved in formulating the details of the oath, and he may have been assisted in this by Sir Christopher Perkins, a former Jesuit who became a civil lawyer.

R. G. Usher suggested that the oath had already been largely drawn up before the Gunpowder Plot, and that it was part of an ongoing campaign by Bancroft to divide the Jesuits from their opponents among the Catholic priests. He argued that it was prepared by Bancroft after consultation with the leading secular priests (that is to say, priests who were not in any special order or society).[9] The evidence for this is unconvincing, for the Appellants and the Jesuits had patched up their quarrel in May 1603, and secular priests in fact petitioned the King, Parliament, and the Earl of Salisbury against the oath.[10] Many of the seculars had not approved the Protestation, and of the thirteen who had signed it only two took the oath, while another two suffered a traitor's death rather than swear it. The oath may have been based on the Protestation in the broad sense that it was an assertion of loyalty to the Crown and a condemnation of violent policies for restoring the faith. But, as we have seen, it went much further than the earlier document in utterly rejecting the papal deposing power. Furthermore, the swearer of the oath was required to abjure 'as impious and hereticall' the 'damnable doctrine' that 'Princes which be Excommunicated or deprived by the Pope, may be deposed or murthered by their Subjects, or any other whatsoever'.[11] As we shall see, some modern historians have vastly exaggerated the importance of this clause. They insist that if it had been dropped the majority of English Catholics would have had no compunction about taking the oath. This is incorrect, but the clause certainly did go far beyond anything in the Protestation.

Though the oath was a more uncompromising condemnation of papal claims than the Protestation, it was nevertheless a more moderate document than some Members of Parliament had at first proposed. Catholics commonly claimed that anyone baptised as a Christian was subject to papal jurisdiction. The oath did not reject this idea, and Catholics who defended the measure adopted the view that popes had power over secular rulers in *spiritual* matters, though not in temporal ones. There is evidence that some Members of Parliament initially contemplated an oath which would have rejected not just the pope's authority to depose monarchs, but also his power to use spiritual sanctions against them, and in particular the sanction of excommunication. James I himself claimed that the Commons had initially included in the oath a clause asserting that 'the Pope had no power to excommunicate, which I forced them to reform'. It has been suggested that 'the king and parliament ... held starkly different views of what the Oath was meant to achieve', with the king intending it 'to marginalize the more extreme Jesuits', while 'Parliament' wanted to use it as 'another weapon in the drive to flush out recusancy'. But there is no evidence that the King and the House of Lords disagreed on the oath, and the Commons put up no perceptible resistance when James asked them to drop the clause on excommunication. Jacobean Houses of Commons were quite capable of making their disagreements with the King known, but on this occasion they did not do so, and we have only the King's testimony for his victory over them on the oath. Moreover it is difficult to see how an oath intended to be taken by recusants could flush out recusants. If flushing out secret Catholics was its purpose, then it would surely have made sense to tender it to apparent non-Catholics, not to known recusants.[12] The idea that the King pursued a long-term policy of tolerating loyal Catholics, and that the oath was part of this policy, is also questionable, since he and his chief advisers frequently denounced toleration.[13] They stressed the King's clemency in not taking severe action against all Catholics, implying that he could do so if he chose. The King's treatment of recusants varied in accordance with his wider domestic and, especially, foreign policies. The oath resulted from the Gunpowder Plot and was intended to target those who, like the plotters, believed that heretical rulers could (at least in certain circumstances) be deposed or killed by their subjects. The policy of treating such people more severely than other Catholics was a continuation of Elizabethan precedent, and did not at all imply that papists who took the oath would win full toleration. Nor does it seem likely that the oath was intended 'to marginalize the more extreme Jesuits' since it seems certain that people of the theological acumen of Bancroft and even James I were well aware that a great many Catholics, and not just a few extreme Jesuits, would find the oath unpalatable. And so it proved.

The Catholic establishment did not welcome the new English oath. Pope Paul V set up a commission of theologians, including the highly influential controversialist Cardinal Bellarmine, to report on the oath, and when they pronounced it unlawful, he issued a breve against it in September 1606.[14] Safe in Rome, he could do so with impunity. Things were not so easy for Catholic priests and layfolk in England. There, the penalties of praemunire awaited refusers of the oath. Not surprisingly, some Catholics devised ways of interpreting it which permitted them to take it while adhering to the very principles which it was intended to condemn. The leader of the secular priests, Archpriest George Blackwell, initially condemned the oath as unlawful, but soon changed his mind, arguing that, although the pope did indeed have the power to depose secular sovereigns, he could exercise it only if doing so would benefit the Church; in current circumstances, it would harm the Church if the pope deposed James I, and so it was lawful to swear an oath saying that he could not do so. Some priests endorsed Blackwell's position, and a number of Catholics acted on it by taking the oath. When he heard about the papal breve, Blackwell changed his mind on the oath, and condemned it. Then the English

Protestant authorities captured him, and he changed his mind back again. He was persuaded to take the oath of allegiance, and to write to Catholics telling them to do so as well. The royal printer published this letter along with a detailed account of his interrogation, in which Blackwell repeated the gist of his earlier arguments for taking the oath.[15] In response, the pope issued another breve against it on 13 August 1607, and on 18 September Bellarmine himself denounced it in a letter to Blackwell.[16] By November, James I was at work on a response to Bellarmine's letter, and in February 1608 the king's printer published *Triplici nodo, triplex cuneus, or an Apologie for the Oath of Allegiance*, in which His Majesty defended the oath against Bellarmine and the papal breves. Thus began the controversy. In the next few years, scores of books and pamphlets debated the oath. Lancelot Andrewes, John Donne, and others took the King's side, while the pope's supporters included Bellarmine, the great Spanish philosopher and theologian Francisco Suárez, and English priests such as the Jesuit Robert Parsons (or Persons) and the secular Matthew Kellison, president of the college at Douai. All these Catholics shared the same broad political outlook, which is surveyed below.

PAPALIST POLITICAL THOUGHT

Bellarmine, Suárez, and their followers adopted a set of political views that were derived from the thinking of Aquinas and other medieval scholastics, which was itself a Christianised version of Aristotelianism. They held that God had designed human nature, and given people certain goals. The ultimate goal was spiritual union with God, but in order to achieve this there were some subordinate goals that had first to be attained. The simplest of these was survival. Humans would not reach their religious objectives if their race died out. For human survival to occur, people had to procreate, and parents also had to look after their children, at least until they were old enough to look after themselves. In other words, the preservation of the species requires that people live in families. Thomists like Bellarmine, Suárez, and the rest argued that God had created human nature in such a way that family life was necessary for us. Nature, they said, does nothing in vain. So the family must possess the power which it needs in order to attain its objectives. They argued that by nature males are superior to females, and that parents are authorised to govern their young offspring, concluding that power over the wife and children within the family ought naturally to belong to the husband and father. Aristotle distinguished between families and political communities, and the Thomists did likewise. They claimed that the family provides for human survival but that our nature is geared not just to the preservation of the species but also to a greater degree of material welfare. Without a considerable measure of temporal prosperity, people would be severely handicapped in the pursuit of their ultimate spiritual objectives. In order to attain temporal welfare, they needed an institution larger and more complex than the family – namely the 'perfect community' (*communitas perfecta*), or commonwealth, or state. Within the family, the father was naturally authorised to command, but within the first states there had been no one with any natural claim to superiority over the rest. In his *The Right and Iurisdiction of the Prelate, and the Prince*, the secular priest Matthew Kellison summed up the conventional Catholic wisdom when he affirmed that 'in respect of imperfect societies, to wit, families, the good man of the house, by the law of Nature is superiour ... but when families increasing, men met together in Cities and commonwealthes, then none in particular had authoritie to governe that new communitie, and so the power was resident in the communitie'.[17]

This notion of the original sovereignty of the people was widely accepted by Catholics, though it was interpreted in slightly different ways. According to Suárez, the initial form of government was direct democracy. He held that this was not usually a very convenient way of ruling, and recommended that the originally sovereign people grant authority to one or a few people, thus instituting aristocracy or monarchy.[18] Kellison likewise claimed that the first commonwealths had been empowered either to govern themselves or to make over their authority to one or a few magistrates: 'as the Communitie ... hath power to governe itself; so hath it power to choose that government which it liketh best'.[19] Edward Weston, another secular priest who wrote against the oath, took the same line.[20] On the other hand, Bellarmine argued rather differently, asserting that the first community did not have sovereign power to govern itself, but merely the power to institute a government.[21] The influential Spanish Jesuit Luis de Molina had adopted a similar position.[22] Marc'Antonio De Dominis – a Catholic Archbishop who came to England and wrote against Suárez and Bellarmine – noted the difference of opinion among papalists on this point, but few other people paid much attention to it, and it is probably of little significance. It is true that after the French Revolution a number of Catholic theorists tried to distance themselves from the theory of Suárez, which seemed to them alarmingly democratic. Not all did so. Around 1920 the question of whether Catholic tradition favoured popular sovereignty and rights of resistance to an unpopular government, or acquiescence in the status quo, became highly topical in Ireland. Alfred O'Rahilly vigorously asserted 'that popular sovereignty is the traditional political theory of Catholic philosophy' and declared that 'Bellarmine stands practically alone in maintaining that the people are bound by the law of nature to transfer their power'.[23] On the other hand, John Fitzpatrick declared that 'the Suaresian theory' was not 'the official teaching of the church', suggesting that such democratic notions were 'a help to the enemy' rather than 'a defence against him' – the enemy in this case being the proponent of 'ultra-liberal ideas'.[24] Similarly, Gabriel Bowe looked to Bellarmine rather than Suárez as the true representative of Catholic orthodoxy.[25] Arguably, however, the difference between the theories of the two theologians was not great. Both agreed that kings originally derived their powers from the commonwealth. The implication was that in certain circumstances the commonwealth can discipline its ruler. James I took Bellarmine to task on this very point, claiming that the Cardinal had said that the people 'doe but so transferre their power in the Kings person, as they doe notwithstanding retaine their habituall power in their owne hands, which upon certaine occasions they may actually take to themselves again'. Bellarmine quite rightly responded that he had here been quoting another Catholic theologian. But there is little reason to suppose that he dissented from the words he quoted, and Suárez specifically endorsed them.[26]

While James I and his supporters maintained that royal authority comes from God alone, all or almost all of the Catholic writers against the oath argued that it is derived from the people. The Jesuit John Floyd rejected the idea that royal power comes from God alone as 'a paradox which scarce any Christian Devine houldes', and insisted that it was 'the consent of the commonwealth' which made kings. Even a conqueror had no royal rights over a conquered people 'till they consent'. Once they had consented, he became their monarch, with power to govern them 'according to the lawes and conditions agreed upon: which conditions if he neglect, he is no lesse subiect and corrigible by the Commonwealth, then Kings made by election'.[27] Weston held that in order to find how much authority a particular king had, it was necessary 'to return in our minds to the origin of his power, that is to the will of the commonwealth, and frequently this has been set down in some written law'.[28] Royal authority, he held, is derived from the original contract between the commonwealth and the king. This 'first contract' retained 'a kind of moral permanence', and the initial king's descendants remained bound by the conditions on which he had been granted the crown.[29] Kellison noted that the power of kings varied from country to country, asserting that in France and England royal authority was limited, for legislation there required the consent of 'the Parlament of states'. He thought it was most unlikely that monarchs themselves had introduced such limitations, and concluded that they had been brought in by the people when it first gave power to a ruler: 'as the people gave the king his authoritie; so it was the people that thus limited and restrained him for their owne preservation: for to the same Authoritie that giveth power, it pertaineth to restraine it'.[30] Weston and Suárez said much the same thing.[31]

Papalists insisted that once the community has granted authority to a king, it cannot recover it on a whim, or whenever it likes. As Parsons put it, all 'learned Catholiks' agreed 'that a King when he is made by the people, cannot be deposed by them againe at their pleasure'. But he added – very significantly – 'so long as he conteyneth himselfe within the nature of a King'.[32] Things would be very different if the king unkinged himself by acting as a tyrant. After the assassination of Henry IV of France by a Catholic fanatic in 1610, papalists tried to distance themselves from such crude statements on tyrannicide as that of the Jesuit Juan de Mariana, whose *De rege* was condemned by the Sorbonne and the Parlement of Paris.[33] But although they sometimes toned down their views, many Catholic writers continued to argue that there were circumstances in which the people could resist and depose their kings. If the king turned into 'an intollerable Tyrant', said Kellison, the commonwealth was authorised to depose him, 'for then the common opinion holdeth, that the Authoritie, which the people had in the beginning to create him, returneth againe by devolution to depose him'.[34] Floyd asserted that rulers ought not to be 'called to account nor punished, much lesse deposed for ordinary and personall offences, or for their deeds injurious only to few', but he permitted the commonwealth to remove tyrants whose activities caused wider public harm.[35] Even in this case, Floyd insisted that a Christian people ought to consult the pope before it took so drastic a step as deposing its king: 'Papists teach that a Christian Commonwealth may not proceed against their Christian Prince, though he be a tyrant, without the advise and consent of the supreme Pastor of their soules'.[36] It is unlikely that this piece of information did much to comfort James I, or to persuade him to drop the oath of allegiance.

The reason why Floyd claimed that commonwealths ought to consult the pope before deposing their rulers was that in his opinion – and that of other papalists – the pope had God-given power to provide for the spiritual welfare of Christians, and such power was superior to the mere temporal authority of kings and peoples. Any change in a country's affairs as major as the deposition of a king was likely to have repercussions in the spiritual and ecclesiastical realms, and therefore fell within the pope's competence. Catholics believed that the state – or 'perfect community' – enabled humans to fulfil their secular objectives, but that another institution was needed to lead them to eternal felicity. This was the Church. Using reason alone, pagans had been able to perceive the virtues of having a priesthood, but it was only with the coming of Christ that people had been able to obtain really accurate and reliable information about the church and its authority. Christ had established an ecclesiastical hierarchy under the leadership of St Peter and his successors, the popes. In the Middle Ages and early modern period, a number of Catholics asserted that Christ had given the pope not only spiritual but also temporal power, so that he was a kind of super-king with straightforward secular authority over other monarchs, or at least Christian monarchs.[37] But the papalists who wrote against the Jacobean oath adopted the rather milder doctrine that the pope's authority is not directly temporal. Rather, it is spiritual. However, the soul is superior to the body, and spiritual matters are more important than temporal ones. Where the spiritual good is at issue, then, the pope is authorised to intervene in temporal affairs, for instance by deposing a king. Kellison typically insisted that the pope could use temporal punishments to get erring Christians to do their duty, but added that this power 'is not Temporall but spirituall'.[38] Parsons declared that no Catholic could 'with safety of his Conscience' deny that the pope was empowered to depose kings 'in certeyne urgent cases ... for the universall good of Gods church'.[39] According to Weston, the pope 'cannot order or command princes in civil things to a civil end', but he can give temporal orders if the end is spiritual.[40] The Jesuit Anthony Hoskins contrasted the pope's unlimited power to depose bishops with his more limited authority to remove princes, which was restricted to cases where it was 'necessary for the health and salvation of souls'.[41] It was the pope who judged the necessity. Unlike kings, popes got their powers directly from God. Kings could intervene in the life of individual families if this was for the good of the commonwealth. Popes could interfere in the affairs of states if doing so promoted the interests of that higher community, the Church.

Papalists were usually insistent that kings may only be deposed by the public authority of the Church or commonwealth. Private individuals could not take it upon themselves to oust a ruler if he had not been publicly judged by the pope or the representative assembly of his subjects. When the Gunpowder Plot was discovered, Archpriest Blackwell moved rapidly to condemn it, writing a letter to the English Catholics denouncing it on 7 November. His main objection to it was that it had taken place on private, not public, authority: 'our divines do say that it is not lawful for private subjects, by private authority, to take arms against their lawful king, albeit he become a tyrant'.[42] As the Earl of Salisbury observed, the Archpriest 'bestowed many thundring words, against those which shall attempt against Princes by private authoritie, and yet reserveth thereby a tacite lawfulnesse thereof, in case it be directed by publicke warrant'.[43] Occasionally, papalists modified the principle that only a public decree can depose a king. In a book of 1592, Parsons claimed that the pope could depose heretical rulers but also argued that 'it is certain and an article of faith' that if the monarch's heresy is obvious, subjects could resist without even waiting for the pope to issue a formal sentence of deposition: 'if any Christian prince manifestly turns away from the Catholic faith and tries to take others with him, he at once loses all power and authority, by both human and divine law, and all subjects are freed from their oaths to him, even though the pope has pronounced no sentence against him'. Indeed, his subjects could use violence to remove him, and if they possessed sufficient forces they had a duty to take up arms against him.[44] At the trial of the Gunpowder Plotters, Sir Edward Coke quoted this passage at length and also drew on a work by the plotter Francis Tresham, which expressed similar views.[45] During the oath controversy, most papalists – including Parsons – were more circumspect. But Leonardus Coquaeus, the confessor to the Grand Duchess of Tuscany, asserted that there was no need to await a papal sentence of deposition if the faith was in imminent danger.[46]

Papalists based their claims about the deposibility of kings on a theory of Church-state relations which had been worked out in the course of the Middle Ages, and which was given its most complete and precise formulation in the writings of Bellarmine, Suárez, and their associates. These thinkers also drew on history, claiming that the papal deposing power had been widely recognised and frequently exercised in the past. One problem they encountered in discussing the early history of the church was that although there had been a number of persecutions and some unpleasant Roman emperors, the first popes had not deposed them. The usual papalist explanation of this phenomenon was that the Church at that time had lacked the force needed to carry out a deposition. As Floyd put it, 'there wanted at that time meanes to unite the whole Empire in the business of deposing hereticall Emperours', and 'the Empire was so mixed of heathens and Christians, that this power could not be conveniently exercised'.[47] Bellarmine claimed that early popes had not possessed the forces necessary to effect a deposition. Attempts at deposing wicked emperors would have failed, and would have backfired on the Church. In the ancient Roman period 'severity would have been profitless' against pagan emperors, so it had been sensible for popes 'to exercise patience rather than authority'.[48] In the opinion of another papalist, deposing the Roman emperors would have been 'over great impudency and folly ... not only unprofitable, but absolutely pernicious to the Christians ... For it is not sufficient to say, that the Church is bound to doe some thing, because she may lawfully do it, unless she also can doe it with prudence and profit.'[49] A version of this sort of principle underlay Blackwell's notion that it would damage the Church if the pope deposed James I, and that it was therefore possible to take an oath denying that he could do so. Most papalists rejected Blackwell's case on the grounds that the oath ruled out the deposing power completely, and not just in some particular circumstances.

THE OATH, THE PAPALISTS, AND MODERN
INTERPRETATIONS

The political theory of Jacobean papalists was not very far removed from the ideas of such Catholic monarchomachs as Mariana and Jean Boucher, who had advocated violent resistance to regimes which tolerated heresy. After Spain and England made peace in 1604, it became increasingly less likely that the Catholic faith would be restored in England by force. Catholics shifted to a policy of de-emphasising – though not rejecting – rights of resistance and the papal deposing power, in order to win concessions and perhaps even toleration. A venerable tradition in Catholic historiography plays down the importance of the theory of the deposing power for early modern papalists. According to Bellarmine's Jesuit biographer James Brodrick, the Cardinal's theory really had no place for the deposing power, but he 'mistakenly' thought he 'had an obligation' to defend it, since Pius V had deposed Elizabeth. Bellarmine, he informs us, 'rather ruined his theory of the indirect power by tacking on to it a direct power of deposition in cases of extreme emergency'.[50] According to J. C. Murray, the deposing power had indeed been 'claimed and exercised' by the church in the Middle Ages, but by James' reign medieval times had come to an end, and the oath of allegiance debate really manoeuvered Catholics 'into a false position' in 'defense of an outpost that in 1606 could well have been abandoned'.[51] According to Adrian Morey, 'the deposing power was not a formal part of Catholic religious belief but rather a subject of discussion and argument among theologians'.[52] In asking recusants to take the oath of allegiance, so the case goes, the Jacobean authorities were not really interested in testing the loyalty of Catholics, but instead aimed at mounting a religious persecution of them. In Brodrick's opinion, it was 'intended to suffocate Catholicism in England'.[53] According to Gordon Albion, the oath resulted from 'a misguided hatred of popery'.[54] A. F. Allison maintained that king and his advisors made the oath 'the principal instrument of its campaign to break Catholic resistance'.[55]

The latest and in many ways the most persuasive version of this sort of line was recently put forward by Michael Questier. He claims that the oath 'was no mere loyalty test', and argues that 'the government could hardly have thought that real political extremists would either reveal or jeopardize themselves by refusing the oath openly'. 'There was', he declares, 'quite enough casuistical theory around to permit virtually anyone to take any oath in any situation'. So, even if Catholics had in fact been disloyal to the Crown, they could easily have disguised this and taken the oath. The problem which the oath caused for Catholics did not, Questier affirms, arise from the fact that it was a test of loyalty, and that some of them held disloyal views. Rather, it was caused by 'the novel "impious and heretical" clause rejecting the "damnable doctrine" that excommunicated or deprived princes "may be deposed or murdered by their subjects"'. It was this single clause, he proceeds, and not the deposing power itself, which lay at the centre of Catholic objections to the oath. Indeed, the doctrine of the deposing power had never been more than 'a matter of legitimate debate among Catholics', and the notion that the Jacobean authorities intended to use the oath 'to find and eliminate those who thought the deposing power was *de fide*' is without foundation, for John Almond thought that the deposing power 'was not a matter of faith' and that 'Catholics could either accept it or reject it', and yet he refused the oath and underwent execution as a result. Questier concludes that the oath was not a test of civil allegiance, but an instrument of religious persecution. At the time, Catholics sometimes alleged that the oath of allegiance was really just a disguised version of the oath of supremacy, which struck at papal claims to spiritual power over the church by declaring that the monarch was its supreme governor in England. Protestant defenders of the oath, says Questier, 'were generally happy to affirm' that 'the oath of allegiance of 1606' was 'the ideological equivalent of the oath of supremacy'. In short, the oath of allegiance was designed by a bigoted but subtle government to try to force Catholics to acknowledge the King's supremacy over the church under the guise of requiring them to swear temporal allegiance.[56]

Like Questier, J. H. Pollen stressed the importance of the clause condemning the deposing power as heretical and damnable. To swear to this clause, he declared, 'was what no God-fearing adherent of the old Faith, who knew what he said and to whom he spoke, could conscientiously do'. Again, W. K. L. Webb asserted that 'the crucial objection' to the oath was the inclusion of this clause, and not its rejection of the deposing power, and Ann M. C. Foster claimed that it was this clause which made the oath 'unacceptable to the majority of English Catholics'.[57] Brodrick took a similar line, but added the observation that the clause in effect acknowledged that the King was empowered to define what was, and what was not, heresy. So the oath tacitly granted the King supremacy in religion, and therefore no Catholic could conscientiously take it. Arnold Pritchard likewise portrayed the clause as the oath's 'most objectionable feature', stating that it allowed 'a Protestant temporal ruler to define heresy'.[58] According to Brian Magee, 'many Catholics whose loyalty to the crown was a permanent factor in Stuart politics felt themselves unable to subscribe' to the oath because of this intentionally offensive clause. Although the oath 'was in the main unexceptionable', said David Mathew, this clause 'stuck in the gizzard' of Catholics.[59]

The arguments mounted by Questier and the rest are not supported by much evidence, as we shall see in what follows. It is, of course, easy to grasp why Catholic historians should attempt to demonstrate that their co-religionists in seventeenth-century England were loyalists who were persecuted for religious reasons. It made sense for Catholics in Jacobean England themselves to put forward such claims. They were much more likely to win sympathy if they said they were suffering for their religious beliefs than if they publicly declared that they thought the pope could deprive King James of his crown, and that if Catholics possessed sufficient forces they could then use violent means to carry out the pope's sentence. Some priests who refused the oath of allegiance suffered execution, and we might expect that as they went to their deaths they would have told the crowds about their purely religious grounds for not taking the oath, and said less about the deposing power. It would not be surprising if priests in scaffold speeches had laid emphasis on the 'impious and heretical' clause, even if they privately believed that what was really objectionable about the oath was simply its denial of the deposing power. More generally, it would be reasonable to expect that papalist writers who strongly endorsed the pope's authority to discipline erring rulers would nevertheless tone down their discussion of papal rights, and lay weight on the 'impious' clause - especially, perhaps, after the assassination of Henry IV in 1610, when the position of the Jesuits in France was under threat. As we saw, papalists did indeed make an effort to move away from the cruder ideas of the monarchomachs, though the Parlement of Paris none the less condemned works related to the oath controversy by both Bellarmine and Suárez.[60] But the writings of Catholics against the oath of allegiance place remarkably little emphasis indeed on the 'impious' clause. In fact, not a single surviving contribution to the Jacobean controversy over the oath places the clause at the centre of its arguments, and most give it scant attention.[61] Questier, whose knowledge of the archival sources on the oath is probably unrivalled, was able to find just a couple of priests who said anything much about the clause. One of these was the Gallican William Bishop, and Questier admits that his 'main reason' for refusing the oath was not the clause, but a desire to stay on the good side of Rome and thus strengthen his position in his quarrels with the Jesuits. This does very little to support the notion that the bulk of the English Catholic community would have been happy altogether to reject the papal deposing power, but that they could not bring themselves to take the 'impious' clause.[62]

There are also major difficulties with the idea that papalists had a relaxed attitude towards the deposing power, viewing it as merely one of a number of equally plausible doctrines. As we saw, Questier strongly rebuts the suggestion that the oath was intended 'to find and eliminate those who thought the deposing power was *de fide*', and he rightly observes that not all the priests who were executed after refusing to swear in fact deemed the papal powers *de fide*.[63] This does little to show that the Jacobean authorities concocted the oath as an instrument of religious persecution. Arguably, the King was interested in finding out whether Catholics held principles which were likely to result in him being murdered. He was less concerned with whether people believed that the principles in question were articles of the Catholic faith, or just probably true. You end up equally dead whether your killer acts on a probable or a *de fide* principle. In fact, many leading Catholics *did* hold that the doctrine of the deposing power was *de fide*. The doctrine was an integral part of the theory of church-state relations of Suárez, Bellarmine, and other intellectual leaders of the church. The notion that it was an optional extra which Bellarmine tacked on to his theory at the last moment in order to defend the actions of Pius V is without foundation. The committee of theologians which condemned the oath in 1606 included Bellarmine. Reporting opinion in Rome to Henry Garnet, Parsons asserted that there were many reasons why theologians there held that it was unacceptable, 'but all reduced to this that the

Popes authoritie in chastineing princes upon just cause is *de fide*.[64] William Bishop – the Gallican priest who did stress the 'impious' clause – at one time claimed that Bellarmine regarded the deposing power as only a 'most probable' opinion. The Catholic authorities forced Bishop to revise this, since the doctrine was certain and not just probable.[65] A book by Bellarmine and the German Adam Schulcken trenchantly declared that the doctrine was 'not an opinion but a certainty' and stated that to deny it was 'heretical, or at least erroneous and temerarious'.[66]

While J. H. Pollen claimed that Jacobean Catholics were God-fearing people who would not swear falsely, Michael Questier has more recently suggested that they might easily have found casuistical justifications for taking pretty well any oath, and therefore that the Jacobean government could not really have hoped that the oath of allegiance would reveal political extremists – since it knew they were likely to use such evasions. This somewhat Clintonian approach to the topic of oath-taking is problematic. Questier claims that there 'was enough casuistical theory around to permit virtually anyone to take virtually any oath in any situation'.[67] But if that is so, it is hard to perceive why Catholics did not employ such theory to take the oath of allegiance, while evading the apparent implications of the 'impious' clause. Yet Questier tells us that the oath, and that clause in particular, caused them great difficulties. Perhaps the argument is that only political extremists within the Catholic community resorted to casuistical evasions, while Catholics who were loyal to the Crown insisted on swearing without any deceptions. The evidence for this is weak. Catholics – including both moderates and extremists – held that it was always wrong to deny the Christian faith. No one was entitled to use equivocations if doing so involved dishonouring God by saying things contrary to true Christian doctrine. The Jesuit Henry Garnet wrote a book in defence of the occasional use of equivocation, by which Catholics said things that were not straightforwardly true in order to mislead the Protestant authorities. He insisted that any oath which was 'scandalous or manifestly contrary to Christian dewtye' could never be taken, even with equivocation. Parsons had written against James' succession and in favour of violent resistance to heretical governments. Though he moderated his public statements once James had become King of England, in 1608 he was still privately suggesting that the pope depose the King, and that the Spanish government aid an Irish rebellion against him.[68] Like Garnet, he argued that an oath containing things contrary to Christian faith could never be taken, and denied that equivocation was ever justifiable in 'confession of faith'.[69] And he spelled out that this meant the oath of allegiance could not be sworn, even with equivocation. When the oath was first introduced, he stated, some Catholics in England were moved by compassion to think up arguments which could justify taking the oath 'in some sense'. As we saw, this was what Blackwell did. 'Yet', Parsons added, none abroad were 'of that mynd: For that they allowed not of any sort of Equivocation in matters touching faith & religion'.[70] The Jesuit Hoskins argued similarly, claiming that the oath was directly contrary to the Catholic faith, and asserting that the papal deposing power was 'not ambiguous & doubtfull, nor such as the contrarie therof may with probability be maintayned: but so certaine, as without prejudice of faith it cannot be denied'.[71] Another Jesuit, Michael Walpole likewise claimed that the oath contained much that was 'opposite to Catholike fayth and doctrine', and that 'all Catholike Authours' condemned the use of equivocation in such cases.[72]

So, a number of leading Catholics, including the pope, major intellectual authorities like Bellarmine and Suárez, and prominent English priests such as Parsons, held that the deposing power was certain, that denying it was heresy or something close to it, that the oath of allegiance struck at central tenets of the faith, and that it could not be taken even with casuistical evasions. It looks very much as though the oath was rather well-designed to ferret out people who adhered to this set of ideas – people who shared the ideology of Bellarmine and Parsons. The oath's defenders insisted that the measure was intended as a test of civil allegiance, and not of religious conviction. From the very beginning of the controversy, James emphasized that he 'onely desired to be secured' of the Catholics 'for civill obedience', and his adherents stuck to the same line throughout.[73] Questier's claim that the oath's Protestant defenders were happy to equate it with the oath of royal supremacy over the church is unfounded. Nor is there much reason to argue that the principles which underlay the oath led in some *indirect* way to the royal supremacy and Protestantism. Venetian and French Catholics eschewed both, but also often rejected the deposing power. In 1606, disputes on church-state relations led the pope to place Venice under interdict. During the debate on the interdict, the Venetians adopted ideas which had a very great deal in common with those of the English defenders of the oath, and one of them – Marc'Antonio De Dominis – later came to England and there published writings against the thinking of Bellarmine and Suárez. In France, Gallicans also rejected the papal deposing power. A book against it by William Barclay (a Scot who had settled in France) was published in England as a contribution to the oath controversy, and Barclay's Catholic son John came to England, assisted the King in the debate, and defended his father's views against Bellarmine himself. Though the Sorbonne was under strong pressure from French papalists to condemn the oath of allegiance, it refrained from doing so, perhaps through the efforts of the ultra-Gallican Edmond Richer.[74] It is clear enough, then, that it was possible to be a Catholic and yet reject the deposing power and take the oath.

It is sometimes suggested that if the Jacobean establishment had really been interested in testing the loyalty of Catholics they would not have designed an oath which focused on the obsolete old medieval deposing power.

But it is difficult to show that they knew it was obsolete. The leaders of the Catholic church were certainly not prepared to declare that it had fallen out of use. Some English Catholics may indeed have been willing, as Questier contends, to swear loyalty to the King irrespective of whether the pope had excommunicated him.[75] As we saw, Blackwell himself took this line. But Blackwell held that we can make this kind of commitment only so long as it would be contrary to the interests of the church for the pope to exercise his powers over the King. We should be loyal to excommunicated kings as long as the faithful are not strong enough to oust them. If the times change, however, and Catholics grow stronger or acquire powerful foreign assistance, we have a duty to obey the pope and not the King. James wanted more than assurances that Catholics would remain loyal to him for the moment, or as long as they found loyalty convenient. He wanted a full rejection of the deposing power. The papalists were unwilling to give him this, and it is only with hindsight that their doctrine appears anachronistic. Indeed, it is arguable that it came to seem outmoded only after James, and his Gallican and Venetian allies, had conducted a largely successful propaganda campaign against the papalists. The interpretation of the oath offered by Pollen, Questier, and the rest invites us to believe that most English Catholics were scrupulously loyal to the crown, and that the troubles they encountered during the oath controversy were brought upon them by a bigoted government intent on persecuting them for religious reasons. The evidence for this is thin, and the evidence that in the wake of the Gunpowder Plot the Jacobean government felt sure that the greater number of Catholics were unswervingly loyal is thinner. There is very little reason to suppose that James or his counsellors thought that on central questions of papal power the large majority of English Catholics differed profoundly in attitude from the pope himself, or from Bellarmine and Suárez. But even if they did suspect this, and even if it was true – which is exceedingly doubtful – it still remains the case that the uncomfortable situation in which English recusants found themselves stemmed not only from the government's policies but also from the intransigence of the pope and papalists.

Commenting in 1611 on the contributions of Bellarmine to the debate on the oath, St Francis de Sales remarked that he 'did not at all like them ... not that I agree or disagree', but because 'dangerous disaffection' was likely to result if 'kings and princes are given a bad impression of their spiritual father as if he lay in wait to deprive them of the their authority'.[76] It was to avoid such disaffection that papalists fell silent about the deposing power, and that the fashion grew of portraying virtually all Catholics past and present as unswervingly loyal to the state. Before the dispute on the oath, however, it had seemed to many thoughtful and principled papalists that there were loyalties higher than those which we owe to the state, and that if governments misruled too egregiously they could be called to account. Arguably, they were right.

NOTES

I am very grateful to Margaret Sena for reading and commenting on an earlier version of this chapter.

1 Charles Howard McIlwain (ed.), *The Political Works of James I* (Cambridge, Mass., 1918), pp. lvi–lviii.

2 C. J. Ryan, 'The Jacobean Oath of Allegiance and English Catholics', PhD dissertation, St Louis University, 1941; J. V. Gifford, 'The Controversy over the Oath of Allegiance', DPhil dissertation, Oxford University, 1971; J. P. Sommerville, 'Jacobean Political Thought and the Controversy over the Oath of Allegiance', PhD dissertation, Cambridge University, 1981.

3 Among many important works that discuss aspects of the oath are Thomas Clancy, 'English Catholics and the Papal Deposing Power', *RH*, 6 (1961–2), 114–40, 205–27; *RH*, 7 (1963–4), 2–10; Thomas Clancy, *Papist Pamphleteers: The Allen-Persons Party and the Political Thought of the Counter-Reformation in England, 1572–1615* (Chicago, 1964); W. B. Patterson, *James VI and I and the Reunion of Christendom* (Cambridge, 1997); Michael C. Questier, *Conversion, Politics and Religion in England, 1580–1625* (Cambridge, 1996); and Michael C. Questier, 'Loyalty, Religion and State Power in Early Modern England: English Romanism and the Jacobean Oath of Allegiance', *HJ*, 40 (1997), 311–29.

4 Donna B. Hamilton, *Shakespeare and the Politics of Protestant England* (New York, 1992).

5 3 & 4 Jac. I, c. 4, in *Statutes of the Realm*, ed. T. E. Tomlins et al., 11 vols (London, 1810–28), 4: 1071. In 1606, lords were exempted from having to swear, but a new statute of 1610 ended this exemption, and greatly broadened the category of those required to take the oath, who now included officials of all sorts, lawyers, physicians, and anyone getting a university degree: 7 & 8 Jac. I, c. 6, in *Statutes of the Realm*, 4: 1162.

6 The Protestation of 31 January 1603 is printed in M. A. Tierney (ed.), *Dodd's Church History of England*, 5 vols (London, 1838–43), 3: clxxxviii–cxci.

7 Persons' memorial to Bellarmine, 18 May 1606, in Ibid., 4: cxxxv–vi.

8 Thomas Preston (alias Roger Widdrington), *A New-Yeares Gift for English Catholikes* (London, 1620), p. 11.

9 R. G. Usher, *The Reconstruction of the English Church*, 2 vols (New York, 1910), 2: 93–109.

10 Usher, *Reconstruction*, 2: 89–90; John Bossy, 'Henry IV, the Appellants and the Jesuits', *RH*, 8 (1965–6), 80–122, at 93–4. Richard Broughton, *English Protestants Plea, and Petition, for English Priests and Papists* (St Omer, 1621), pp. 47, 62–88; James Pateson, *The Image of Bothe Churches. Ierusalem and Confusion* (Tournai, 1623), pp. 344–5; William Udall to Salisbury in P. R. Harris (ed.), 'The Reports of William Udall', *RH*, 8 (1965–6), 192–287, at 214–15.

11 3 & 4 Jac. I, c. 4, in *Statutes of the Realm*, 4: 1071.

12 James I, *Premonition*, p. 9, in his *An Apologie for the Oath of Allegiance ... Together with a Premonition of his Maiesties* (London, 1609). The second issue of this book replaces the harsh 'forced' with the softer 'caused'. Further evidence that a clause rejecting papal spiritual jurisdiction was originally included in the oath is in John Hayward, *A Reporte of a Discourse Concerning Supreme Power in Affaires of Religion* (London, 1606), pp. 2–3; *Commons Journal*, 1: 275; BL Royal MS 17. B. xxx, fo. 2a. The latter source (an

anonymous Jacobean treatise on the oath) states that it was resolved to drop the clause, since the oath's purpose was to 'declare their civill duetye to their Prince' and not their 'spirituall duetye'. Importantly, it does not mention the King's role in the affair. Anthony Milton, *Catholic and Reformed: the Roman and Protestant Churches in English Protestant Thought, 1600-1640* (Cambridge 1995), 257–8.

13 Salisbury and Northampton in *A True and Perfect Relation of the Whole Proceedings against the Late Most Barbarous Traitors* (London, 1606), sigs. N2a, M2b. In February 1606 James vehemently and at length denied that he had ever intended to tolerate Catholics: *The Letters of John Chamberlain*, ed. N. E. McClure, 2 vols (Philadelphia, 1939), 1: 204. The suggestion that the oath was part of a long-term policy of toleration may be found, with varying emphases, in D. H. Willson, *King James VI and I* (London, 1972), pp. 227–8; W. K. Jordan, *The Development of Religious Toleration in England from the Accession of James I to the Convention of the Long Parliament (1603–1640)* (Gloucester, Mass., 1965), pp. 72–6; Hörst Witte, *Die Ansichten Jakobs I von England über Kirche und Staat* (Berlin, 1940); Joel Hurstfield, 'Church and State 1558–1612: The Task of the Cecils', in his *Freedom, Corruption and Government in Elizabethan England* (Cambridge, Mass., 1973), p. 112; Kenneth Fincham and Peter Lake, 'The Ecclesiastical Policy of James I', *JBS*, 24 (1985), 170–206, at 171, 185–6.

14 The breve is printed in English translation in James VI and I, *Triplici nodo, triplex cuneus, or an Apologie for the Oath of Allegiance*, in his *Political Writings*, ed. Johann P. Sommerville (Cambridge, 1994), pp. 88–91. The commission is discussed in Thomas Fitzherbert, *The Reply of TF* (St Omer, 1614), p. 215, which states that Bellarmine was a member.

15 Tierney (ed.), *Dodd's Church History of England*, 4: cxxxvi–vii; Thomas Preston and Thomas Green, *Humillima supplicatio* (London, 1621), pp. 29–30; Antoine le Fèvre de la Boderie, *Ambassades de Monsieur de la Boderie en Angleterre*, 5 vols (Paris, 1750), 1: 231. Blackwell's letter and his justification of the oath were printed in George Blackwell, *Mr. George Blackwell (Made by Pope Clement 8. Arch-priest of England) his Answeres upon Sundry his Examinations* (London, 1607). Later, the government discovered that Blackwell did not unconditionally reject the papal deposing power, and he was interrogated anew. He finally agreed to the absolute rejection which they wanted, basing his revised thinking on the arguments of Gallican theorists like Major and Almain, works by whom had been published in Edmond Richer's 1606 edition of Gerson. See *A Large Examination Taken at Lambeth of M. G. Blackwell* (London, 1607), especially pp. 63–4. There is further interesting evidence on the efforts of Catholics to interpret the oath in such a way that they could take it while evading its principles in BL Additional MS 39,829 (Tresham Papers, vol. II), fo. 17r; I am very grateful to Margaret Sena for this reference.

16 The second breve is printed in James VI and I, *Triplici nodo*, in his *Political Writings*, pp. 97–8, and Bellarmine's letter is translated at pp. 99–102.

17 Matthew Kellison, *The Right and Iurisdiction of the Prelate, and the Prince*, 2nd ed. (Douai, 1621), p. 44. For the Elizabethan background to papalist thinking, and to English Catholic political thought in general, the fundamental work is Peter Holmes, *Resistance and Compromise: The Political Thought of the Elizabethan Catholics* (Cambridge, 1982).

18 Francisco Suárez, *Defensio fidei Catholicae*, III, 2, 8, in his *Opera omnia*, 28 vols in 30 (Paris, 1856–78), 24: 208–9.

19 Kellison, *Right and Iurisdiction*, p. 45.

20 Edward Weston, *Iuris Pontificii Sanctuarium* (Douai, 1613), pp. 197–8.

21 Robert Bellarmine, *De laicis*, III, 4, in his *Opera omnia*, 6 vols (Naples, 1856–62), 2: 317.

22 F. B. Costello, *The Political Thought of Luis de Molina, S.J.* (Rome, 1974), pp. 40–4.

23 Alfred O'Rahilly, 'The Sovereignty of the People', in *Studies*, 10 (1921), 39–56, 277–87, at 42, 56. His case is amplified, with extensive reference to primary sources, in 'The Catholic Origin of Democracy', *Studies*, 8 (1919), 1–18; 'The Sources of English and American Democracy', *Studies*, 8 (1919), 189–209; 'Some Theology about Tyranny', *Irish Theological Quarterly*, 15 (1920), 301–20.

24 John Fitzpatrick, 'Some More Theology about Tyranny: a reply to Prof. O'Rahilly', *Irish Theological Quarterly*, 16 (1921), 1–15.

25 Gabriel Bowe, *The Origin of Political Authority: An Essay in Catholic Political Philosophy* (Dublin, 1955), pp. 43–7, 94–5. A similar argument is in C. N. R. McCoy, 'Note on the Origin of Political Authority', *The Thomist*, 16 (1953), 71–81, at 72–3.

26 James I, *Premonition*, in McIlwain (ed.), *The Political Works of James I*, p. 117; Bellarmine, *Apologia*, in his *Opera omnia*, 4, part 2, p. 399. Bowe, *Origin of Political Authority*, asserts that Bellarmine did not endorse this doctrine, but provides no evidence in support of this contention, and gives no reason why Bellarmine would have quoted this passage without criticising it if he in fact disagreed with it. Bellarmine was certainly cautious in his statements about the people's power over kings (see Jakob Gemmel, 'Zur Staatslehre des Kardinals Bellarmin', in *Scholastik: Vierteljahresschrift für Theologie und Philosophie*, 4 (1929), 166–88, at 186), but 'his words leave little doubt that he recognised the right of the community to depose the king for a just cause': R. W. Carlyle and A. J. Carlyle, *A History of Medieval Political Theory in the West*, 6 vols (New York, 1903–36), 6: 404; Suárez, *Defensio fidei Catholicae*, III, 3, 3.

27 John Floyd, *God and the King* (St Omer, 1620), pp. 32, 29. Though usually attributed to Floyd, the Jesuit Joseph Creswell may also have had a hand in the composition of this work. There is much useful information on this book and other writings by Floyd, Creswell, and Kellison in A. F. Allison, 'The Later Life and Writings of Joseph Creswell, S. J. (1556–1623)', in *RH*, 15 (1979–81), 79–144, and 'Richard Smith's Gallican Backers and Jesuit Opponents', in *RH*, 18 (1987), 329–401; *RH*, 19 (1989), 234–85; *RH*, 20 (1990), 164–206.

28 Weston, *Sanctuarium*, 225: 'ut sciamus quoto gradu aucthoritatis imperet princeps quicunque, recurrendum animo ad originem, scilicet voluntatem reipublicae, plerum-que lege aliqua scripta consignata'.

29 Ibid., 207: 'illud primum pactum Reipublicae, quo sancitum, huic primo conferendam regiam dignitatem, morali quadam permanentia durat'.

30 Kellison, *Right and Iurisdiction*, p. 54.

31 Weston, *Sanctuarium*, p. 199; Suárez, *De Legibus*, in his *Selections from Three Works*, ed. G. L. Williams et al., 2 vols (Oxford, 1944), 2: 386.

32 Robert Parsons, *A Treatise Tending to Mitigation towardes Catholicke-Subiectes in England* (St Omer, 1607), pp. 232–3; Robert Parsons, *A Quiet and Sober Reckoning with M. Thomas Morton* (St Omer, 1609), p. 453.

33 *Arrest de la Cour de Parlement* (Paris, 1610), translated into English as *The Copie of a late Decree of the Sorbone at Paris* (London, 1610). The assassination and its aftermath is discussed in Roland Mousnier, *The Assassination of Henry IV*, trans. Joan Spencer (London, 1973). Jesuit reactions are the subject of P. Blét, 'Jésuites et Libertés Gallicanes

Johann P. Sommerville

en 1611', *Archivum Historicum Societatis Jesu*, 24 (1955), 165–88; and P. Blét, 'Jésuites Gallicanes au xviie Siècle', *Archivum Historicum Societatis Jesu*, 29 (1960), 55–84.

34 Kellison, *Right and Iurisdiction*, pp. 51, 53.

35 Floyd, *God and the King*, p. 83.

36 Ibid., p. 91.

37 An excellent discussion of medieval theories is Michael Wilks, *The Problem of Sovereignty in the Later Middle Ages* (Cambridge, 1963).

38 Kellison, *Right and Iurisdiction*, p. 178.

39 Robert Parsons, *The Iudgment of a Catholicke English-Man* (St Omer, 1608), pp. 16–17.

40 Weston, *Sanctuarium*, p. 163: 'summus Pontifex non potest praecipere aut mandare Principibus in rebus civilibus in ordine ad finem civilem'.

41 Anthony Hoskins, *A Briefe and Cleare Declaration* (St Omer, 1611), p. 40. This work is an abstract of Leonardus Lessius, *Defensio potestatis summi pontificis* (St Omer, 1611). Lessius and Hoskins are discussed in A. F. Allison, 'Leonardus Lessius of Louvain and his English Translator', in S. Roach (ed.), *Across the Narrow Seas: Studies in the History and Bibliography of Britain and the Low Countries, Presented to Anna E. C. Simoni* (London, 1991), pp. 89–98.

42 Blackwell to the Catholic clergy and laity of England, 7 November 1605, in Tierney (ed.), *Dodd's Church History of England*, 4: cxi–cxii. The Plot was condemned for the same reason by the Jesuit Oswald Tesimond alias Greenway: *The Gunpowder Plot: The Narrative of Oswald Tesimond alias Greenway*, ed. Francis Edwards (London, 1973), pp. 80–1.

43 Robert Cecil, *An Answere to Certaine Scandalous Papers, Scattered Abroad under Colour of a Catholicke Admonition* (London, 1606), sig. C3r–v.

44 Robert Parsons, *Elizabethae Angliae reginae haeresim Calvinianam propugnantis saevissimum in Catholicos sui regni edictum ... per D. Andream Philopatrum presbyterum* (Rome, 1593), pp. 199–200, 195–6: 'est certum & de fide'; 'quemcunque principem Christianum, si a religione Catholica manifesto deflexerit, & alios avocare voluerit, excidere statim omni potestate ac dignitate, ex ipsa vi iuris tum humani, tum divini, hocque ante omnem sententiam supremi Pastoris ac iudicis contra ipsum prolatam, & subditos quoscunque liberos esse ab omni iuramenti obligatione, quod ei de obedientia tanquam principi legitimo praestitissent, posseque & debere (si vires habeant) istiusmodi hominem, tanquam Apostatam, haereticum, ac Christi Domini desertorem & reipub. inimicum hostemque ex hominum Christianorum dominatu eijcere'. The book appeared in a number of editions in 1592–93, funded by Philip II as part of his propaganda efforts against England: A. J. Loomie, 'Philip II and the Printing of "Andreas Philopater"', *The Library*, 24 (1969), 143–5.

45 *A True and Perfect Relation of the Whole Proceedings against the Late Most Barbarous Traitors*, sig. F4r–v.

46 Leonardus Coquaeus, *Examen Praefationis Monitoriae* (Freiburg-im-Breisgau, 1610), p. 172. As the renegade Catholic priest Richard Sheldon noted, Coquaeus' doctrine is a shade less radical than that of Parsons / Philopater, for he did not pronounce it an article of faith: Richard Sheldon, *The Motives of Richard Sheldon, Pr. for His Iust, Voluntary, and Free Renouncing of Communion with the Bishop of Rome* (London, 1612), first count, pp. 66–7.

47 Floyd, *God and the King*, pp. 87, 71.

48 Bellarmine, *Apologia*, in his *Opera omnia*, 4, part 2, 411; Bellarmine, *De potestate summi pontificis*, in his *Opera omnia*, 4, part 2, 274: 'severitatem ostendere nihil profuisset, ideo patientia potius adhibenda fuit quam auctoritas'.

49 Jacques Davy, Cardinal Du Perron, *An Oration Made on the Part of the Lordes Spirituall, in the Chamber of the Third Estate* (St Omer, 1616), p. 81.

50 James Brodrick, *Robert Bellarmine: Saint and Scholar* (London, 1961), pp. 280, 271.

51 J. C. Murray, 'St. Robert Bellarmine on the Indirect Power', *Theological Studies*, 9 (1948), 491–535, at 531.

52 Adrian Morey, *The Catholic Subjects of Elizabeth I* (London, 1978), p. 91.

53 Brodrick, *Robert Bellarmine*, p. 269. A similar position is adopted in C. J. Ryan, 'The Jacobean Oath of Allegiance and English Lay Catholics', *Catholic Historical Review*, 28 (1942), pp. 159–84.

54 Gordon Albion, *Charles I and the Court of Rome* (Louvain, 1935), p. 248.

55 Allison, 'The Later Life and Writings of Joseph Creswell', p. 93.

56 Questier, 'Loyalty, Religion and State Power in Early Modern England', pp. 318–19, 321.

57 J. H. Pollen, 'Oaths', in C. G. Herbermann et al. (eds), *The Catholic Encyclopedia*, 15 vols (New York, 1907–12), 11: 177–80, at p. 178; W. K. L. Webb, 'Thomas Preston O. S. B., alias Roger Widdrignton', *RH*, 2 (1954), 216–68, at 261; Ann M. C. Foster, 'The Real Roger Widdrington', *RH*, 11 (1971–72), 196–205, at 199.

58 Brodrick, *Robert Bellarmine*, pp. 269, 271; Arnold Pritchard, *Catholic Loyalism in Elizabethan England* (Chapel Hill, 1979), p. 213 n. 3.

59 Brian Magee, *The English Recusants* (London, 1938), p. 43; David Mathew, *Catholicism in England*, 2nd ed. (London, 1948), pp. 71–2.

60 The decree of 1610 against Bellarmine is printed in English translation in E. Le Jay, *The Tocsin, or Watch-Bell* (London, 1611), sigs. G2a–G4b. The decree of 1614 is discussed in A. J. Rance, 'L'Arrêt contre Suarez', *Revue des Questions Historiques*, 74 (1885), 594–608, and is printed in Thomas Preston (alias Roger Widdrington), *Appendix ad disputationem theologicam de iuramento fidelitatis* (London, 1616), sigs. B1a–B3a.

61 Thomas Preston, *A Theologicall Disputation Concerning the Oath of Allegiance* (London, 1613), p. 70, refers to an English dialogue entitled *The Iudgement of Protestancie, and Puritanisme, Both Highly Displeased at this Passage in the Oath*. This dialogue, which does not survive, may be the same as 'the late idle Pamphlet, of the *Puritan* and *Protestant Sister*, communing against the Oth of Allegiance', referred to by Richard Sheldon, *Motives*, second count, p. 23. John Donne, *Pseudo-Martyr*, ed. Anthony Raspa (Montreal, 1993), pp. 254–5, asserts that most of those who wrote in defence of the oath of allegiance did not bother to discuss the 'impious' clause 'because perchance they did not suspect, that any would stumble at that clause'. Donne claims that when he discussed the oath with 'some *Catholiques*', they named the 'impious' clause as a particularly clear instance of the oath's rejection of the pope's *spiritual* power, for they interpreted the clause as effectively denying that the pope alone is authorised to determine what doctrines are heretical. Moreover, they contended that the papal deposing power had been endorsed by many learned Catholics, and that it was therefore improperly bold for any private person to style it heretical (p. 255). Donne responds that

some principles are so contrary to Christian faith that they can reasonably be called heretical even without a formal declaration by the church, and observes that the Parlement of Paris had in fact condemned as heretical ideas which justified regicide (p. 257). Donne denied that the oath declared the papal deposing power heretical, insisting that it was the murdering of kings that it branded as impious and heretical (p. 266). Thomas Preston argued similarly in *Theologicall Disputation*, pp. 74–9. Neither Donne nor Preston attached much weight to quibbles about the clause, and they devoted little space to it.

62 Questier, 'Loyalty, Religion and State Power in Early Modern England', 319; Michael Questier (ed.), *Newsletters from the Archpresbyterate of George Birkhead*, Camden Society 5th series, vol. 12 (Cambridge, 1998), p. 111.

63 Questier, 'Loyalty, Religion and State Power in Early Modern England', 318.

64 Quoted in Clancy, 'English Catholics and the Papal Deposing Power', *RH*, 6, 227.

65 Allison, 'The Later Life and Writings of Joseph Creswell', 104.

66 Adolphus Schulckenius, *Apologia Adolphi Schulckenii Geldriensis* (Cologne, 1613), pp. 629, 259: 'quod Summus Pontifex possit Principes haereticos deponere, non est opinio, sed res certa'; 'Haereticum, vel certe erroneum et temerarium est dicere: Pontificem ... non habere potestatem privandi Principes'. This is a revised version of a book by Bellarmine; the original was printed but not published: Maurus Lunn, 'The Anglo-Gallicanism of Dom Thomas Preston', in D. Baker (ed.), *Schism, Heresy and Religious Protest*, Studies in Church History, 9 (Cambridge, 1972), p. 243 n. 3.

67 Questier, 'Loyalty, Religion and State Power in Early Modern England', 318.

68 Henry Garnet, *A Treatise of Equivocation*, ed. David Jardine (London, 1851), pp. 105–6, 88, 56. Garnet's authorship is demonstrated in A. F. Allison, 'The Writings of Fr. Henry Garnet, S.J. (1555–1606)', *Biographical Studies*, 1 (1951), 7–21. Parsons' memorandum on Ireland is discussed in Francisco Suárez, *De Iuramento Fidelitatis. Estudio Preliminar. Conciencia y Politica*, ed. L. Pereña (Madrid, 1979), p. 96.

69 Parsons, *A Treatise Tending to Mitigation*, p. 548; Robert Parsons, *A Discussion of the Answere of M. William Barlow* (St Omer, 1612), p. 30. The secular Richard Broughton – very much more of a political moderate than Parsons – endorsed the same standard view: Richard Broughton, *A Plaine Patterne of a Perfect Protestant Professor* (n.p., n.d., but c. 1609–10), p. 21.

70 Parsons, *The Iudgment of a Catholicke English-Man*, p. 9.

71 Hoskins, *A Briefe and Cleare Declaration*, pp. 46–7, 27.

72 Michael Walpole, *A Briefe Admonition to All English Catholikes* (St Omer, 1610), p. 124.

73 James VI and I, *Triplici nodo*, in his *Political Writings*, p. 86.

74 P. E. Puyol, *Edmond Richer*, 2 vols (Paris, 1876), 1: 137–8.

75 Questier, 'Loyalty, Religion and State Power in Early Modern England', p. 319 n. 38.

76 Quoted in Joseph Lecler, *Toleration and the Reformation*, trans. T. L. Westow, 2 vols (New York, 1960), 2: 411.

Chapter 8

'Furor juvenilis': post-Reformation English Catholicism and exemplary youthful behaviour

Alison Shell

R eaders of literature on childhood and youth in early modern England
might be forgiven for thinking that the old faith was primarily attractive
to old people.[1] It has always been rare, outside specialised studies in the field
of recusant history, for scholars in this field to give sustained consideration to
the Catholic experience – though, as this article will demonstrate, the gap is
not caused by want of source-material.[2] Even when England became a Protestant country, Catholicism was passed down through the generations; and
Counter-Reformation stirrings among the English, as for all Europe, were
nowhere more evident than in education. The architects of the post-Reformation
English mission realised the need to persuade each succeeding generation of
the truth of Catholicism, and utilised the most advanced pedagogical theory to
help them. This article will argue that they were repeatedly successful in their
aim of winning over children and young people, but also that many youthful
converts were proactive in seeking out Catholicism, defining themselves
against a religious norm just as their forbears had done in the earliest years of
the English Reformation. In addition, the notion of youthful ardour was
central to the exhortatory programmes and imaginative self-definition of
many post-Reformation English Catholics: clerical and lay, male and female,
parents and celibates, old and young.[3]

The evidence for this is diverse. The healthy number of children and youths
passing through the Continental schools and seminaries certainly testifies
that Catholic parents were keen to procure an orthodox education for their
children, but the biographical details in the registers of these institutions also
reveal something else: that a significant number of ardent youthful Catholics
came of households prepared to compromise with the Protestant status quo,
or – more strikingly still – had run away to school in the teeth of full-scale
parental opposition. Ambitious blueprints for youthful holiness were laid
down in the autodidactic dramas which were part of Catholic education for

boys at the English colleges, and these form a continuum with poetic representations of juvenile sanctity. Evidence for domestic religious education, particularly relevant to the experience of young girls, can also be gleaned from the didactic stratagems in specific families. Though inevitably such stratagems were imposed from the top down, they are often suggested, to a striking degree, by the behaviour of the children themselves. Exemplary childish behaviour made an impact on adults, both within and outside families, and this is sometimes taken into account by the children themselves. Moreover, there is evidence for religious activity which, while obviously deriving from what children had been taught, was developed to a conspicuous degree by children themselves: literary activity on the one hand, and on the other, gangs and secret societies to promote the true religion.[4]

YOUTH AND EXEMPLARY ANECDOTE

If one considers it normal in this period for parents to exhort their children rather than the other way round, then youthful Catholics routinely overturned expected familial hierarchies.[5] The Jesuit Robert Southwell is perhaps the most famous example of this. His written justification to his family of his vocation, *An Epistle to his Father*, was a much-circulated and much-copied text, which came to be imitated by other Catholic sons in time.[6] The editor of one such imitation, explaining how he came by a copy and justifying his decision to print it, gives a painful glimpse of a parent publicly obsessed by his son's apostasy: 'the Father more prodigall than the Sonne himselfe, carried the Originall continually about him, making no dainty at all to shew it to him in *St. Pauls* ... and in many other places at his pleasure, he making it his common Table-discourse in Tavernes and Ordinaries: by which meanes I obtained a Coppy.'[7]

The Douai student John Typpet, having been apprehended in London and sentenced to whipping and branding, wrote a letter to his heretic father Mark which illustrates well the tone of respectful exhortation adopted by youthful Catholics obliged to set themselves against the demands of filial obedience. 'Now tell me, dear Father, how this confident bravery has grown in the midst of these terrible torments? Certainly I do not know, because at first I had it not, unless it has been granted me through the merits of the holy blood of our new martyrs ... They perhaps have this virtue of enkindling the love of the Catholic faith in the hearts of us boys and children, as the excessive desire of worldly goods has the power of stifling it in the hearts of you old folk.' The letter continues, demonstrating as well as any Jesuit drama the role of exemplars in heightening Typpet's zeal, but drawing on the Bible as well as more recent history.

If the words written in your letter are really your own, namely that you will no longer be to me a father, unless I abandon the Catholic faith ... then God alone shall be my Father, whose holy Providence will not fail me. As you called me 'boy', I will take to myself the words of the youngest and most boyish of the Machabees,[8] and will finish my letter with them as he finished his life. They were these in effect: 'I will not obey the command of the king or of the emperor or of any earthly father whatsoever, but only the command of God and his Holy Church.' ... For this reason you must hold me excused ... I will not cease to pray continually for your salvation.[9]

A recent writer on child psychology has commented that children and young people embrace religious stories 'because they are quite literally inspiring – exciting their minds to further thought and fantasy and helping them become more grown, more contemplative and more sure of themselves'.[10] Postmodernism's awareness of the role of the imagination in shaping human behaviour, especially via role-models, should by now have given us the tools with which to approach an account like this. But even so, both historians and literary critics find this kind of exemplarity difficult to handle. It poses aesthetic problems for the literary critic, trained to value complexity and contradiction in character. For the historian, though, its difficulties are evidential: how far can one believe in accounts of exemplary behaviour when these accounts are written by the subject, or by a supporter? The problem is certainly real, but is compounded by the fact that accounts of exemplary actions need not, necessarily, be *untrustworthy* as evidence. Some hagiographies are exuberantly fictional, but certainly not others; the genre of hagiography is biased towards giving a good account of its subject, yet some subjects would defeat the most cynical and ingenious debunker. It is surprisingly common for historians to treat hagiography as if fictions and ideals never impinged on real life – an attitude which is of little help in understanding saints, still less in understanding children and young people.[11]

Some historians of childhood and youth act upon what is still, essentially, a Romantic view of their subject. This can result in typifying as authentic only that behaviour which runs counter to usual adult demands, or – at least – gives some evidence of internal struggle and development. Biographical accounts showing this type of behaviour are likely to receive more credence than anecdotes of unwavering juvenile sanctity, fictional accounts of it are more likely to be praised as realistic. These assumptions, though, are problematic for two reasons. Firstly, recent mainstream educationalists have confirmed that, even in the twentieth century, children can reflect on religious matters to a sophisticated level, from a very young age.[12] Secondly, realism is itself a literary mode, and one which gives imaginative prominence to inconsistency and bad behaviour. Accounts of steadfast youthful goodness may *seem* to be tainted by fiction, but can contain authenticable material; accounts of immaturity and change may *seem* more real than the former, but to regard them as necessarily less subject to generic convention would be a bad mistake.

At all times, we should be asking ourselves which generic conventions are acting on us.[13] To say that a story seems unreal can often be no more than an admission that we have been aesthetically conditioned into finding such accounts boring, chilling, or distasteful. Certainly, the possibility that some early modern children might have enjoyed didactic literature is ruled out by anachronistically judgemental accounts such as Warren Wooden's: 'while many seventeenth century children were certainly *subjected to* the Puritan tracts and various godly instructional manuals aimed at them ... [they] also made their way into the literary marketplace and *devoured* the chapbook adventure stories, popular ballads and fairy lore'.[14] Believing that didacticism is always dreary tends, for literary-historical reasons, to reinforce a linked assumption that exemplary tales are always suspect. Fiction about children, especially children's literature, has long been waging a war with its earlier didactic self, and – just as in the adult novel – naughty children, or children with a mixture of good and bad qualities, are perceived as being more true to life than exemplary ones.[15] This is a literary set of criteria, but it has had a considerable impact on historians' evaluation of evidence. We should not automatically assume that an account of children playing marbles during a sermon is truthful reportage, and one of children listening to a sermon with rapt attention has been hagiographically improved upon – but the prejudice runs deep.

Historians tend to distrust accounts of children who, in Keith Thomas's phrase, seem 'too good to live ... spending much time in the company of adults, and displaying largely adult thoughts and emotions': a bias all the odder because, as Thomas himself points out in the same article, children in the early modern period – or at any other – are constantly imitative of adult behaviour.[16] Children are likely to play childish games, or to try and impress their peer group by daring behaviour likely to be disapproved of by adults; but different children, or the same children at different times, are just as likely to act in a way designed to win approval from their family or teachers. Early modern children, moreover, were given every opportunity to develop their conscience, and behave in a manner pleasing to God, independently of specific adult direction. Some did this freely, others – as will be suggested below – experienced peer group pressure to do so. Lastly, one would not always have earned general adult approval by one's religious precocity; what was youthful exemplarity in Catholic eyes would have looked like profound disobedience to a Protestant parent or tutor, and, even while giving full respect to religious motivation, one should not overlook the possibility that in some cases pious and disobedient urges might have had a symbiotic relationship.

Developing a personal opinion about religious matters would have been inseparable from reaching adulthood in early modern England, but the age when it happened would have varied enormously. Separating childhood and youth is never easy for the early modern historian, nor is it always desirable; and the notion of precocity, especially *religious* precocity, problematises the attempt still further.[17] But there is no reason not to admit that some children would have leapt ahead of the class, at a remarkably young age. Precocity of all kinds is not prima facie unlikely; this was an era when precocious academic achievement was not uncommon, and religious precocity would have been available to many more children. This article has taken the view that while specific accounts of childish piety and fervour would have been very welcome to the English Catholic community, they would also have been as open as any other claim to disproof in the public arena. One is on even safer ground with adolescent and youthful subjects, especially where they are old enough, and eloquent enough, to give testimony themselves: Typpet is likely to have been in his teens, and whether or not he was the sole author of the letter which bears his name, one can assume that he would have endorsed its sentiments.

Few of the English Catholics' anecdotes about heroic children seem impossible, or even unlikely, given a culture of intense religious conditioning from an early age; but, since fact and interpretation cannot be easily separated, one also needs to ask what purposes were served by their preservation. Crucial to exploiting this evidence, therefore, is an awareness of the generic context in which exemplary actions are described, and of the audience being addressed. This type of biographical evidence comes from a number of sources: typically, admissions registers for schools and colleges, the Annual Letters of the Jesuit order, and hagiographical accounts of those who died young. Each of these genres invokes different expectations, makes different use of biographical material, and plays to a different audience. For instance, admissions registers such as the *Responsa Scholarum* at the English College, Rome, were a record of the pupil's history to date, primarily for in-house use. An anecdote of juvenile heroism which comes from one of the Annual Letters, intermixed with news of local religious conditions and shifts in missionary personnel, is obviously being used as an index of the church's success in the area; but even so, the modesty of the claims is striking. Typically, a Letter may include one or two examples of sanctity, presented as praiseworthy precisely because they are unusual. When the usual allowance has been made for early modern tolerance towards supernatural and providential narrative, an Annual Letter tends to read less like a golden legend than like the annual report of any organisation: upbeat in tone wherever possible, tending to place blame for underperformance on external rather than internal factors, but not outrageous in its claims, and recognising the obligation to make statements that can be independently verified.

One is perhaps most likely to incur ridicule if one cites hagiography or panegyric; but again, since the evidence is there, one needs to ask how it should be read. Hagiographical memoirs of the recently dead are written from several different motives.[18] But when their subject is too obscure and dies too young to be politically important, he or she is even more likely than usual to inspire a tribute which, whether singly or jointly authored, takes its inspiration straightforwardly from popular acclaim and a general sense of loss. These memoirs were, besides, not something which was accorded to everyone. Plenty of young students died at the colleges overseas; only a few seem to have inspired biographical tribute.[19] One can also assume that the authors would have addressed an audience keenly aware of the subject's moral and spiritual desert, relative to others of the same age; and, even if one were to take an approach to juvenile spirituality more uniformly sceptical than the evidence warrants, one could hardly argue away the general attentiveness among Catholics at this date to the exemplary value of youth.

EDUCATORS AND THE ENGLISH COUNTER-REFORMATION[20]

This was an attentiveness which both Catholics and Protestants shared, for good practical reasons. From the early Tudor period, English reformers made a direct strategic appeal to youth, and a number of recent studies have advanced the idea that early support for the Reformation was particularly high among the young.[21] But since all accounts of Protestant innovation in England need – to a greater extent than many currently display – a systematic alertness to Catholic counter-example, it is not to query the findings of these particular studies to suggest that one should look, as well, at the other side.[22] Direct addresses to youth were not undertaken only by Protestants; from Elizabeth's reign on, Catholics were to become well aware of the need to instruct each succeeding generation in the faith from an early age. In the medium to long term, their educators became both willing and able to address the special needs of the young in an up-to-date manner; and as Elizabeth's reign advanced, a significant level of enthusiasm for Catholicism among children and young people was thereby aroused and maintained.[23]

These statements should be truisms; but at present, they are not. The classic study of post-Reformation English Catholic education, A. C. F. Beales's *Education under Penalty* (1963), has had surprisingly little impact outside denominational history – proof, if added proof were needed, that mainstream historians of education are often less conscious than they should be of English activity outside England. But, since such an educator as Cardinal William Allen, founder of the English College at Douai, is seldom spoken of in the same breath as Richard Mulcaster and William Lilly, Beales's findings are worth re-emphasising. Catholic acculturation of children by adults could be accomplished in both a clerical and a lay context: through parents and tutors at home, as well as through schoolmasters and schoolmistresses working within a network of illicit Catholic schools in Britain, and abroad, tutors within seminaries and convents. Both boys and girls could have attended schools run by lay Catholic schoolmasters, or been taught by lay or clerical Catholic tutors within households that could afford to maintain them. Not dwelt on at length by Beales, but well worth further study, are the many Catholic children who would have received their education at mainstream establishments, and who developed various stratagems to maintain their religious and cultural separateness.

To avoid such compromises, both sexes among the upper echelons of society might well have been sent abroad: boys to the schools at Douai, St Omer, or elsewhere, as a preparative for ordination at one of the English seminaries overseas or as a means of acquiring a gentleman's education; girls, increasingly, might be sent to the schools attached to English convents, or the convents themselves. At the most basic level, the setting up of these schools – still more, their survival in various forms throughout England's penal times – testifies to a successful collaboration between the Catholic clerisy who ran them and Catholic parents or guardians who sent their children abroad to be educated. Judging from their entrance registers, they also indicate something more: the desire of the children themselves to be educated in the Catholic religion. These were, after all, schools which it was illegal to attend and risky to get to. In Elizabeth's reign especially, officialdom was alert to the 'crafty Catholic Childrene Abroade in every quarter or Coaste in Englande', to quote the priest-hunter Richard Topcliffe.[24] The phrase bears witness to a common contemporary perception that the children were not passive victims of family pressure, but were actively co-operating in being sent overseas.

Parties of boys were escorted by tutor- or schoolboy-chaperons along recognised safe routes; sometimes parents and children fled together; and yet others made their way to the schools by their own efforts.[25] Writing to Sir Robert Cecil in 1594, Thomas Jefferies reported how students got out of England in Flemish ships or disguised as soldiers.[26] This might or might not have been at the bidding of their parents or guardians, or with priestly aid. At the age of eleven, Henry Clayton's mother sent him to London 'by round-about-ways, all the roads being guarded', then to St Omer disguised as a sailor.[27] But a letter written in 1644 by Thomas Rob, the Rector of the Scots College in Douai, mentions the arrival at college of three boys who had travelled to the school without the knowledge of their heretic parents.[28] Sometimes such families positively opposed their children's plans – if seldom in such draconian style as Robert Walker's, the young seminarian of Valladolid whose father attacked him with a knife on hearing of his intention to go abroad.[29]

One can postulate a huge, irrecoverable oral culture in which children and young people swapped travellers' tales about themselves on arrival at their destination. But stories of this kind are also preserved in the written records of continental schools, seminaries and convents. No doubt this was often done for practical pastoral reasons, since they often denote what sort of a family the individual came from and suggest something of his or her early life. But they would also have set up expectations for the future, governing to some extent how that individual was regarded by his or her teachers. It is, then, hardly surprising that the masters at the English colleges seem often to have contemplated the boys in their charge with an intense, almost reverential respect. It was certainly counterbalanced by the absolute obedience that they demanded of their charges; there was a distinction, as in all Jesuit education, between the mind and the will, developing the former by a process of active self-education while training the latter to an unquestioning obedience to superiors and complete self-renunciation.

In this enterprise, fact and fiction were not distinct concepts. Since historians have traditionally dealt with facts and literary critics with fictions, to claim that fiction can be used as a means of modelling future fact might once have seemed perverse, the responsibility of neither discipline. But even blatantly fictional biographical incidents can become true when someone copies the behaviour of the saint, and the tendency towards biographical idealisation of youth, shared by many English Catholic educators, was as much an attempt to programme the future as to interpret the past.

Exemplary anecdotes are designed to facilitate the remodelling of the hearer's future, and I have suggested elsewhere that the same was true of religious drama: an important educational tool across early modern Europe which was much practised in Catholic schools, particularly those run by the Jesuit order.[30] Jesuit education laid especial stress on the role of the imagination in bringing about saintliness, and schools and colleges were an important potential arena for imaginative acculturation, boys being more privileged in this respect.[31] Jesuit dramas were among the earliest school plays; they were educative, teaching boys the elements of physical and oral self-presentation, training them in memory skills, and indoctrinating them in the faith in a way particularly suited to their tender age. The subject matter of these plays was frequently juvenile sanctity, in the tradition of the Catholic Church's celebration of child saints and martyrs: the Holy Innocents, the baby martyr Cyriac, St Pancras, St Hugh of Lincoln, and others. But the use of those stories for imaginative didactic purposes, to be read, viewed, learnt, rehearsed, performed, and internalised, was one of the most remarkable manifestations of the new impetus towards child-centred learning across early modern Europe. Though an important part of the curriculum, Catholic school drama was not just a top-down mode of teaching. Catholic children and youths were active participants in their own religious instruction, perhaps even helping to write the plays on occasion.[32]

English Catholic educators, both within and outside the Jesuit order, also found school plays useful for a more culturally specific reason. Plays could become a form of role-playing directly relevant to the experience of a persecuted minority, and could be used as a means of training the youthful actors – as well as the audience and even the authors – to exhibit exemplary behaviour during real-life moral crises. Plot-wise, therefore, English Jesuit drama has a distinctive emphasis on situations that could be paralleled with the experience, past or present, of persecuted Catholics in England. Heroes in these plays, as with all Jesuit drama, are often of childish years. Typical is Joseph Simons's tragedy *Vitus*, performed at St Omer in 1623 and re-telling the story of a youthful early Christian saint who suffered at the hands of the emperor Diocletian for his beliefs. With his skill in theological disputation, Vitus would have invited comparison with such youthful controversialists as the boy whose conversion is related in the English College, Seville's Annual Letters for 1597: 'Sent by Prince John Andrew Aurik to the College to be instructed in his catechism ... he was so remarkably precocious and skilled in heretical controversy, as to be a match for all not well instructed in that science. He was at length handed over to a veteran Father ... After some time the child, with shame and tears, confessed himself vanquished, saw the fallacy of Anglicanism, and was received into the Church.'[33]

Vitus's predicament, that of being held captive by a monarch who tries to make him apostasise, would also have reminded any viewer well informed in past confessional history of a policy originated by Lord Burghley and implemented for a time in the 1580s, whereby Catholic children were forcibly abducted. The story of four boys from the Worthington family came to have a conspicuous exemplary force in this context, being related in John Gibbons's *Concertatio ecclesiae Catholicae* and elsewhere.[34] In 1584 they were seized at a house near Warrington, and the youngest boy, John, aged twelve, and the eldest boy, Thomas, aged sixteen, were taken off to be questioned by the Earl of Derby and the Bishop of Chester. John was kept without food, though plied with wine which he persistently refused, while Thomas refused a bribe from the earl to hear a Protestant sermon. When they and the other two boys had been examined, they were confined in a house in Manchester and treated kindly for a month. Then their food was reduced because of their obduracy; and they were eventually pronounced guilty of treason, flogged, and separated from each other. The two older boys refused the Protestant catechism at school and set out instead to convert their schoolmates, while John engaged in disputations with the bishop.[35] Then, angered that they were regarded as conforming after they were escorted to a Protestant church under guard, they began to escape separately. After a number of setbacks, including the imprisonment of Thomas, they all crossed to Douai. Later, all four were ordained – John and Laurence as Jesuits – and two of them returned on the English mission.

Vitus has to justify his faith before the emperor just as the Worthington boys did before the bishop. This is not the only real-life story illustrating how youthful Catholics were, at some periods, felt to be opponents worthy of a bishop's attentions: on entering the English College, Rome in 1611, James Griffiths gave an account of how, some years previously, he and twelve of his Catholic schoolfellows had been summoned to the palace of the Bishop of Hereford and interrogated as to their motives for separating themselves from Protestant worship.[36] However, there is also a crucial difference between Vitus's predicament and the Worthingtons'. The brothers suffered as hostages for their parents' faith, whereas Vitus sets an example to his real father, a pagan who is upset by his son's Christianity.[37] This situation is paralleled in Act IV Scene 2 of Simons's play, when Diocletian's son Valerius becomes converted to the true faith, and Diocletian rages at him.

These episodes would have invited practical application wherever a St. Omer son, home for the vacation, could act as conscience to a wavering recusant or heretic father. Only a short time after the performance of Simons's play, the Annual Letter from St Omer for 1624/5 reports the valiant manner in which one of the pupils stood up to the attempts of a time-serving father to make him apostasise: the boy was called home and first sent to the archbishop of Canterbury, then turned out of the house for a period, and subsequently received back and sent to Cambridge under the care of a heretical tutor.[38] Boys were well aware how their parents, facing temptation back in England, could be more spiritually vulnerable than they themselves were; the St Omer Annual Letters for 1680, reporting on how the news of the Popish Plot was received at the College, stress that sons who heard of their parents falling into the hands of pursuivants were primarily anxious that they should bear their misfortune with a proper disposition of soul.[39]

YOUTHFUL EXEMPLARITY WITHIN THE HOUSEHOLD

Even in the most committed Catholic families, differences could arise about the appropriate level of religious commitment for a son or daughter. Some families would have been delighted at the idea of their children developing religious vocations: Peter Giffard's mother prayed that one of her sons might become a priest and one of her daughters a nun, a desire that clearly had a shaping effect on the children, since Giffard himself became a Jesuit, and his sister Joyce a nun at St Monica's, Louvain.[40] But parents could have other plans; and the story of Lady Catherine Vere illustrates how obstacles to youthful religious fervour could be presented by family and friends. She was

> by her friends much urged to marry, and also had many occasions presented, but ever was in trouble of mind when they were like to happen, and our Lord also concurred to make the intended matches crossed by some means or other ... So that

at length after much ado she got her father's consent to come over to be a religious, although he had long denied her. Upon an occasion that happened, whereby he began to fear she might in time chance to marry against his mind, for there was then one very earnest in the pursuit of her whom he could by no means like of (he gave her leave to enter religion). She thereupon set up a Father of the Society of Jesus to strike the iron whilst it was hot to procure his grant, which having obtained, she willingly bade the world farewell.[41]

Catherine Vere's story is narrated in a way that shows her passively resistant, but obedient. Though it would have been difficult for girls to run away to their vocation as boys could, they also had more proactive ways of making their feelings felt. Elizabeth Plowden's Jesuit uncle, who lived with her and her parents,

> would sometimes speak to his niece Elizabeth of religion, but she had no mind thereto. Yet it pleased Almighty God to call this child by such means as He Himself ordained – letting her fall into such discontent of mind, as she determined to get away from her parents over seas. Speaking first to her father, who liked it not, but bade her go to her mother, which she did, saying first that she would go over to learn qualities and language; but her mother answered that she might learn all she would in England. Whereupon she told her she would be religious, who, learning that, said, 'Nay, child, then I will not hinder thee,' being a pious woman. She told her uncle of it, who said there was even the next Sunday a good opportunity to depart, and would himself bring her over.[42]

Elizabeth Plowden's is a story suggesting that, on such questions as a child's religious vocation, the structures of authority within a family need not have been straightforwardly patriarchal. Father defers to mother on the topic, despite his own dislike of the idea, and though both parents were staunch Catholics, Elizabeth's sense of vocation seems likeliest of all to have been stimulated by her uncle. George Duckett, whose parents were schismatics but who was converted at the age of around ten by his Jesuit uncle Richard Holtby, demonstrates even more strikingly how conscientious cross-currents within a family could lead to children looking to authority figures other than their parents.[43]

It is no coincidence that both uncles were priests, and that they were both Jesuits may also be significant. Where parents asked different things from priests, the child had to discriminate between two conflicting authority figures, and where priests were also senior relatives, their preferences would have been still harder to disregard. Writing of Counter-Reformation Italy, Oliver Logan has suggested that this up-ending of normal familial hierarchies is a characteristically Jesuit stratagem, designed to assert the authority of a child's religious calling over against the rulings of a unsympathetic parent.[44] What was visible among Catholics in Catholic countries across Europe assumed a different importance in officially Protestant countries, where the opportunity for familial schism was greater. In England, one can distinguish between orthodox parents, who had nothing against the religious calling except in the case of their own son or daughter, and schismatic or heretic parents whose objections ran deeper.

Since anti-Catholic polemicists thought Jesuits were near relatives to Satan, they would not have been surprised by the young girl who found an ally less close to home, and whose case is described in the Lancashire district's Annual Letters for 1655. Taking her inspiration from a recent local spate of exorcisms performed on young children, she 'prayed earnestly to God that power might be given to the devil over her body, on condition that it should be the means of an interview with a priest, and of becoming a Catholic'. Accordingly, she was possessed by the devil, and a priest came to perform the exorcism. When she was cured, her father 'insisted again on her abjuring her faith, and returning to heresy. She, having found the tyranny of the devil more endurable than that of her father, renewed her prayer, and again ... had the devil as a temporary lodger in her body, that she might have God for her habitation for ever in her soul.' The Annual Letters report that she was eventually successful, by this means, in converting her whole family.[45]

It is hard, and perhaps not especially helpful, to distinguish between creative self-deception and deliberate pious fraud in cases like this. But playing on superstitious fears might well have been a more effective means than many of converting one's family, given the difficulties faced by other juvenile conscientious objectors within the household. After the domestically catastrophic conversion to Catholicism of Elizabeth Cary, Lady Falkland, her sons 'were desirous to refuse to go to church, though they should be never so much whipped for it', while another boy hid in the woods to pray rather than accompanying his family to church.[46] The youthful Alice Harrison, who converted herself by reading Catholic books, was 'severely persecuted, corporally chastised, and when this would not reclaim her, was turned adrift by her father'.[47] Another young girl, whose story is told in the Scottish Catholics' Annual Letters for 1664, was converted to Catholicism at around the age of fifteen by her aunt. Her prayer and fasting were noticed by her family, who had her whipped and imprisoned. When she told her father that if he dragged her to church she would make public profession of Catholicism, he confined her in a secret chamber for two years. She was not permitted to read Catholic books, but retained, so the Letters tell us, 'a little collection of meditations and prayers on loose sheets which one of our Fathers managed to get conveyed to her secretly, and which she carefully concealed in the plaits of her hair and in her shoes'.[48]

Orthodox households present a much happier picture, but one which can also be surprising in the extent to which children take the moral lead. A playlet designed for young children, written in the Blundell family in the 1660s and reprinted in a volume of Blundell papers, has occasionally been glanced at both by historians of education and Catholicism, and yields very interesting evidence as to how Catholic girls were acculturated into appropriate forms of adult spirituality.[49] It begins with Blundell saying to his daughter Mary, or 'Mall', that he is not satisfied with her deportment and other aspects of her behaviour, the whole being put in a distinctively Catholic framework when Blundell reminds Mall that the promise to amend these faults is something that has been monitored by her confessor. She promises to mend her ways; he says in response, 'but how oft have you broke your promise and been whipped and penanced, and promised and broke again, and been whipped again?' She retorts, politely but definitely, 'Sir, my duty makes me to think that you are a good man, yet perhaps you may have displeased God oftener than one time in committing the same fault.' Blundell is taken aback – 'Umph. This is a new mode of pleading. Who taught you this?' – but recognises the justice of her reproach. In the second half of the playlet, Father goes out and Mall reflects: 'I never came off thus in all my life when my father was so angry ... Now I'll pray and mend.' Her two sisters Frances, 'Franke', and Bridget come in, Franke driving Bridget 'tied like a horse with a string in her mouth'. Mall reproves them, 'Fie, sister Franke, fie! This is too childish for one of your years. We should now be grave and womanly.' Bridget, who is given all the childish lines, asks 'Sister Mall – I pray you, sister Mall, will not knowledge of cockle bread and turning the cat in the pan [i.e. somersaults] bring a body to heaven?' Mall responds: 'Oh, by no means, love. They know their way to Purgatory, but not to Heaven.'

Though this text certainly shows the severity of girls' upbringing in early modern England, its egalitarian quality is far more remarkable.[50] Obviously scripted by an adult – probably William Blundell himself – it is nevertheless designed to be appealing to children, perhaps actually recording games which Blundell had seen his daughters playing. The family relationship it presupposes is strikingly interactive, showing a father who is open to the idea of being exhorted by his child, in a piece probably written by that father. The degrees of formality, and of affectivity, present within the early modern family have been a topic of keen debate for some time. Missing from the argument, though, has been consideration of occasions such as these, where a parent lays him or herself open to correction from a child – perhaps because such occasions, however autobiographical, tend to be rendered in genres associated with imaginative literature, such as poetry and drama. Yet if this play was written to be performed within the family, one cannot write it off as a rhetorical exaggeration, whose whole point is its removedness from normally acceptable familial structures; it must give a clue as to how parents sometimes actually thought of their children, and to how children knew that their parents sometimes thought.

A child's saintly behaviour, as well as their exhortatory words, could also evoke a humbled response from a parent. Catharine Aston of the Tixall circle –

the scribal community of Catholic men and women centred around Tixall, Staffordshire, during the Civil War – wrote a poem 'To my daughter Catherine, on Ashwensday, 1654, finding her weeping at her prayers, because I would not consent to her fasting.' The second half of the poem, if it is to be read as a record of an actual conversation as well as an authorial self-reproach, suggests that Catherine Aston saw her self-denial as atoning for her mother's sins as well; and if so, she prompts comparison with such children as William Hart, a schoolboy at St Omers who consecrated himself to Christ and the Virgin Mary at the age of eleven with a vow of perpetual chastity, as a means of making reparation for blasphemers.[51]

> But you reply, 'tis fit you sigh and grone,
> Since you have made my miseries your owne;
> You feel my faults as yours, so them lament,
> And expiate those sins I should repent.
> O cease this sorrow doubly now my due,
> First for my self, but more for love of you.
> Ile undertake what justice can exact
> By any penance, if you will retract
> Those sorrows you usurp, which doe procure
> A payne I only cannot well endure.[52]

Though youthful longings to weep and fast were certainly not restricted to girls, arenas of spiritual excellence were more circumscribed for women, and weeping and fasting tends to have a greater visibility in the lives of female saints.[53] This could be seen as a particularly female remodelling of Lent, with a young girl undertaking Christ's undeserved, expiatory fasting and prayer. The daughter is assumed to be atoning for her mother's sins by weeping, to the point where the mother vows to take 'any penance' upon herself rather than see her daughter suffer further. The idea of an innocent sacrifice plainly derives from the doctrine of the Atonement; but if the daughter can be read as Christ, the mother's position is more ambiguous. She is, obviously, a sinner; but as well, one needs to be attentive to the familial relation of addressor to addressee. The writer, mother of the subject, assumes in herself a propensity to sin, combined with a motherly tenderness towards her faultless offspring: the ideal posture of the ordinary believer when contemplating the Christ-child, and an admission that the Church must adopt a maternal protectiveness towards Him.

Aston's daughter is the ostensible addressee of the poem. If her mother intended her actually to see it as well, then the poem would be even more of a counterpart to the Blundell playlet. Both, in any case, demonstrate how little girls could be seen as possessing moral authority within the home, up-ending conventional familial hierarchies and re-channelling the directions of instruction. This problematising of the authority of the home in favour of religious claims, always inherent in the Gospel message and particularly emphasised by the Jesuit order at this date, is visible in many generically distinct kinds of Catholic writing, and echoed in English Catholic writers of religious verse.[54] Moreover, sympathetic parents from all denominations, finding themselves guilty of a lack of insight or humbled by their child's religious fervour, could have found a model for their reactions in the scenes in the Gospels where Christ overrules his parents, especially the episode from St Luke where Joseph and Mary search for the twelve-year-old Jesus and find him teaching in the temple.[55]

CONCLUSION

But was this real-life attentiveness of adults to lessons to be learnt from children a reversal particularly characteristic of Catholicism? Certainly, it begs comparison not only with the role-reversals of Jesuit drama but with such aspects of the medieval church as the boy-bishop ceremony, which – as so often with carnival – gave a temporary, ludic power to subordinate members of the community.[56] In general, from the theological point of view, Catholics may have found it easier than Protestants to be edified by children. A mid-seventeenth-century poetic miscellany in the Bodleian, generally attributed to the Catholic Fairfax family and containing a good deal of religious verse, preserves two carols attributed to the young Anna Alcox, and a piece of adult poetic commentary on them:[57]

> This Anna Above exprest, As yo^w shall understand
> is A little mayd of six yeares old, who writ it wth her hand[58]
> Gods mighty workes, in her Appeare
> he water with his Grace
> his gracious gifts in her begunne
> And let her see his face, Amen

The writer of the above picks up on the notion of grace, addressing perhaps the most conspicuous difference between Catholic and Reformed theology in how children were perceived. God's gracious gifts, he or she asserts, have already begun in Anna, and are made visible by her unlikeness to ordinary children. On the face of it, this celebration of literary and spiritual precocity seems characteristically Catholic: recognisably akin to medieval notions of child-sanctity and to Counter-Reformation theories of a child's moral independence from its parents, very alien to the Reformers' stress on infant depravity. Yet this would not be quite the whole story: as Alexandra Walsham says in her article on the puritan child-prophet William Withers, 'People in the early modern period were seemingly predisposed to perceive childhood as a stage of life in which one might be afforded at least flashes of startling divine insight',[59] and many adult auditors, particularly those of puritan sympathies, would have been attentive to instruction from the lips of child-prophets. The difference of emphasis, though, remains striking. God's grace is shown in the early acquisition and conscious command of adult capacities to celebrate God's glory, not in a revelation of God for which the speaker is merely being used as a conduit.

One of the most powerful interdisciplinary studies on the early modern English child remains Leah Marcus's *Childhood and Cultural Despair* (1978).[60] Drawing particularly on seventeenth-century literary sources, she contrasts conformist nostalgia for prelapsarian innocence with puritan suspicion of the childish unconverted soul. Had the book also encompassed a sustained consideration of English Catholic writing, though, she might have sent it out under a more optimistic name. A practical and relatively benign view of youthful capability, whether this ran with or against the theological grain, could also be a source of comfort for religious movements which would have gained from a change in the status quo. As C. J. Sommerville has said, 'When people organise for change ... it is never long before they recognize that the rising generation will be central to their enterprise. ... the image of the child will inevitably figure in the movement's ideology.'[61] Childhood could, in other words, be a focus not for cultural despair but for cultural optimism.

Sommerville is, of course, not discussing Catholics but puritans; but the two groups have a good deal in common, not least an emphasis on education which was enhanced by religious dissent. It is commonly assumed, and not just by historians of puritanism, that puritans were the first to pay attention to children's education from the child's point of view;[62] but the more one sees over the edge of the denominational fence, the harder this is to sustain. We know a good deal, for instance, about the puritan contribution to early children's literature; but despite the fact that much English Jesuit drama falls into this category, I am aware of no discussion of it in those terms. As a genre that was popular in the English colleges overseas from the late sixteenth century onwards, Jesuit drama even pre-dates seventeenth-century puritan children's books. The distinctiveness of Counter-Reformation educational theory and practice is something which, when dealing with evidence from officially Catholic *countries*, historians have had no trouble in admitting; but they have been slower to see that it had implications for some citizens, both youthful and adult, in an officially Protestant country like England.

The notion that discipline was necessary because of children's innate sinfulness is generally, and with reason, thought of as distinctively puritan. Despite the admission that God could act early on a child, this tended to reinforce the idea of authority as necessarily flowing from the elder to the younger.[63] But Catholics and puritans shared an unusually intense, theologically generated concern with the disciplining of children, and contemporary Catholic – particularly Jesuit – ideas on intellectual, moral, and spiritual pedagogy arose from a more optimistic notion of grace, and a model of authority which was potentially more interactive.[64] Hence, in real life as in Jesuit drama, children could be seen as providing examples to adults.[65] The emphasis on adult authority was still there, but regularly shifted from father and mother to tutor, priest, or another theologically orthodox individual. Discipline could be seen in terms of discipleship, and the demands of spiritual family units could sometimes trump the authority structures within biological ones. More generally, Catholics' and puritans' differing notions of sanctity would have given Catholics of all ages a larger library of youthful exemplars than their Protestant counterparts. Given that children and young people are actively imitative, at this date or at any other, one should not be surprised that these exemplars fed into real-life behaviour, and were widely noticed and commemorated.

NOTES

I would like to thank the Leverhulme Trust, for funding a period of research during which this article was written; Elizabeth Clarke; Arnold Hunt; John McKinnell; Mary Phillips; Michael Questier; Alexandra Walsham; Margaret Sena; and Ethan Shagan. An early version of some sections was presented at the 'Gendered Spirituality' conference at Reading University, April 1999.

1 Important works in the field include P. Ariès, *Centuries of Childhood: A Social History of Family Life*, trans. Robert Baldick (New York, 1962); K. Thomas, 'Age and Authority in Early Modern England', *Proceedings of the British Academy*, 62 (1976), 205–48; I. Krausman ben-Amos, *Adolescence and Youth in Early Modern England* (New Haven, 1994); and the essays by M. J. Tucker, E. W. Marvick, and J. E. Illick in Lloyd deMause (ed.), *The History of Childhood* (New York, 1974). Recent literature, while severely qualifying Ariès's formulations, tends broadly to agree that an emphasis on the abstract nature of childhood, and on its importance, increased in the early modern period: e.g. the introductions to R. Houlbrooke, *The English Family 1450-1700* (London, 1984), and L. Pollock, *Forgotten Children: Parent-Child Relations from 1500 to 1800* (Cambridge, 1983). A recent authoritative study is P. Griffiths, *Youth and Authority: Formative Experiences in England, 1560-1640* (Oxford, 1996).

2 However, see I. Pinchbeck and M. Hewitt, *Children in English Society*, 2 vols (London, 1969), I: 260–2; W. W. Wooden, 'The Topos of Childhood in Marian England', *Journal of Medieval and Renaissance Studies*, 12 (1982), 179–94, reprinted in W. W. Wooden, *Children's Literature of the English Renaissance*, ed. J. Watson (Lexington, 1986). N. Wood, *The Reformation and English Education: A Study of the Influence of Religious Uniformity on English Education in the Sixteenth Century* (London, 1931) gives Catholicism a more sustained consideration than most scholars, observing: 'There can be no doubt that the recusant movement was revived, given new life and turned into an important national problem chiefly because of the seminaries, which, by a systematic and well-organised educational training, provided the men who gave the stimulus to a moribund cause' (p. 302).

3 Literary exploitation of the heroic child-exemplar was common in Catholic writers: e.g. 'Hymn to St Teresa', in Richard Crashaw, *Poems*, ed. L. C. Martin (Oxford, 1927); the sequence on the life of the Virgin Mary and Christ in Robert Southwell, *Poems*, ed. J. H. Macdonald and N. Pollard Brown (Oxford, 1967); and the discussion of Jesuit drama below. While most of my examples are drawn from sixteenth- and seventeenth-century sources, the importance of the heroic child exemplar continued at least into the eighteenth century: e.g. H. Foley, *Records of the English Province of the Society of Jesus*, 7 vols (London, 1875–1883), [hereafter Foley], 5 (Series XII): 697.

4 For an example of a Catholic boys' gang, see the biography of Edward Throckmorton: Foley 4 (Series IX–XI): 288–330. Throckmorton also features in Foley 6: 96–7 (Annual Letters for 1582, mentioned together with two other students who died that year, Thomas Bennett and Ralph Shirley). See also Christopher Devlin, *The Life of Robert Southwell, Poet and Martyr* (London, 1956), pp. 18–21.

5 Father-son letters and dialogues were also employed by Lutheran writers. See S. Brigden, 'Youth and the English Reformation', *PP*, 95 (1982), 37–67, at 64; Steven E. Ozment, *The Reformation in the Cities* (New Haven, 1975), pp. 82–3. I am grateful to Margaret Sena for these references.

6 For the most recent list of surviving contemporary copies of Southwell's *Epistle*, see P. Beal (compiler), *Index of English Literary Manuscripts*, 4 vols (London, 1980), 1, part 2: 296–306. The comments of N. P. Brown, in 'Paperchase: The Dissemination of Catholic Texts in Elizabethan England', in P. Beal and J. Griffiths (eds), *English Manuscript Studies, 1100–1700*, (Oxford, 1989), pp. 120–43, are suggestive of how exemplary writing can move from the biographically particularised to the general: Southwell's *Epistle*, which commonly begins with father's and son's names in other manuscripts, has in the MS compilation of Peter Mowle the superscription 'An excelent Epistle (perswasitorie) from a Childe to his father: disswading him from scissmn and from vices' (p. 128). See also Brown's edition of the 'Epistle' in *Two Letters and Short Rules of a Good Life* (Charlottesville, 1973), pp. xxi–xxiv, xlvii–viii; P. Janelle, *Robert Southwell the Writer* (London, 1935), pp. 148, 155, 228–32.

7 N. N., *An Epistle of a Catholicke Young Gentleman, (Being for His Religion Imprisoned) to His Father a Protestant* (1623). The author compares himself to St Francis of Assisi, also cast off by his father (p. 36) and stresses God's superior claims to fatherhood (pp. 4–6).

8 Typpet is paraphrasing 2 Maccabees 7: 30–1. A mother who has seen all but one of her sons murdered for refusing to abandon Jewish law is urged by the king to plead with her youngest son, but he stands firm nevertheless. Cf. G. Avery, 'Intimations of Mortality: The Puritan and Evangelical Message to Children', in G. Avery and K. Reynolds (eds), *Representations of Childhood Death* (Basingstoke, 2000), esp. pp. 95–6.

9 Catholic Record Society, *Miscellanea II* (London, 1906), pp. 71–4 (pp. 80–2 for translation); Foley 5 (Series XII): 695–6.

10 R. Coles, *The Spiritual Life of Children* (London, 1992), ch. 5, esp. p. 121.

11 Paul Griffiths, for instance, refers to the description of youthful exemplary behaviour as 'something which may raise our suspicions' (Griffiths, *Youth and Authority*, p. 183).

12 Elizabeth Ashton argues that 'The depth of reflection of which the youngest child is capable should not be underestimated': *Religious Education in the Early Years* (London, 2000), p. 61. Ronald Goldman has postulated five developmental stages: pre-religious thought (up to 7–8), sub-religious thought 1 and 2 (7–9, 9–11), and personal religious

thought (11–13, 13+): *Religious Thinking from Childhood to Adolescence* (London, 1964), discussed in D. Bastide, *Religious Education 5–12* (London, 1987). See also B. Watson (ed.), *Priorities in Religious Education: A Model for the 1990s and Beyond* (London, 1992), esp. ch. 5, and B. Watson, *The Effective Teaching of Religious Education* (London, 1993), esp. ch. 6; D. H. Webster, 'Spiritual Growth in Religious Education', in M. F. Tickner and D. H. Webster (eds), *Religious Education and the Imagination* (Hull, 1982), pp. 85–93.

13 C. J. Sommerville, *The Discovery of Childhood in Puritan England* (Athens, Ga, 1992), ch. 2, discusses the link between puritan children's writing and early literary realism, stressing the didactic antecedents of the latter.

14 Wooden, *Children's Literature*, p. x (italics mine).

15 Patricia Demers, *Heaven upon Earth: The Forms of Moral and Religious Children's Literature to 1850* (Knoxville, 1993), p. 3, comments on the 'critical animus toward the moral tradition in children's literature'.

16 K. Thomas, 'Children in Early Modern England', in G. Avery and J. Briggs (eds), *Children and Their Books* (Oxford, 1989), p. 49. For this distrust in action, see Avery, 'Intimations', p. 102: 'The spiritual records that the young were sometimes encouraged to keep rarely carry much conviction; the writers so often seem to be parroting their elders. But very occasionally genuine emotion surfaces.'

17 On the common preference for precocity in this period, see Thomas, 'Age', p. 210. Griffiths, *Youth and Authority*, and ben-Amos, *Adolescence*, discuss some of the difficulties involved with distinguishing the categories of child, adolescent and youth. On the topic of adolescent religious conversion, see ben-Amos, *Adolescence*, pp. 184–5. Adolescence is still recognised as the time when religious commitment often takes place: see (e.g.) K. E. Hyde, *Religion in Childhood and Adolescence: A Comprehensive View of the Research* (Birmingham, Ala., 1990), p. 186.

18 Peter Burke emphasises the growing stringency of standards for official canonisation at this date: 'How to Become a Counter-Reformation Saint', repr. in D. M. Luebke (ed.), *The Counter-Reformation* (Malden, Mass., 1999).

19 Edward Throckmorton's biography is cited above; see also the mention of verses written for Christopher Owen's obsequies at the English College, Rome, in the Annual Letter of 1580 (Foley 6: 70).

20 For the debates surrounding the term 'Counter-Reformation' and its various alternatives, see J. W. O'Malley, *Trent and All That* (Cambridge, Mass., 2000).

21 E.g. Brigden, 'Youth'; P. Tudor, 'Religious Instruction for Children and Adolescents in the Early English Reformation', *JEH*, 35 (1984), 391–413. S. J. Wright, 'Confirmation, Catechism and Communion: The Role of the Young in the Post-Reformation Church', in S. J. Wright (ed.), *Parish, Church and People: Local Studies in Lay Religion, 1350-1750* (London, 1988) discusses conformist practices; Griffiths, *Youth and Authority*, discusses godly practices among the youthful (ch. 4, esp. pp. 181–3). See also T. Watt, *Cheap Print and Popular Piety* (Cambridge, 1991), pp. 99, 138, 162, 190, 248; and M. Spufford, *Small Books and Pleasant Histories* (Cambridge, 1981), pp. 202–3.

22 Demers, *Heaven upon Earth*, ch. 4, discusses Catholic and Protestant catechisms in tandem. However, Ian Green's fine recent study of Reformation English catechetical techniques lists approximately 4 dozen *post*-Reformation Catholic catechisms in an appendix but makes no attempt to integrate them into his main discussion: *The*

Christian's ABC: Catechism and Catechizing in England c.1530-1740 (Oxford, 1996). On post-Reformation Catholic catechising, see also Marian Norman, 'John Gother and the English Way of Spirituality', *RH*, 11 (1972), 306–19.

23 Wooden, 'Topos of Childhood'.

24 Foley 1 (Series I): 356. For an account of state intervention to prevent the growth of popery among the children of recusants, see Pinchbeck and Hewitt, *Children*, 1: 261.

25 K. R. Wark (ed.), *Elizabethan Recusancy in Cheshire* (Manchester, 1971), pp. 78, 108–9, 111, 114; Edwin Benson (ed.), *Registers of the English College at Valladolid, 1589–1862*, CRS, 30 (London, 1930), pp. 33–4; Foley 7 (1): xxii. For a detailed account of a boy being transported overseas, see Ann M. C. Forster, 'The Venerable George Errington', *Biographical Studies*, 3 (1956), 322–33.

26 Cited in Hubert Chadwick, *St Omers to Stonyhurst: A History of Two Centuries* (London, 1962), p. 32.

27 Foley 7 (1): xxxi.

28 William Forbes Leith, *Memoirs of Scottish Catholics during the XVIIth and XVIIIth Centuries*, 2 vols (London, 1909), 2: 223–4.

29 A. C. F. Beales, *Education under Penalty* (London, 1963), p. 58 (cf. the story of John Maxey). For a similar attempted murder of son by father, see Foley 7 (2): 1158.

30 Alison Shell, 'Autodidacticism in English Jesuit Drama: the Writings and Career of Joseph Simons', *Medieval and Renaissance Drama in England*, 13 (2001), 34–56. For religious drama in English Protestant schools, see Paul Whitfield White, *Theatre and Reformation* (Cambridge, 1993), ch. 4; for a typical Protestant school dramatist, see Matthias Wilhelm Senger, *Leonhard Calmann* (Niewkoop, 1982).

31 However, the lost plays performed by Mary Ward's pupils at her successive educational foundations might have done something similar for Catholic schoolgirls: see Henriette Peters, *Mary Ward: A Life in Contemplation*, trans. H. Butterworth (Leominster, 1994).

32 The issues are discussed in Shell, 'Autodidacticism'.

33 Foley 7 (1): xxxi.

34 Originally conceived as an extension of the royal prerogative, this measure was put before Parliament unsuccessfully in 1593. For the Worthingtons, and other instances of children being seized, see Beales, *Education*, pp. 58–64.

35 For an example of a boy being punished for avoiding Protestant catechetics, see Foley 3 (Series V–VIII): 124.

36 Foley 4 (Series IX–XI): 429–30.

37 His subsequent experimentation with Christianity is treated in Act III Scene ii.

38 Foley 7 (2): 1160–1.

39 Farm Street, London: Foley MSS, Vol. 2, fo. 64v. See also the letter from Thomas Stapleton, then rector of St Omer, transcribed at fos. 63v–64r, where he testifies how calmly the students reacted to bad news about their families, desiring only to suffer with them.

40 Foley 7 (1): 302.

41 Dom Adam Hamilton (ed.), *The Chronicle of the English Canonesses Regular of the Lateran, at St. Monica's in Louvain* (Edinburgh, 1904), p. 158.

42 Extract from the Chronicle of St Monica's Convent, Louvain: Foley 4 (Series IX–XI): 549.

43 Interrogatories of the English College, Rome: Foley 4 (Series IX–XI): 404.

44 Oliver Logan, 'Counter-Reformatory Themes of Upbringing in Italy', in D. Wood (ed.), *The Church and Childhood*, Studies in Church History, 31 (Oxford, 1994), 275–84. See also E. W. Marvick, 'Nature versus Nurture: Patterns and Trends in Seventeenth-Century French Child-Rearing', in deMause (ed.), *History of Childhood*.

45 Foley 2 (Series II–IV): 21–2 (summarising the College of St Aloysius's Annual Letter for 1655).

46 'The Lady Falkland: Her Life. By One of Her Daughters', appended to Elizabeth Cary, Lady Falkland, *The Tragedy of Mariam, the Fair Queen of Jewry*, ed. B. Weller and M. W. Ferguson (Berkeley, 1994), p. 249; Foley 6: 89–91. The Annual Letter of the English Mission for 1614, describing the sudden death of a widowed mother who had started attending Protestant services, mentions in passing how her little daughter had refused to join her in church: Foley 7 (2): 1072.

47 See J. Kirk, *Biographies of English Catholics in the Eighteenth Century*, ed. J. H. Pollen and Edwin Burton (London, 1909), pp. 11, 111–12, 262–3. Some of his stories about Dame Alice Harrison come from her ex-scholars (see pp. 262–3).

48 Leith, *Memoirs of Scottish Catholics*, pp. 105–7.

49 M. Blundell (ed.), *Cavalier: Letters of William Blundell to his Friends, 1620–1698* (London, 1933), pp. 304–12. See John Bossy, *The English Catholic Community, 1570–1850* (London, 1975), pp. 166–7.

50 On the harshness of the punishments, see Pinchbeck and Hewitt, *Children*, 1: 303.

51 Foley 3 (Series V–VIII): 185.

52 A. Clifford (ed.), *Tixall Letters*, 2 vols (London, 1815), 1: 158–9.

53 See C. W. Bynum, *Holy Feast and Holy Fast: The Religious Significance of Food to Medieval Women* (Berkeley, 1987).

54 For ways in which religious discourse could empower women, see most recently David Como, 'Women, Prophecy and Authority in Early Stuart Puritanism', *Huntington Library Quarterly*, 61 (1999–2000), 203–22.

55 E.g. B. Cabilliavus, *Venatio Sacra, Sive Puer Amissus* (Louvain, 1642).

56 See Wooden, 'Topos of Childhood', and his 'Childermass Sermons in Late Medieval England', repr. in his *Children's Literature*.

57 Bod. MS Eng. poet, b. 5, p. 69. This manuscript is associated with the Fairfax family: see *Bodleian Library Record*, 3 (1950–51), 50, under 'Notable Accessions'; F. M. McKay, 'A Seventeenth-Century Collection of Religious Poetry: Bodleian Manuscript Eng. poet. b. 5', *Bodleian Library Record*, 8 (1970), 185–91. Alcox's authorship is endorsed in Peter Davidson and Jane Stevenson, *Early Modern Women Poets* (Oxford, 2000).

58 This may mean that the copy sent to the compilers of the miscellany was in Alcox's own handwriting, though Deborah Aldrich-Watson expresses scepticism in *The Verse Miscellany of Constance Aston Fowler: A Diplomatic Edition* (Tempe, 2000), pp. lx–lxi. The periods of a young girl's life tended to be divided up duodecimally (6, 12, 18: end of innocence, age of discretion, majority). See Thomas, 'Age and Authority', p. 222.

59 Alexandra Walsham, '"Out of the Mouths of Babes and Sucklings": Prophecy, Puritanism and Childhood in Elizabethan Suffolk', in Wood (ed.), *Church and Childhood*, p. 295. The genre of anecdote in which children see eucharistic visions (e.g. Foley 2 (Series II–IV): 647; Foley 7 (1): 389) demonstrates how Catholics too believed children could have an unusually acute sense of the Divine; cf. William A. Christian, *Apparitions in Late Medieval and Renaissance Spain* (Princeton, 1981), pp. 36, 198–9, 215–22 (I am grateful to Alexandra Walsham for this reference). Ben-Amos, *Adolescence and Youth*, contrasts medieval and Protestant ideas of childhood while also stressing the continuities, arguing that Protestant theology may sometimes actually have muted ideas of youth's propensity to sin (pp. 12–16, 31). S. R. Smith, 'Religion and the Conception of Youth in Seventeenth-Century England', *History of Childhood Quarterly*, 2 (1975), 493–516, discusses puritan exhortations of children and youthful conversions.

60 Leah Marcus, *Childhood and Cultural Despair: A Theme and Variations in Seventeenth-Century Literature* (Pittsburgh, 1978), esp. ch. 2.

61 Sommerville, *Discovery of Childhood*, p. 10. However, for problems with Sommerville's view that the Puritans 'discovered' childhood, see Griffiths, *Youth and Authority*, pp. 1–2.

62 The phenomenon of the puritan child-saint has been much discussed: see G. Avery, 'The Puritans and Their Heirs', and N. Smith, 'A Child Prophet: Martha Hatfield as *The Wise Virgin*', in Avery and Briggs (eds), *Children and Their Books*; Walsham, '"Out of the mouths of Babes and Sucklings"'.

63 Pollock, *Forgotten Children*, ch. 4, discusses the perceived necessity to make children realise the sinfulness of their actions.

64 Kathryn Sather comments that 'during periods of social tension for minority faiths, child-rearing is likely to involve increased discipline which may appear excessive by normal standards': 'Sixteenth- and Seventeenth-Century Child-Rearing: A Matter of Discipline', *Journal of Social History*, 22 (1989), 735–43, at 739.

65 John Gother, *The Spiritual Works of the Rev. John Gother*, 16 vols (Newcastle, 1792?) codifies the Counter-Reformation emphasis on education, and on the child's autonomous will: see 1: 88–90; 2: 351–3; 4: 178, 278–9, 281, 357–8; 5: 102–3; 11: ch. 25. Groups other than Catholics would have admitted in certain contexts that religion lay outside the bounds of parental authority: Houlbrooke, *English Family*, p. 168.

Index

Index

Houliston, Victor, 82
Howard, Henry, 80, 155, 157
Hughes, Ann, 12
Hughes, Philip, 22
humanism, 23, 53, 128
human nature, 167
Hunt, William, 36
Huntingdon, Earl of, 81, 86, 142
Hurault, André, 72
Hussey, Lord, 30

Ingram, John, 112

James I, 13, 69, 82–3, 86–8, 146, 150–
    6, 162–78, 194
James V of Scotland, 29
Jefferies, Thomas, 191
Jesuits, 13, 71, 74, 76, 83, 87–8, 99,
    103–20, 164–6, 175, 192–6,
    199–201
Jesus Christ, 170
John Foxe Project, 95
Jones, Francis, 112
Jones, Richard, 62
Jones, Robert, 119
Jonson, Ben, 87, 129–33, 137, 143–56
Joye, George, 38

Kamen, Henry, 18
Kellison, Matthew, 167–71
Keys, Thomas, 62
King's Book, 32, 34

Lake, Peter, 2, 11, 14, 82, 87
Lambton, Joseph, 112
Langdale, Thomas, 107
Lascelles, John, 41
Latimer, Hugh, 36, 63
Laud, William, 17
Lee, Edward, 36
Lee, Rowland, 34
Leicester, Earl of, 80–6, 98, 140–3, 149
Leicester's Commonwealth, 80–7, 138–
    43, 155
Leland, John, 29

Lennox, Countess of, 62
Leslie, John, 77
Lewis, Owen, 106
Leyburn, James, 73–4
Lisle, Lord, 34
Lister, Thomas, 110
Loades, David, 95
Loarte, Gaspar, 16
Logan, Oliver, 195
Lollards, 27
Longland, John, 15, 51
Longley, Katherine, 72–3
Loomie, A.J., 10
Lowre, William, 55
Luria, Keith, 18
Luther, Martin, 25
Lyle, John, 52

McClendon, Muriel, 13
McCoog, Thomas, 71
MacCulloch, Diarmaid, 5, 23
Machiavellian statecraft, 135–41, 155–7
McIlwain, C.H., 162–3
Magee, Brian, 174
Marcus, Leah, 200
Mariana, Juan de, 170, 172
Markland, Robert, 108–9
Marotti, Arthur, 73
Marshall, Richard, 28
Marshall, William, 31
Martin, Gregory, 114
martyrologies, 95–6, 100–6, 116–20
Martz, Louis, 16
Mary, Queen, 53, 61–2
Mary, Queen of Scots see Stuart, Mary
Matthew, David, 174
Matthewe, Simon, 30
Mayne, Cuthbert, 96
Mayr, J., 104
Melusine, 24
Mendoza, Bernardino de, 102
Mercurian, Everard, 99
Messenger, E.C., 22
Michell, Christopher, 52
Mildmay, Thomas, 61